WORLD DIRECTORS SERIES

Film retains its capacity to beguile, entertain and open up windows onto other cultures like no other medium. Nurtured by the growth of film festivals worldwide and by cinephiles from all continents, a new generation of directors has emerged in this environment over the last few decades.

This new series aims to present and discuss the work of the leading directors from across the world on whom little has been written and whose exciting work merits discussion in an increasingly globalised film culture. Many of these directors have proved to be ambassadors for their national film cultures as well as critics of the societies they represent, dramatising in their work the dilemmas of art that are both national and international, of local relevance and universal appeal.

Written by leading film critics and scholars, each book contains an analysis of the director's works, filmography, bibliography and illustrations. The series will feature film-makers from all continents (including North America), assessing their impact on the art form and their contribution to film culture.

D1354669

Other Titles in the Series

KITANO TAKESHI

Aaron Gerow

First published in 2007 by the
BRITISH FILM INSTITUTE
21 Stephen Street, London W1T 1LN

The British Film Institute's purpose is to champion moving image culture in all its richness
and diversity across the UK, for the benefit of as wide an audience as possible, and to create
and encourage debate.

Set by Fakenham Photosetting Limited, Fakenham, Norfolk
Printed in the UK by The Cromwell Press, Trowbridge, Wiltshire

British Library Cataloguing-in-Publication Data
A catalogue record for this book is available from the British Library

ISBN 978-1-84457-166-6 (pbk)
ISBN 978-1-84457-165-9 (hbk)

CONTENTS

ACKNOWLEDGMENTS

Since this book has been several years in the making, there are a number of individuals and institutions that have helped along the way. My editors at the *Daily Yomiuri* provided me with the initial opportunity to review Kitano's work and the Japanese journal *Eureka (Yuriika)* gave me the chance to write my first lengthy study, an abridged version of which was published in the Italian anthology *Kitano Beat Takeshi* and then in *Asian Cinema*. Mark Selden and Laura Hein asked me to write about Okinawa and Japanese film, including Kitano's work. Darrell W. Davis first introduced me to this book project and my editors at the British Film Institute have shown both patience and understanding along the way. Three readers of the first draft provided valuable comments. The Liguria Study Centre in Italy funded a workshop where I first presented my research on *manzai* and *Getting Any?*, and I would like to thank the Centre as well as the other participants, Linda Ehrlich, Millicent Marcus, Dario Tomasi, Michael Raine and Rebecca West, for their help and questions. Versions of various chapters were presented at the Society for Cinema and Media Studies, at the Center for Japanese Studies at UCLA, and at the IIAS at the University of Amsterdam, and I express my gratitude to the organisers and participants. Along the way, I received important help and/or advice from Shinozaki Makoto, Aoyama Shinji, Hase Masato, Abé Markus Nornes, Dennis Doros, Roberta Novielli, Ichiyama Shōzō and Dudley Andrew. I should also express my appreciation to the webmasters of two internet sites, <KitanoTakeshi.com> and <TakeshiKitano.net>, that have proved quite useful in the production of this book. Finally Yale University and my colleagues there have been most supportive as I worked to complete this book.

A note on Japanese names: this book follows Japanese custom by placing the family name first, except in cases of Japanese who have been mostly active abroad. It also uses modified Hepburn romanisation. Thus it is Hisaishi Jō, not Joe Hisaishi.

INTRODUCING TWO TAKESHIS

The title of the film *Takeshis'* (2005) emphasises plurality first of all. It initially refers to the two characters from the movie named Takeshi: the successful film and television star Beat Takeshi and a down-and-out actor named Kitano Takeshi. An encounter between these largely identical men generates a dreamlike and increasingly absurd narrative as the latter, chancing upon some yakuza guns, becomes more and more like the action star until he eventually tries to murder, Beat Takeshi. This becomes ironic not only because this Kitano proves to be just the product of the star's fanciful if disturbed reverie, but because *Takeshis'* is directed by a real individual named Kitano Takeshi, who also stars in the film under the moniker Beat Takeshi, which he has used as a stage name since starting the comedy duo the Two Beats in the 1970s, eventually becoming one of the most famous Japanese television personalities. The doubling in front of the camera is doubled by another behind it. The film's title screen

'Beat Takeshi' in *Takeshis'*

'Kitano Takeshi' in *Takeshis'*

emphasises this mirroring by first showing the reflection of the title in blue before revealing what is reflected, the word 'Takeshis'' in red.

The fact that the reflection comes before what it reflects and takes on a different colour, underlines that this is not merely a duality of the real and its mirror image. What seems to be a distinct half of a pair can itself involve multiple identities. For instance, the action star Kitano the actor emulates – the one with blond hair and dark sunglasses – is not the same Beat Takeshi as the dark-haired individual in the TV studio. Multiplicities proliferate as most of the actors play three or four different roles in the movie. The posters of the film summarise rather than explicate this plurality. There are not one, but two official posters: one featuring a large close-up of the Beat Takeshi character with the title in blue, the other the Kitano character with *Takeshis'* in red. Interestingly each face is composed of hundreds of smaller images, the grand majority of which are of Takeshi, but not necessarily from the film (some are from earlier works such as *Hana-Bi* [1998] and *Zatoichi* [2003]), and there is at least one photograph of each of the other characters in the movie. Visually, the posters underline not only Takeshi's two identities, but also how each of these identities is an amalgam of many Takeshis and the people that surround them.

Representing multiple 'Takeshis' is not unique to *Takeshis*'. From his first directorial effort, *Violent Cop* (1989), Takeshi has credited 'Kitano Takeshi' with direction and 'Beat Takeshi' with acting. Given how many films concluded with the death of the character played by Beat Takeshi, Abe Kashō, in his book from 1994, *Kitano Takeshi vs Beat Takeshi*,[1] focuses on the films up until *Sonatine* (1993) as a battle between the televisual Beat Takeshi and the cinematic Kitano, where the latter is attempting to break down the body of the former. More recently, Daisuke Miyao has pictured the two as embodying 'the gap between cinephilia and telephilia', a means by which 'Kitano problematizes the inevitable coexistence between TV and cinema in Japan'. Miyao argues that 'the telephilic media conditions in recent Japan' may have in effect absorbed the cinematic Kitano Takeshi as just another TV personality.[2]

These shifts and divisions may not be so simple. Takeshi has used his real name, 'Kitano Takeshi', from before he began directing, as character names in comedy skits in the groundbreaking show *We're the Clown Tribe* (*Oretachi hyōkinzoku*) or when publishing books. He in fact made a strategy of offering different versions of himself as one means of negotiating the televisual world. Just as he would later talk of television as 'insurance' allowing him to do very different work in cinema, he spoke of his popular programmes as 'insurance' permitting him to do more daring television comedy elsewhere.[3] The divisions in his identity have thus never been easily reducible to the television/cinema split.

This is also not the division between the real person, Kitano Takeshi, and the fictional 'Beat Takeshi'. Takeshi has often spoken of these two characters as dolls (*ningyō*) that he, a third, presumably 'true' identity, manipulates.

I'm having fun with Beat Takeshi and Kitano Takeshi. If I'm asked who I am, I can only answer, 'I'm the man who plays Beat Takeshi and Kitano Takeshi.' Every once in a while, I call out to myself, 'You must be tired', and ask, 'So what should we do Take-chan?' It's a classic case of a split personality.[4]

He says he swings back and forth between these characters like a pendulum, a metaphor he also uses to describe his cinematic shifts from the romantic

(*A Scene at the Sea* [1991]) to the violent (*Sonatine*) to the comic (*Getting Any?* [1995]). Such statements indicate that, at least in Takeshi's mind, his different personalities remain separate, strategic positions for managing the Japanese entertainment world. His producer and the president of his entertainment company, Office Kitano, Mori Masayuki emphasises how central this is to their business strategy, where they make a point of not selling Kitano's films on Beat Takeshi's popular television programmes.

> If you casually place something of quality in a mass-produced consumer product, the customer is not going to go to it since they know better. Our experience up until now is that people will not consider it worth going to a movie sold only as a film made by Beat Takeshi. That is why we want to create absolutely no confusion on this point. We don't want the film director Kitano Takeshi and the TV talent Beat Takeshi treated within the same frame.[5]

Perhaps the specifics of this policy have changed now, but the general marketing plan has not, especially as Kitano has become a global phenomenon. Takeshi first became known abroad as Kitano Takeshi, with 'Beat Takeshi' operating largely as a footnote explaining what Kitano does in another space. 'Beat Takeshi' was encompassed within 'Kitano Takeshi', such that the personalities were often melded into a single name, ' "Beat" Takeshi Kitano'[6] (a phenomenon unheard of in Japan). That has tended to downplay Beat Takeshi's status as 'a mass-produced consumer product', rendering it merely an extension of the auteur Kitano Takeshi. With Office Kitano now producing the works of other directors, including Jia Zhangke's *The World* (*Shijie*, 2004), Mori 'wants to create the image that Office Kitano's K logo stands for high-quality works with an auteurist stance' on an international scale.[7] The names Beat Takeshi and Kitano Takeshi, earning different emphasis at home and abroad, are kept separate partially because of product differentiation.

How does one approach a star director who bears different names in different media, producing various meanings in various locations? Kitano's case poses interesting questions first for the study of stardom. *Takeshis'* is partially Kitano's reflection on being a star. Although 'Beat Takeshi' and

'Kitano Takeshi' are physically identical, the former has fame and women while the other does not. 'Beat Takeshi' behaves like the new elite, but the ease with which 'Kitano' is mistaken for the star (by the fan, by the chauffeur, etc.) only reminds us that stars differ little from ordinary people. In fact, what raises 'Kitano's' status is the pure accident of acquiring a gun, a fact that seems to endorse the notion that stardom is 'attributed', not 'achieved' or 'ascribed'.[8] The constructed nature of stardom is evident from the fact that the elements that compose 'Beat Takeshi's' screen persona, such as the blond hair, are identified as imitable.

Takeshis', if not Takeshi's own star status, acknowledges the polysemous and often contradictory nature of star identity. Many have theorised modern stardom as being a product of bourgeois society. Richard Dyer writes that 'one of the types that stars embody is the type of the "individual" itself; they embody that particular conception of what it is to be human that characterises our culture'.[9] Such ideological functions overlap with economic ones as a unique and consistent individual identity is also important for selling stars. But just as the economic sphere has shifted from fixed capital towards flexible accumulation in the postmodern world, so stars have increasingly become flexible entities, being either subject to a variety of readings by different consumers, or themselves increasingly embodying the disjointed and often schizophrenic flow of images.[10] Takeshi presents an interesting case of a star who not only represents, but apparently is conscious of these shifts, foregrounding his own polysemy through multiple identities, ones that also exceed national boundaries. He thus encourages the knowing, perhaps even ironic form of star appreciation that Joshua Gamson discusses.[11] But just as we can ask if fans vicariously and self-consciously consume the relations between Takeshi's various personae, if not also his self-critical attitude towards celebrity culture, we can ask whether Takeshi's foregrounding of the apparatus actually reintroduces the star as the figure rising above the postmodern flow, someone who can both play with and criticise it.

Takeshi's star persona has often been sold as a 'genius' (*tensai*) who stands above the crowd of '*tarento*' (talents) in the Japanese entertainment industry. Abroad, this has translated into the image of a Renaissance man who not only acts and directs, but writes novels, poetry and political criticism. In Japan this image is subject to self-parody as some of his sillier shows, such as *The Genius Takeshi's Enlivening TV* (*Tensai Takeshi no genki ga deru terebi*), sport 'genius' in the title. Seemingly his genius lay not merely in his intelligence, but in his ability to simultaneously be a clown and a genius. Mitsuhiro Yoshimoto has analysed Japan's unique *tarento* system, in which the display of known personalities playing 'themselves' in variety and quiz shows has become central to nightly programming. *Tarento*, to Yoshimoto, are the currency of contemporary Japanese television, where wealth is measured not in terms of real talent, but in exposure and exchanges with the audience.[12] As often the master of ceremonies of these shows, Takeshi appears both as a *tarento* and as someone who manages this currency.[13]

The posters for *Takeshis'* embody this. Although composed of multiple photos, they are not a true image mosaic like Chuck Close's self-portraits, where the individual images are arranged and manipulated according to their relative hue and tone so that, viewed from a distance, they meld into a larger image. The posters are just large images of Beat Takeshi or Kitano Takeshi imposed over the multiple smaller photographs. The plurality here is less an inherent multiplicity behind a larger fiction ('fiction' because it is the product of perception only), one available to those who look closely, than a duality offering Takeshi as both a single, overarching identity and an accumulation of distinct instantiations. We can say it is this duality, one which allows Takeshi to both 'have his cake and eat it too' – to be both a *tarento* and someone who transcends it, a polysemous intertextual entity and a singular artistic genius, a Japanese *tarento* and an international star – that distinguishes his star image.

This also relates to his image as a film auteur. Since this book concentrates on his directorial career and not on his activities in other media, it is his image as an auteur that is the foremost concern. The two – being a star and being an auteur – are related because Takeshi, along with Clint Eastwood, Charlie Chaplin, Buster Keaton and a few others, is one of the few stars to concurrently succeed as a director. His star image was used to sell at least his first film, *Violent Cop*, and the tension between his star and auteur images has fuelled his subsequent film career. He often spoke of the frustration he felt when Japanese audiences, expecting the comedian Beat Takeshi, laughed at his first major film role, the brutal Sergeant Hara in Ōshima Nagisa's *Merry Christmas, Mr Lawrence* (*Senjō no merī kurisumasu*, 1983).[14] His cinematic work is partially aimed at combating the star image obstructing his film identity; his directorial work, whether or not actively opposing the televisuality of that image, aspires to multiply the possibilities of his identities. Yet it was inevitable that he would have to coordinate the two: although the blond hair he sported in *Zatoichi* was one of the ways he rewrote this established character, he actually dyed his hair months beforehand so that Japanese audiences could get used to it on TV and not laugh when they saw him in the film. When Kitano's work travels abroad, this coordination is more difficult and more flexible (since he is less burdened with an extra-cinematic star image). He has both taken advantage of and fallen victim to these transnational differences.

Creating a distinct image as a director was one of the aims of his cinema, and that was further augmented by the control he seemed to have over the production process. The structure of Japanese film production has often been director-centred, even during the studio era. Kitano, too, quickly created a 'Kitano-*gumi*' (Kitano crew) composed of regulars like the actors Ōsugi Ren, Watanabe Tetsu, Kishimoto Kayoko and Terajima Susumu. An unusual production schedule designed to fit Takeshi's TV obligations and the lack of complete scripts encouraged improvisational creation on the set and made production dependent upon the director's decisions. Even though Kitano is well known for rarely giving his actors specific instructions, this is less to encourage their expressive talents, than to have them not act, and thus better fit his overall scheme. Often credited not only for directing and acting, but also for screenplay and editing, Kitano appears to have undeniable personal artistic control over his films. This apparently confirms the impression, in the words of Tony Rayns, of

> the singularity of the position Kitano has carved for himself as a director. No film-maker currently active . . . gives less thought to the impact of individual films on his or her career. Kitano has no impulse to build on past successes, or to go any significant distance towards meeting audience expectations.[15]

It is common in studies of film directors to announce the caveats to the auteur theory. Surely one must not fall into the illusion that Kitano's films are 'clearly recognizable as the work of one man'.[16] We cannot ignore the significant contributions of artists such as cinematographer Yanagijima Katsumi,[17] lighting designer Takaya Hitoshi, set designer Isoda Norihiro, composer Hisaishi Jō or even script supervisor Nakata Hideko, who maintained order as Kitano changed the script from day to day. Yamamoto Yōji's designs for *Dolls* (2002), for example, were so bold that Kitano ended up changing his plans for the film. Arguably the most significant presence in Kitano's work is his producer Mori Masayuki, who has been with him on every single film, on the set and in the editing room, making decisions on what project to film and when. He, for instance, came up with the title for *Hana-Bi*. Such varied contributions are hard to account for, which is why it sometimes makes more sense, *à la* auteur-structuralism, to consider the auteur's name as designating less a single creator than the sum total of forces that shape, unify and sometimes disrupt the texts. Some of these forces include the social and industrial conditions of production and the processes of reception. Kitano's films appeared at a time of readjustment in the Japanese film industry, after the end of the studio era and on the cusp of a wave of independent productions increasingly aimed at foreign festivals and markets. Japan was also suffering from the bursting of the economic bubble of the 1980s, a rethinking of postwar culture, and the rise of nationalism, just as it pursued reforms to make it more globally competitive. On an international level, Kitano's films were important texts in reappraising the relation of genre and art cinema in what could be termed a post-classical age of cinema, trends that were not unrelated to changes in how Japan was consumed abroad.

Within all this, fans played an important role in supporting Kitano's work and shaping it. This is not only because Kitano, contrary to Rayns's appraisal, admits to decisions made to satisfy his audience, but also because the expectations spectators brought to his films constantly interacted with them. The example of fans laughing at *Merry Christmas, Mr Lawrence* reveals Kitano's awareness of the power of reception to manipulate a film's significance. What is intriguing from the standpoint of auteurism is the strategy

Kitano took against this. Instead of attempting to satisfy the demands of his consumer base, he fought against them and the persona Beat Takeshi itself. This helped create a subversive or an auteur, who ignores commercial considerations to undermine convention. But this was a peculiar image for an auteur: as film audiences would get used to a 'Kitano Takeshi' who was not Beat Takeshi, he would then, for instance, undermine that label with a film the posters said was 'directed by Beat Takeshi' (*Getting Any?*). Throughout his film career, Kitano has shifted, sometimes radically, between different film styles and narratives.

One of the hallmarks of the auteur theory, if not the spark for its inception, was the perception that works by the same director shared certain traits. They were so consistent it was said that all the movies of an auteur constituted a larger single work. What is interesting about Kitano is that while there are those who insist this is true of him – that despite the apparent changes, there remains an unmistakable 'Kitano' quality to all his work[18] – many have declared that if there is anything unchanging about Kitano, it is that he is always changing. To Horike Yoshitsugu,

> The moment one utters a word to describe him, he is no longer in the place that word describes. That is, there is no place where he exists himself as Kitano Takeshi; he rather seeks his identity in always becoming something other.[19]

This is a different conception of the auteur from that focusing on the single, expressive subject creating a consistent textuality. Post-structuralism declared the 'death of the author' because it identified operations of language and textuality that deferred or deconstructed such unities, as well as argued for the liberating effects of freeing the polyphony of language from a restrictive solitary source. In that vein, one can point to the contradictions and fissures of Kitano Takeshi's works as proof that they exceed and undermine the enunciation of a single genius director. But to do that with the aim of disproving the existence of 'Kitano, the auteur' is to miss the point: just as Takeshi acknowledges the polysemy of his star identities, Kitano consciously performs the contradictions of any authorial identity ascribed to him by continually becoming different auteurs, evading attempts to define him. This could be the postmodern authorship analogous to his schizophrenic manipulations of star identity. This may not be Kitano's final, self-conscious deconstruction of authorship. We should remember that one of the impetuses for his performance of change was precisely to avoid mistaken readings. It was in some ways a realist stance, trying to prevent audience impressions from overwhelming his real message. But combating audience expectations can also become a strategy to oppose spectator power. Pulling the rug out from under the viewer gives the author an advantage in the struggle over meaning. Again, as with his star identity, the knowing subversion of authorial identity can allow for the auteur to re-emerge through the back door, where now the flaunting of change and cynical resistance to expectations are taken as emblematic of a more authentic auteur. As such, the continuous Kitano and the discontinuous Kitano may in fact be two sides of the same auteurist coin. It is thus important to examine Kitano's work not only for the signs of these consistencies or diffusions, but also for marks of a strategy to manage and manipulate authorial identity in a postmodern age after the death of the author.

As star or auteur, Takeshi ultimately emerges as a juggler managing multiple identities and meanings, all the while performing a tap dance around the borders of genres and categories that may work to define him and his cinema. In this acrobatic act, Takeshi usually swings between two poles. Just as Jean-François Buiré has identified the contrapuntal as a central figure in Kitano's film-making 'fugue',[20] so we can see him playing two sides of a pair against each other, starting with 'Beat Takeshi' and 'Kitano Takeshi', but continuing with comedy and violence, life and death, convention and subversion, seeing and being seen, words and silence, motion and stillness, masculine and feminine, visibility and invisibility. The figure of the pair can be traced to the *manzai* vaudeville comedy that initially brought him fame, one usually performed, as Takeshi did with his partner Beat Kiyoshi, in a two-person team. It multiplies throughout his work, however, as we see pairs of characters in every film, from Azuma and Kiyohiro in *Violent Cop* to Shigeru and Takako in *A Scene at the Sea*, from Shinji and Masaru in *Kids Return* (1996) to Nishi and Horibe in *Hana-Bi*, from Yamamoto and Denny in *Brother* (2001) to Beat Takeshi and Kitano Takeshi in *Takeshis'*. One of the issues I will pursue in this book is how Kitano portrays these dualities, asking particularly whether he proliferates their contradictions or instead finds frames that, while distinguishing the pairs, ultimately renders them part of a greater unity.

Given the deft dance we see in Kitano's oeuvre, one could argue, as Nakano Midori has, that 'theorising Takeshi' (*Takeshi-ron*) is impossible.[21] This argument is a central plank in a critical platform that has supported Kitano's cinema, but it also is a 'Takeshi-ron'. We must consider the foundations for such an assertion and what kinds of analyses it enables and disenables. I think it is incumbent upon us to swing between such assertions and their critique, while also seeking a frame – albeit not always the one Kitano might offer – that offers us a different perspective on this process, one connecting it to larger problems in Japanese and global culture.

The methodology and structure of this study will therefore borrow a page from Kitano's book and utilise the figure of the pair, while also considering frames for reappraising it. I will refrain from predetermining the 'Kitano as consistent' versus 'Kitano as ever changing' debate by dividing the book into two main sections: one devoted to summarising accounts of the stylistic and thematic consistencies in his work, relating and sometimes problematising them through historical and biographical context, and another that analyses each film from *Violent Cop* to *Zatoichi* for its uniqueness – as well as for the problems it poses to the vision of the ever-changing auteur. Book-ending these dual sections will be an introduction (this chapter) and a conclusion that use his twelfth film, *Takeshis'*, as a frame to provide perspective on this particularly self-conscious film-maker, but without solving all the contradictions and inconsistencies this inherently divided account will provide. I hope the reader can frame them as representing the contradictions and inconsistencies of Kitano's cinema itself.

This task will not be easy, as I myself will have to juggle multiple Takeshis, offering his different identities and my own analysis of them, but taking care not to force a single opinion on a figure whose definition paradoxically includes resistance to definition. With Takeshi problematising efforts to name him, the very issue of what terms to use becomes difficult.

In this introduction and elsewhere, I allot different names to different figures, particularly using 'Beat Takeshi' for the star persona, 'Kitano Takeshi' for the director, and 'Takeshi' for what is often an amorphous, and not necessarily real 'other' entity perhaps above, perhaps between, but always somehow around the other two. These are only provisional terms, so I enjoin my readers to try juggling them themselves.

Another problem will be my own position *vis-à-vis* Takeshi. Although I have no personal connection to him, I lived in Japan through many of the years of his directorial career, and participated in the debates about his work and his contemporaries, writing criticism and analytical articles in English and Japanese. Although it is important to frame Takeshi in a global perspective, juggling his domestic and international activities, my natural bias is towards the debates in Japan that are most familiar to me. Since those are also the issues unfamiliar to most readers of this book, my emphasis will be on explicating this neglected pole – the discourses and conditions in Japan that attempted to define and make possible his film-making and its reception – so as to get a fuller picture of Takeshi's position between the local and the global. This bears a critical aspect because it involves intro-ducing domestic criticism of his work that is largely unknown abroad, and which may alter his international image. Negotiating these different views, Kitano's voice and the voices of others, will be an important aspect of this work. Emerging in a 'World Directors' series, and limited by length, this book will also concentrate on Kitano the director, covering other aspects of Takeshi mainly as they are pertinent to the film-maker.

An obstacle faced when writing about Takeshi is the mythology that sur-rounds his personae. Some of what is said about him is simply untrue, but nonetheless takes on a life of its own, especially as fans latch on to certain narratives that support their vision of him. For example, even up until *Zatoichi*, commercially his most successful film, it was common to say that Kitano's movies were not successful at home. That is false. Takeshi is some-times to blame for these myths, as he has admitted to lying to interviewers on more than one occasion,[22] but the endurance of such myths says more about those believing them than about their accuracy. I will take a critical stance towards Takeshi's various images, one that may overturn fan illusions. But I do not think this is necessarily alien to this project, since he often acknowledges the made-up nature of his tales even as he utters them. Again, we must weave our way between the myths, understanding how they operate and why, and the factual truths, analysing the game that Takeshi himself plays between these two realms.

That does not mean this book will offer a cold debunking of the Takeshi myth. It is important to stake out a mobile position between hagiography (which is what many of the books written on Kitano have been) and polemical criticism, one that appreciates his artistry, that of his films and his image production, and critically examines its historicity and ideology. This book is not concerned with evaluative appraisals. Given Takeshi's own dual status as intellectual and buffoon, the language of this book stands between scholarly analysis and popular criticism (with reduced theoretical jargon, but also unfortunately without much Takeshi-like humour). Against a director who is still swinging his pendulum, what I offer is a critical approximation of that motion, with thoughts on its conditions and future direction. Where it goes from now is up to Takeshi and, I believe, all who view this unique cinematic performer.

Part I

Kitano Takeshi: The Auteur

Despite statements that Kitano is 'constantly rejecting [his] previous film while making the next one',[1] a number of commentators insist that his work evinces the same concerns from *Violent Cop* in 1989 to *Takeshis'* in 2005. Even those who focus on Kitano's seemingly constant effort to reinvent himself still identify 'trademark' elements, from themes to stylistic figures, that render them recognisably 'Kitano films'. I want to explore these elements, less in order to confirm their basis in the texts, than to consider the image they create of Kitano and the problems they raise, especially with regard to the relation between the cinematic and the extra-filmic (personal biography, cultural context and politics) and to the politics of style and periodisation, both within Kitano's oeuvre and in Japanese film as a whole.

Between Biography and Fiction

Auteurist accounts of Kitano Takeshi almost always begin with a biographical summary. This is not simply because auteurism often tries to secure the unities of a film corpus in the biographical experiences of the director; nor just because Kitano often claims a biographical basis to episodes in his work. It is because he has made his life a public spectacle. Kitano has repeatedly narrated moments in his life in books like *Yes, Takeshi!* (*Takeshi-kun, hai!*), *Asakusa Kid* and *Kikujiro and Saki* (*Kikujirō to Saki*), which then became popular television shows or movies. His life is seemingly an open book, inviting viewers to connect it with his work on TV and film. Many people have done that, seeing the struggle between Beat Takeshi and Kitano Takeshi as rooted in the conflicts with his parents, Kikujirō and Saki,[2] or the style of his humour in his childhood experiences.[3] It is commonplace to credit his near-fatal motorbike accident in August 1994 with a shift in his films' thematics.

Such suppositions are not without merit, but we must be wary of grounding Kitano's films in his life. First, because Takeshi's accounts are not always truthful. Biographers have noted discrepancies between his accounts and those of others, especially those of family members.[4] Takeshi does not necessarily hide that fact: *Kikujiro and Saki*, for instance, features both a disclaimer that it is a work of fiction and an afterword by his brother Masaru noting the events that differ from reality. The 'facts' about Takeshi's life should always be taken with a grain of salt. Second, a flesh-and-blood individual and the textual production of that individual are different entities. Tying interpretation to biographical facts rarely produces fruitful analyses of films because it ignores the rich creativity of both textual production and how texts are read. Takeshi appears to recognise this creativity, making the construction of his biography – its self-conscious fictionalisation – and the creation of alternative personalities part of his productive activities. The case of Kitano Takeshi thus demands that we read his biography not in terms of a one-to-one relation between fact and text, but as the formation of multiple personalities. What is important is not what really happened, but what has been constructed of his life and how it operates to shape his image and readings of his films.

Kitano was born on 18 January 1947 in Adachi Ward, Tokyo, to Kitano Kikujirō and his wife Saki. The couple had four children quite varied in age: Shigekazu was nineteen when Takeshi was born, Yasuko (his only sister) twelve and Masaru four. Since their father, who failed at most of his business ventures and worked primarily as a house painter, fulfilled few parental duties (he is often depicted as a violent drunkard), Shigekazu served as a substitute father. Saki, however, backed by Ushi, Kikujirō's aunt who lived with them, had undisputed authority over the children, becoming the epitome of the 'kyōiku mama' (educational mother). Takeshi often complained that she refused the children such entertainments as manga and movies and pushed them to become engineers (that being her image of success). In fact, Shigekazu and Masaru both studied engineering at college, the latter becoming a professor of engineering (as well as occasional TV talent). Takeshi too would enter the engineering faculty at Meiji University, but he became the first to rebel against his mother and dropped out. He spent several years doing odd jobs, including taxi driver and bus boy at a jazz club, but spent much of his time in Shinjuku, which was the centre of 1960s' counter-culture. When he became fed up with that life in 1972, he headed to Asakusa to train to be a comedian.

Takeshi is said to have inherited several characteristics from his family, beyond his intelligence. Kitano says that some of the blood of Japan's tra-ditional performing arts flows from Ushi, who performed *musume gidayū* (a narrative form of song accompanied by a *shamisen*, a three-stringed instru-ment);[5] Beat Takeshi reportedly inherited his quick wit and fast tongue from Saki; and according to Masaru, all the boys in the Kitano clan devel-oped their father's sense of embarrassment (*tere*).[6] Although a performer known for his loquaciousness, Takeshi in person is shy and repeatedly cites 'embarrassment' as a reason for not doing something in a film.[7] Some have even speculated that his predilection for violence stems from his bashful-ness.[8]

Another influential factor was growing up in Adachi Ward. Adachi is part of Tokyo's *shitamachi*, and not too far from Asakusa. *Shitamachi* is the 'downtown', populated mostly by lower-class workers and merchants, opposed to the 'uptown' of high-class Yamanote. *Shitamachi* is often said to possess a distinct culture, one that was popularised by Yamada Yōji's *It's Tough to Be a Man (Otoko wa tsurai yo)* series featuring Tora-san, an itiner-ant peddler who wanders the country, occasionally returning to his family in Shibamata in Tokyo. Begun in 1969, the series represented Shibamata as a friendly *Gemeinschaft* oasis within the modern city. Kitano had long criti-cised this representation, stating not only that Shibamata was not *shita-machi* (if Adachi was marginal to *shitamachi*, Shibamata was the boonies), but that *shitamachi* was actually harsh, detached and discriminatory.[9] Kitano states that far from representing that culture, his films 'are shot from the feeling that I hate *shitamachi*'.[10] Nevertheless, he often says his worldview emerged from Adachi Ward, where yakuza and other socially ostracised figures lived nextdoor. Kitano's family itself may have been a member of such a group.[11] This context may be the basis for the marginal and socially underprivileged characters that populate his films: gangsters, the handicapped, the ill, the menial labourers.

More importantly, his stories of childhood in Adachi have become a central source for Takeshi's adult image as a rambunctious, misbehaving child (*warugaki*). Takeshi's narration of his life mostly elides the process of becoming an adult and focuses on his adolescence and the period he learned comedy. In *Yes, Takeshi!* and *Asakusa Kid*, these are eras viewed with sentiment, nostalgia and a certain degree of continuity: even though *Asakusa Kid* is set in the 1970s, it is a world seemingly left over from the 1950s in *Yes, Takeshi!*. Some have criticised Takeshi's worldview as being stuck in the 1950s,[12] but Beat Takeshi often treads the line between creating a sentimental *shitamachi* and criticising it. That duality is part of his pranksterism, an aspect of the childishness he located in 1950s' Japan. The childish Takeshi is one of the most attractive aspects of his persona. As one critic put it, Takeshi 'turned his back on life as a "sensible adult" and chose instead to keep on acting like a child. . . . His theory that "owarai [comedy] is like a never ending move [sic: endless motion]" can be interpreted as "Keep being a cheeky, naughty child who plays pranks, then runs off." '[13] Beat Takeshi himself stressed that, 'the basis [of my stance] is to not become an adult. I am trying to live with the same sensibility I had when I did bad things in lower and middle school.'[14] His primary way of doing that was comedy.

Framing the Clown

When Takeshi decided to end his wandering and become a comedian, it is significant that he chose Asakusa. Asakusa was the entertainment capital of Japan before World War II, the place where Tokyoites went to see a movie or popular theatre, vaudeville and comedy. There was a long, illustrious line of Asakusa comedians starting with Enomoto Ken'ichi before the war and continuing after the war with Hagimoto Kin'ichi, now famous on TV. By the time Takeshi arrived in 1972, however, Asakusa was mostly run down, and so Takeshi counts himself among 'the last generation of the traditional Asakusa comedian'.[15] He may have picked Asakusa because of its familiarity, but it may have also matched his class outlook and nostalgic perspective.

The narrative of how he became a comedian is famous. Liking the work of Fukami Senzaburō, he wanted to work under him at the France-za, a club that had long featured comedians between strip shows, including Atsumi Kiyoshi

(who played Tora-san) in the 1950s. Takeshi started out as an elevator oper-
ator but eventually began appearing on stage in comedy skits. Fukami was an
Asakusa comedian in the prewar mould and he made Takeshi learn tap dancing and other arts. He was the only one Takeshi ever called 'teacher' (*shishō*)
and his influence was considerable. As the owner of the France-za wrote,

> The special trait of Fukami Senzaburō's skits was to put down and ridicule impu-
> dent country bumpkins and people acting like tin gods. When Takeshi became
> Beat Takeshi, that's the kind of comedy he did too. After Beat Takeshi started
> becoming popular, Hagimoto Kin'ichi was impressed and remarked, 'He's
> exactly like Fukami'.[16]

Fukami's comedy refused to curry favour with spectators and Takeshi mas-
tered the 'technique of dragging the customer down from his position as
customer and grabbing a laugh'.[17] The philosopher Nibuya Takashi has seen
this battle with the audience as fundamental to Kitano's cinema. Customers

The Two Beats: Beat Takeshi and Beat Kiyoshi (Courtesy of The Mainichi Newspapers)

Tsukkomi and *boke* in *Kids Return*

at the France-za did not pay to see comedy but naked girls; they were drunk
and either rejected the comedy or laughed at anything, even what was not a
joke. Fukami, and later Takeshi, fought that 'cruelty' with comedic talent
(*gei*), but talent rarely mattered. To Nibuya, this audience later made its way
into Kitano's films in the form of an awareness of the 'essential violence' of
the audience/camera, which is a 'machine that enjoys taking in what goes on
before it with disinterest'. Learning the violence of comedy from Asakusa
audiences, Kitano made films that are 'shot against the camera, against the
violence itself that is inherent in the camera.'[18]

Yet just as Takeshi both sentimentalised and rejected *shitamachi*, he
eventually declared that he was not 'from Asakusa', but came to fame 'after
kicking Asakusa's butt'.[19] He eventually turned his back on Fukami and, on
the invitation of another Fukami disciple, Kaneko Jirō, formed a *manzai*
comedy team in 1974 that was eventually called the Two Beats. It was then
that Kitano Takeshi assumed the persona Beat Takeshi (with Kaneko
becoming Beat Kiyoshi). They first followed the pattern of traditional
manzai using gags written by Kiyoshi, but when that didn't sell, Takeshi took
over the writing and changed the fundamental form of their *manzai*. While

their gags were often racy and dangerous, they rode to fame on the *manzai* boom that took place around 1980, becoming national television stars. *Manzai* is a dialogic style of Japanese vaudeville comedy that often features two performers: a straight man (*tsukkomi*) and a funny man (*boke*). *Tsukkomi* is the one who represents common sense and wields the words of everyday speech. *Boke*, on the other hand, neither follows common reason nor speaks normally. If *boke* is the figure that deviates from accepted structures, *tsukkomi* reminds us of those, interjecting phrases like 'How idiotic!'. By sometimes ending a routine with an 'I can't go on with you!', *tsukkomi* as the purveyor of criticism can reassert the frame and return us to the world of common sense. The frame provided by *tsukkomi* is essential for the production of comedy; without it, the *boke* can simply appear insane, not the safe object of laughter. As Ōta Shōichi argues, *tsukkomi* can be a polyvalent entity.[20] While working to establish the outlines of rational space, it also sets up a situation precisely so that the *boke* can upset it, producing the *boke* as *boke*. *Tsukkomi* embodies forces that specify what is safely funny, enable the abnormal while simultaneously disavowing it, narrate a loss of power and stability while always reassuring us, with a well-timed jab, of the fictionality of that loss, a position that reconfirms our superiority.

This relationship between *tsukkomi* and *boke* can illustrate debates over the nature of comedy. A number of authors ranging from Mikhail Bakhtin to Tsurumi Shunsuke and Yamaguchi Masao have seen comic figures and their spaces, such as carnivals, as alternative figures potentially undermining dominant structures. The *boke*'s actions can be interpreted as engaging in a playful 'deconstructive spirit'[21] that works against the dominant grain. Yet forces like the *tsukkomi* frame comedy, often separating it from such effects. As is evident in Aristotle's famous statement that the events in comedy must be 'painless', the comedic is often insulated from the real world and denuded of true effect. Psychoanalytic interpretations of the comic see it as a safe place for displacing aggression and desire. Many write about comedy involving a narcissistic identification with a position superior to the butt of the joke, but that superiority utilises a narrative of losing and regaining power. To Steve Neale and Frank Krutnik, what distinguishes comedy from horror is the assurance that the monstrous comedian is no threat, laughter

marking 'in each instance the restoration of superiority and power' that was
threatened by the intrusion of the abnormal.[22]

Takeshi first came to fame in this world of framing, encouragement and
superiority. But his *manzai* was not quite like what had existed before. In a
typical Two Beats performance, Takeshi would reel off his lines in a
patented rapid-fire manner, leaving his partner Beat Kiyoshi little time to
insert a 'Quit that!' (*Yoshinasai!*). Here, for instance, is a bit from one of
their famous routines:

TAKESHI: Well, today's a car society. You can score some girls if you've got a car.

KIYOSHI: Can you really?

TAKESHI: I've got a car and the other day, I got three girls in Asakusa.

KIYOSHI: Really? You got three?

TAKESHI: One died instantly, two went to the hospital.

KIYOSHI: That's hitting them with the car, you idiot!

TAKESHI: Well, you've got to be careful driving on dark roads at night. Dogs and
cats will run out in front of you.

KIYOSHI: Yeah, they suddenly jump out.

TAKESHI: The other day when I was driving in Gunma, I hit one – bang! – with the
bumper.

KIYOSHI: That's terrible!

TAKESHI: I like pets, so I thought, 'Oh god, I just killed one!' and got out of the car.

KIYOSHI: And?

TAKESHI: It was OK. Just an old lady.

KIYOSHI: That's not OK! Not at all![23]

The basic structure of *manzai* is still there, with Beat Kiyoshi repeatedly
scolding Takeshi for his violent deviations from social norms. But the *boke*
rapidly changes topics before the *tsukkomi*'s comments can even be registered, or the audience can digest what is going on.[24] Takeshi regularly talks
over the *tsukkomi*'s scolding, rendering it mere rhythmic punctuation.
Kiyoshi stated that his role was 'to put on the brakes and restore balance',[25]
but *tsukkomi* on stage had effectively been hollowed out. It was as if the *boke*
had gotten off the leash.

That was the impression that Beat Takeshi offered at first: the radical, subversive, even offensive comedian who broke social taboos. Famous for his 'poisonous tongue' (*dokuzetsu*), Beat Takeshi's targets were those who had enjoyed respect in postwar society, like the elderly and young women. PTA groups complained and the Two Beats sometimes got in trouble. Some on the left protested that they only targeted the weak and not the powerful of Japanese society.[26] But the Two Beats still enjoyed enormous support. Some justified their humour as social critique. Their most famous gag was a play on Japan's ubiquitous traffic safety slogans:

Red light
If everyone crosses
All will be safe!

This was taken as criticism of a Japanese collective consensus that ignored any absolute sense of right and wrong. Kobayashi Nobuhiko, an authority on Japanese comedy, declared that,

Takeshi was at his best in pointing out the truths that those focused only on climbing the social ladder could not see, while dryly wrapping them in a cachet of the native humour of *shitamachi*. Perhaps we can call them the truths that only a dropout could see. His ability and instinct to smell out the cultural fakes, those who smelled fishy, was unparalleled.[27]

Tsurumi Shunsuke, the famous pop-culture critic, focused on Takeshi's *shitamachi* aversion to the fake and pretentious, to argue that this was comedy that exposed hypocrisy and offered a healthy release of repressed emotions. It took aim at the 'surface democracy' of postwar Japan by offering *honne* (one's true feelings) against the dominant *tatemae* (social façade).[28] This viewed Beat Takeshi as a manifestation of the trickster, one who is subversive and so mobile that 'settling into a set thought pattern is impossible'.[29] His comedy style, then, can be related to Takeshi's desire to evade attempts to categorize him and his cinema.[30]

Beat Takeshi challenged the frames of comedy, but it would be wrong to declare that his comedy totally lacked a frame, or always opposed dominant trends. Beat Takeshi could not have consistently topped surveys of the most popular personalities in Japan if his destructive force was not contained. Some like Horike Yoshitsugu argue that Beat Takeshi the *manzai 'geinin'* entertainer died when he began appearing on television,[31] although others claim his work on shows such as *Kitano Fan Club* or the radio talk show *All Night Nippon* were representative of his poisonous style and helped create his most devoted fans. But even Takada Fumio, Takeshi's partner on *All Night Nippon*, said there was something about his character that excused all the poison:

> Country bumpkins will get mad. Sure they will. Heck, he's saying 'Fuck off Granny!' But in the end, he's charming. No matter how much he flings dirt at people . . . he's still kind of cute, he's got a certain charm. That's one reason people excused him. If he didn't have that, it just wouldn't be funny.[32]

Citing something similar, Yoshimoto Takaaki, arguably the most important postwar intellectual, explained it this way:

> He would call his female fans ugly bitches right in their faces and spit out, like a rapid-fire cannon, cruel, forbidden words abusing old people. Viewers would be stunned for a second, but just before their expressions should have stiffened, they would fall into laughter.
>
> They laughed because they realised that this painfully poisonous tongue expressed all the poison everyone had clogging up their throats but could not spit out even if they tried. Another reason was because his verbal artistry was soaked in a friendly expression and tone, a gentle weakness that could dissolve the poison. It was supplied with the power and timing that could take the black, prejudiced feelings of offence and turn them into smirks and wry smiles, diffusing them into roaring laughter.[33]

Whether it was his talent or his charisma, Beat Takeshi always possessed the ability to deflect the hostility of his audience into laughter. If this was his 'charm', it must also be related to his assumed childishness. Even without a strong *tsukkomi*, he was able to frame his own statements so that viewers could excuse them as 'just a gag', or just the words of a child.

The Two Beats were not alone in transforming *manzai*. According to Ōta, Horike, and a number of other observers, teams like Yokoyama Yasushi and Nishikawa Kiyoshi and Shimada Shinsuke and Matsumoto Ryūsuke changed the relationship between *tsukkomi* and *boke* in ways that significantly transformed the culture of Japanese comedy. The *boke* began to free himself of the *tsukkomi* and, in the cases of Shinsuke and Takeshi, acted like he ruled the show. Ōta argues that not only in *manzai*, but in comedy throughout contemporary Japanese culture, *tsukkomi* has become a weak presence. This, on the one hand, helped create a playful and fantastic performance space in which barely any *tsukkomi* exists to recall the rule of reason. Comedy became centred on a free realm of 'friends' (*nakama*) with humour itself based on inside jokes and keeping up the momentum (*nori*). On the other hand, it prompted the audience to take over the important role of *tsukkomi* in maintaining the comedy, as *tsukkomi* became more an assumption than a presence on stage. This was still weak *tsukkomi* because in many cases, like in impersonation (*monomane*) comedy, the audience was not following a critique or parody (i.e., the performer's *tsukkomi*), but just recognising the object. *Tsukkomi* as mere recognition ('I know who that is!') – what Ōta calls 'tracing' (*nazoru*) – is to him one of the central forms of contemporary comedy.

As the audience supplied the *tsukkomi* essential for comedy, it soon began actively engaging in the comedic performance itself. More shows like Beat Takeshi's *The Genius Takeshi's Enlivening TV* began to feature amateurs. If these people were funny, it was not because they had any talent, but because the performers and the audience read them that way. In this manner, Ōta sees the contemporary TV audience as being both audience (*kankyaku*) and viewers (*shichōsha*), spectators and performers, part of the space of 'friends' and outside it, subjectively engaging in *boke* behaviour and looking at it objectively as *tsukkomi*.

One can relate these transformations in comedy to the emergence of postmodern capitalism, seeing the traced pseudo-space of friends as analogous first to Jean Baudrillard's simulacrum, in which the original has

been replaced by its tracing, and second, to Asada Akira's notion of
'infantile capitalism' in Japan,[34] an adolescent space of playful competition without a goal that to him defined 1980s' Japanese culture. Such a
space was only possible through the benevolent aegis of an invisible presence (Asada assumes the emperor system [tennōsei] but we could substitute the assumed tsukkomi here). Beat Takeshi's TV humour ties into these
social transformations and the redefinition of tsukkomi. The Genius
Takeshi's Enlivening TV was central in the creation of the nakama space,
and We're the Clown Tribe, while offering more poisonous parody than the
almost childish stage slapstick of the Drifters (their initial rival on TV),
was always on the verge of being broken up by personal and adlibbed gags.
Takeshi himself could exemplify the duality of audience and viewers by
always situating himself as part of the space of 'friends' and outside it,
offering his own boke behaviour while providing a cool tsukkomi on the
silly antics of others. To Ōta, Beat Takeshi uses the world of entertainers
(geinin) both to seemingly criticise everything, including his own audience, as well as to disavow that criticism, presenting it as a mere 'comedy
act'. Shows like The Genius Takeshi's Enlivening TV usually featured Takeshi
viewing amateur participants perform various feats. Central to the shows
was his reaction to these actions. While Beat Takeshi was certainly an
expert at tsukkomi he generally did not point out the foolishness of these
amateurs. Ōta reasons it was because to Beat Takeshi, doing a pro tsukkomi
on non-professionals went against his principles as an entertainer.
Instead, he often just made a slight scowl and queried, 'I wonder about
that' (Nanda ka na . . .). To Ōta, this mixed reaction could constitute a
limited critique on Beat Takeshi's part of the incipient space of 'friends',
but only, as Ōta carefully adds, with a 'deeply troubled expression that cannot find anything meaningful to say against it'.[35]

Ōta, however, fails to see the cultural functions of Beat Takeshi's
tsukkomi scowl and how it may account for his immense popularity. Takeshi
doesn't just scowl, he also shrugs. Such a gesture works to frame his own
words and actions, both disavowing their force and dissociating himself
from the situation. This allows him, and his audience, to encourage trans-
gression but with a detachment that helps construct his own authority. It is

important to look at the power relationships within Takeshi's TV shows. Especially in a programme like *Takeshi's Castle* (*Fūun Takeshi-jū*, re-edited and shown abroad as *Most Extreme Elimination Challenge*), Beat Takeshi is the Lord (*tono*), the leader of his own Army. While he may sometimes become the butt of jokes, this is rarely because he lost a game of one-upmanship with another comedian. Just as he invariably beat Akashiya Sanma at the end of the Takechan-man skits in *We're the Clown Tribe*, he always maintained his position of authority over his troupe of comedians (the Army/*Gundan*) in shows like *Super Jockey*, making them not himself suffer the extreme physical comedy (getting into boiling hot baths, etc.). Takeshi's attraction and brilliance lies in his ability to become both the emperor-like detached presence that, in infantile capitalism, protected and authorised the space of play, as well as the ageless *gaki*, the model for that playfulness and the male equivalent of the *shōjo*, the unproductive, adolescent girl who never grows up that many have theorised as the cornerstone of Japan's infantile popular culture in manga, anime, pop music and literature of the 1980s.[36]

The question for many is how Beat Takeshi's experience in comedy shaped Kitano's cinema on a concrete level. Kitano himself has stressed that his comic training, acquiring skills ranging from the ability to trim off excess explanation to using swords, became a fount of experience that was essential to his films. It is clear that the way Kitano edits gags – waiting on a still scene before suddenly cutting to a comedic (and often violent) tableau – is structurally similar to his cinematic depiction of violence. His films have also been self-reflexive, featuring not only comedians, as in *Kids Return*, but also performance situations ranging from the directly theatrical, as in *Dolls*, to a general division between seer and seen in *A Scene at the Sea*. How these situations are framed often influences the core of each film.

Others have approached the question of influence more abstractly. The French philosopher Jacques Rancière has seen Kitano developing a form of tragedy proper to cinema by taking advantage of burlesque's ability to create pathos from stillness, visual power from the suspension of movement.[37] Several authors have attempted to find equivalents of *boke* and *tsukkomi* in Kitano's film form, in the relation either between violence and silence (Saruwatari Manabu) or between his deadpan default style and the sudden outbursts of stylistic violence (Bob Davis).[38] Such attempts are intriguing, but they do not always take into account the historical transformations in *tsukkomi* that are central to Takeshi's conception of comedy.

I believe that it was Takeshi's ability to use frames to play on multiple sides of the comedic equation, to straddle dualities by being both *boke* and *tsukkomi*, the fool and the cool observer, the offensive rebel and the charming kid, that is the aspect that best connects his comedy and his film work. His is a dual existence that tensely plays with the potential to both reinforce and undermine borders and the identities they delineate. His stance shifts during his career. I would argue that Kitano was able to take the weak *tsukkomi* frame of his early *manzai* in radical directions in his first films. *Tsukkomi* is emptied out as reactions by the characters or the camera, which can function as a framing device for actions or statements, are evacuated by a deadpan acting style or a minimalist aesthetics. This is one of the sources of tension in his early work, flowing from the lack of a clear border between stillness and action or comedy and violence. It is as if there is no *tsukkomi* strong enough to contain the insane violence of the *boke*, no transcendental frame to solve the contradictory dualities.

His later work, however, begins to return to the traditional form of *manzai* with a stronger *tsukkomi*, a transcendental frame that contains the violence as art and safely arranges the dualities — a frame that is represented by figures of angels and by the more forceful presence of Kitano the auteur. If the unstable frames and dualities of his early films critiqued mass media and his personality, the later use of frames tends to take advantage of the media. The space Takeshi's TV shows created for wild behaviour encouraged that mass imagination of what Ōta somewhat ironically calls 'conformist individualism' (*dōchō shugiteki kojin shugi*),[39] in which everyone cooperates to stand out, conforming by thinking they are not conforming. In some ways, this mass pursuit of difference, when assured by the authoritative figure of Beat Takeshi, could be analogous to the image of Takeshi himself, being both a product of the mass media, and yet perpetually shifting his identity to become the genius managing the mass media itself. The question in his later films will be how much he is still willing to undermine this new authority.

Evasive Politics

Some appraisals of Takeshi, especially abroad, have been political, asserting that his gags are a rebellious effort to subvert the status quo. Thematic readings of his films have also asserted that they are, for instance, 'an indictment of Japan's institutionalised corruption' (*Violent Cop*), a 'metacritique of the Japanese tension between team play and individual action' (*Boiling Point*), or a 'subtly seething condemnation of . . . the Japanese fondness for all things cute' (*A Scene at the Sea*).[40] The fact that Beat Takeshi has often, when acting on TV or film, portrayed figures ranging from criminals like the serial killer Ōkubo Kiyoshi, to members of the Korean minority like the patriarch in Sai Yōichi's *Blood and Bones* (Chi to hone, 2004) or Kim Hiro (a murderer who used hostage-taking to denounce discrimination against Koreans), signals to some 'his positive concern for those living on the margins of Japanese civil society'.[41] His time in Shinjuku and his admiration for Ōshima Nagisa have also aligned him with the counter-culture they represented.

Such interpretations are not without legitimacy, but we must ask how transgressive his humour could be if it sometimes seemed he was shrugging it off as he was saying it. Comedy need not have a definite ideology, but most conceive of political humour as possessing directionality. If we define a progressive politics as advocating change, pursuing critique with a point, Takeshi's comedy may be conservative if it ultimately subverts its subversions, or equivocal if it appeals to all sides without a consistent stance. That raises the question of how to interpret his words and his performance, especially in relation to the forms of political expression evident in post-1980 Japanese media. The discussion of Takeshi's politics can become quite convoluted when instabilities of language and reading make it difficult to determine what Takeshi really thinks, or how we can ascribe meaning to his often evasive actions.

One way to approach these issues is to simply say there is no need to discuss Takeshi's politics. Just as we have bracketed out his 'real life' to focus on narrations of it, shouldn't we skip his 'real opinions' and just examine the films? That is true, but the films and other texts attributed to him represent certain ideologies we cannot ignore. There is a strong tendency, both in Japan and abroad, to bracket out the question of politics in Takeshi's work – unless it fits under that ambiguous rubric of the 'subversive' – by focusing only on his persona (the 'radical' artist) or his cinematic art. While it would be wrong to reduce his film work to political statements made outside the movies, we should also be aware that the effort to bracket out his politics is itself a politics, one that represents a certain stance towards cinema or a particular position towards postwar Japan. Since I will talk about the former later, I will address the latter here.

The pop-culture writer Tomohiro Machiyama rejects the idea that the famous 'red light' gag is a social commentary. To him, the comedy of the Two Beats bears no political meaning, but is 'like being a child . . . the more your parents tell you not to say certain words, the more you're tempted to shout them out loud'. To him, it is the 'spirit of rock'n'roll – i.e. bollocks to adult common sense and sound judgment'.[42] We can say that is also a politics, but one that in post-1970 Japan rejects politics. Yoshimoto Takaaki found this rejection in Beat Takeshi:

> We have been searching for a foundation on which to build a radical art of estrangement that is elegant and soft, that rejects the anti-moral, that rejects the political, that breaks up the cultural wisdom and the intellectual climate that saw the concept of the radical (the principle) as only achievable through political ideals of trenchant resistance or through a sharp anti-moralism that battles social common sense.[43]

This, in other words, was a radicalism that rejected the doctrinaire politics of the leftwing student movement of the 1960s and early 1970s. Takeshi's own experience in Shinjuku among members of the counter-cultural left is often narrated less as an experience of influence than of rejection, of finding hypocrisy in these radical intellectuals who mostly ended up in corporate jobs. Takeshi was not alone in this. The sociologist Ōsawa Masachi saw the 1970s as a significant shift in the postwar intellectual climate, where the 'age of ideals' (risō no jidai), when Japanese believed in principles and attempted to alter society based on them, gave way to the 'age of fiction' (kyokō no jidai), when people lost faith in ideals and opted for fictional worlds divorced from social reality.[44] That may be too reductive, but incidents such as the Japanese

Red Army's 1971–2 murder of twelve of their own members in the name of intellectual purity did induce a profound distrust of politics among many Japanese. The rejection of politics itself became, like with Yoshimoto, a radical gesture. Takeshi can be put alongside a number of artists who emerged in the 1970s and 1980s, ranging from the novelist Murakami Haruki to the director Morita Yoshimitsu, who experienced the 1960s, but rebelled against it by choosing a lighter, more playful, more postmodern worldview. Kitano and his supporters in Japan have always stressed that his works are not social critiques, partially because of their conception of cinema (as I will show later), but mainly because they distanced these movies from the serious social message films made by the left in the 1950s and 1960s. These were now seen to represent the fakeness or hypocrisy of politics.

The Two Beats' vituperative comedy, uttering all that was discriminatory and politically incorrect, was radical to the degree that it lambasted the arbiters of morality, the politically convinced, the institutions of right in society. Takeshi's honesty/*honne* was an effort to show these groups as not only oppressive, but mistaken, believing in promoting good and equality when the world was really intensely corrupt and amoral. Kitano's works can be considered an alternative realism, one that, in films like *Violent Cop* or *Kids Return*, shows the true corruption or hopelessness of postwar life. The rejection of political ideals was so deep-seated, however, that it became nearly impossible for Takeshi and his contemporaries to offer alternative ideals to cure this corruption and hopelessness. Directing his poison at all, Takeshi embodies Fredric Jameson's conception of the end of parody in postmodernism, in which the loss of secure metanarratives from which to launch a critique undermines the ability to offer a humourous stab at something from outside.[45] The problem, as Ōsawa emphasises, was that the 1980s quickly fell into a culture-wide cynicism that, by criticising all calls for change, descended into conservative immobility. It was into this vacuum, as Yumiko Iida has argued, that nationalism arose in the 1990s, almost as a desperate attempt by many Japanese to find a basis for identity after the authority of so many institutions had collapsed.[46]

The tense relationship between subversion and cynicism in 1990s' Japan makes it difficult to evaluate Beat Takeshi's own statements. After becoming famous as a comedian, Takeshi was increasingly asked to play the role of a public intellectual, albeit in a new vein. As Niizawa Hiroko describes it, Beat Takeshi represented a new intellectual who need not have graduated from an elite university, who talked more than he wrote, who was 'cool' and thus easy to consume – an intellectual who broke down the previous barriers between the masses and the intellectuals.[47] Takeshi's barbs, uttered with the low-class language of Adachi Ward, were sometimes directed at the old-time intellectuals, but his popularity among intellectuals like Tsurumi and Yoshimoto was partially because he solved the dilemma they experienced: wanting to help the masses but by definition not being one with them.[48]

In terms of his voiced opinions, Beat Takeshi was closer to the right wing than the left. Although he differed from traditional nationalists by criticising the stupidity of Japan's plan to win World War II, or its efforts to free Asia by colonising it,[49] he favourably quoted such prominent nationalists as Mishima Yukio and Nishibe Susumu in blaming many of Japan's contemporary ills on the phenomenon of 'postwar democracy' (*sengo minshūshugi*) and the new constitution, which prohibited Japan from having an army.[50] Both were considered the roots of the hypocritical, and thus only superficial, sense of right and wrong he skewered in his comedy. He thus regularly called for the constitution to be changed and for the reinstallation of the Japanese military, both planks central to today's rightwing platform. His most common complaint was against democracy itself. He asked, 'Given that I work this much and pay my taxes, why is my vote equal to that of some lazy, jobless bitch?'[51] He proposed reinstituting restricted suffrage. On an almost visceral level, he criticised the mass society of postwar Japan, opposing it to his older, *shitamachi* world.

> When you go to *shitamachi*, the master carpenter is like the prime minister. You can't say he's a dictator, but he rules over everything from the festival to people's quarrels. It's the opposite of rule by the majority. There are times he asks for too much, but that felt comfortable for my father and other regular people. I don't know if it's the nature of the Japanese, but they can't work if they don't get a leader. I think we Japanese possess this fundamental constitution. . . . That's why when people talk of democracy, it makes me sick.[52]

This was a conceptual move Takeshi often made. While criticising postwar Japan for its bogus side, he never asked people to correct that through a more honest government or by resolving class issues, but rather cited the essence of the nation represented by his 1950s' world, or even the world before the war.[53] His call for honesty also seemed a call to abandon democracy and return to old-fashioned Japanese hierarchy. How much these views have entered his films is debatable but especially from *Hana-Bi* on, he has increasingly used his criticisms of postwar Japan as justifications for narrative choices.[54] Overall, given Beat Takeshi's immense fame, it would not be impossible to see his philosophy helping popularise rightwing ideas in Japanese mass culture – if his fans have been taking his ideas seriously.

It is difficult to be certain if Beat Takeshi is being serious himself. He could criticise democracy on one page, and provide absurd solutions on the next. On his long-running political debate programme, *Takeshi's TV Tackle*, he would often just lean back as the two sides argued vociferously, maintaining his distance by occasionally taking jabs at both. But it is also not certain that he is being humourous, since his political statements never fall into self-parody. There is the danger that this ambiguity over where he stands only feeds on the allergy towards politics, undermining committed calls for change by popularising a detached, but effectively conservative cynicism that ultimately resigns itself to the unchangeable national essence.

Yet the inability to pinpoint Takeshi may also be the result of his media strategy. His deft combinations of humour and *honne*, of poisons directed at the right and left, can appeal to multiple sides, thus achieving support from all. As Darrell Davis says, 'Like a good politician, Kitano plays up different parts of his persona for different constituencies.'[55] Some have criticised him for taking one position for one publication's readership and another for another magazine's audience. The inconsistent logic in his writings can also allow for multiple readings. To some, his popularity is partially due to the pleasure of reading this 'paradoxical rhetoric', something that implies that not a few readers consume him from a detached, even cynical perspective, enjoying the spectacle of language, not its content. What worries some is that this convoluted rhetoric, especially when framed by his humourous irreverence towards pointed political discourse, renders him almost impossible to critique.[56] Charging him with being a nationalist only exposes the accuser to the riposte of being too serious. To a fan like Machiyama, Takeshi's 'theory' 'is just one continuous sequence of running away from everything, of never getting caught'.[57] Takeshi's political stance may then be to perpetually defer a political stance, creating support by forever delaying the closure of his political language.

Takeshi as an Industry

Another problem in evaluating Takeshi's stance is uncertainty over who or what is uttering the words attributed to 'Beat Takeshi'. This is not an abstract structuralist argument, but something more practical: while Takeshi has published over sixty books, he has not really written a single one of them. This is not a secret. Beat Takeshi openly admits that 'I've never written a word myself. I just read what's been written and that's it.'[58] His books are basically 'written' by hired scribes who record his spoken words and compose them in book form. This system raises questions about authorship. The literary critics Fukuda Kazuya[59] and Suga Hidemi have both tried to write analyses of Beat Takeshi's novels, and had to confront the problem of a 'novelist who doesn't write novels', to borrow Suga's phrase. Suga used that as a springboard to question the nature of novel-writing as an institution, but we can use it to start considering Takeshi's industrial nature. To quote Darrell Davis, 'Kitano as media figure is not just an auteur writ large across disparate media, but a cultural production, a little industry in his own right.'[60]

There are probably various reasons why Takeshi does not write his own books, but one is certainly time. In celebrating him as a Renaissance man, many have listed the creative endeavours he has undertaken: TV personality, novelist, political commentator, editor, film director, actor, painter, rock singer, etc. Some he may pursue of his own volition, but most stem from his job as a *tarento*. Mitsuhiro Yoshimoto argues that *tarento* function as the currency of Japanese television, the worth of a programme depending on the *tarento* it uses, and the value of a *tarento* depending on how much she is in circulation.[61] With low production budgets and appearance fees for TV, the pressure on all *tarento* is to increase their exposure by exploiting their image in multiple fields; personalities working in various areas are thus not uncommon. Beat Takeshi is famous for having six to eight regular shows at once, but many popular *tarento* appear in that many programmes a week. Television networks develop numerous variety and information shows because they require less money and fewer rehearsals than dramatic series. This programming centred on talking or participating in situations that do not require practice matches the *tarento*'s desire to appear on multiple shows with minimum expenditure of time and effort. These factors privilege those with improvisatory verbal skills like Beat Takeshi.

If Beat Takeshi was in effect enabled by the Japanese television industry's structure, then most of his activities were shaped by it as well. Methods have arisen to efficiently manage Beat Takeshi's labour time and help produce him and his products as if on an assembly line. Takeshi may check the final products, but he himself is also manufactured, marketed and sold. One of the ideological functions of the Beat Takeshi/Kitano Takeshi split has been to separate the latter from the industrial nature of the former, as an artist free of commercial concerns. However, Kitano Takeshi is also an industry. His recent films are produced by his talent agency and feature many of its contract artists, such as Terajima Susumu, Dankan, Guadalcanal Taka, Ashikawa Makoto, Ide Rakkyo and Great Gidayū. That company has also helped produce films directed by his assistant directors Tenma Toshihiro (*Many Happy Returns* [*Kyōso tanjō*, 1994]) and Shimizu Hiroshi (*Suicide Bus* [*Ikinai*, 1998]), involving Beat Takeshi or other contract performers like Dankan. His films, especially after *Hana-Bi*, are sometimes skilfully tied in to television programming. His new status as a painter segued into the art show *Takeshi's Anyone Can Be Picasso* (*Takeshi no dare de mo Pikaso*), and his turn to colour in *Dolls* linked up with two TV specials on colour sponsored by Canon broadcast around the film's release. Finally, we should never forget that Kitano could not make his films, blessed as they are with certain luxuries, without his industrial position. He enjoys an extremely privileged status no other director in Japan can match.

This status is often credited for creating a film-making space free of industrial concerns, but Kitano's films are fundamentally shaped by his TV work. His peculiar film production schedule, in which he alternates between doing two weeks' worth of shows in one week and one week of film-ing, is overly expensive (since personnel and equipment must be secured even during off weeks) and is only possible because of Kitano's status and the ease of television production. Kitano is also famous for writing a minimal script that is often changed on the set; each film is mostly shot in narrative order, but Kitano can deviate as production progresses and he improvises new ideas. Although Abe Kashō claims Kitano's shooting method constitutes a critique of TV,[62] we should recognise what it shares with television production. Just as Beat Takeshi lacks time to write books, so Kitano Takeshi has little time to produce detailed scripts and storyboards or to conduct extensive rehearsals before filming. Just as he manages multiple TV appearances by improvising, so he shoots his films on the spur of the moment. That is part of his genius, but it is a genius shaped by the television industry. These similarities always threaten to drag his films into the realm of television, and in fact several films, particularly *Sonatine*, *Getting Any?* and *Kikujiro*, have been charged with resembling his television work. Their long sequences of improvised play are emblematic of his cinema, as he often calls film a 'toy' with which he plays with narration and point of view, but they are also an efficient solution to Takeshi's production conditions.

Yet television does not determine the way Kitano produces films. Mori has said it would not be impossible to create a schedule of concentrated film-making (in fact, he had to do that for *Brother*, since it was shot in America).[63] Kitano has opted for his production mode primarily because it offers him time to check and rethink the film's direction. During off weeks, he usually views the rushes and sometimes begins editing. If he senses something is wrong, he may direct his staff to prepare for a re-shoot or for new scenes the next week. His crew also have more time to accommodate those plans. This production mode offers him the same detachment – the opportunity 'to look at myself in the third person'[64] – that he has used in his other activities. It also allows him to focus more on the part of film-making he likes best: editing.[65]

Even if this mode of production shares elements with that of television, it was quite unusual in the context of the Japanese film industry. When Kitano directed his first film, many of the seasoned crew members, who had either started out at the end of the studio era or trained under studio veterans, resisted his shooting style. The Japanese film industry had reached a zenith in 1958 with attendance topping 1.127 billion, and studios had developed a Fordist mode of mass film production that enabled some like Tōei to make more than 100 films a year. The rise of television and shifting population demographics prompted a lengthy slide that culminated with an attendance low of 120 million in 1996. The majors mostly abandoned the studio system, including practices like keeping staff on salary and developing talent. With the big companies no longer making many films, smaller entities were entrusted with the production of product, but not on a scale to enable economies of mass production. Fordist production gave way to a post-Fordist era.

The advent of Kitano symbolised the end of the studio era. The Japanese studio system formulated a strict regimen for becoming a director: college graduates passed a test to enter the studio, after which they worked as an assistant director under established film-makers for a decade or more, writing scripts until finally being allowed to helm their own picture. There were exceptions to this, but exceptions became the rule after the 1970s. Ishii Sōgō and Morita Yoshimitsu directed 35mm features *circa* 1980 with only home-made films under their belt, and established actors such as Itami Jūzō turned to directing as well. In fact, it became so common for stars in other fields to try their hand at directing – mostly with pitiful results – that most critics did not expect much of Kitano. He exemplified this context, but stood out for his achievements.

These accomplishments were the result of his dedication to cinema. Saying that all he did in television was 'supply the brand name Beat Takeshi', he confessed, 'I don't really worry about TV'.[66] He supplied more than that in film. Kitano apparently always has ten or so proposals on hand, from which he selects the next film with Mori. He often says his movies begin with certain images, not stories; recently, he has been putting those together like a four-panel manga, which follows the classical narrative structure of *kishōtenketsu* (*ki* [introduction], *shō* [development], *ten* [transformation], and *ketsu* [conclusion]).[67] The film is fleshed out through a process of deliberation. According to Mori, Kitano meets first with him, and then a number of times with his trusted staff while thinking up the film,

Kitano on the set with Yanagijima

each time explaining the story and obtaining reactions, writing out scenes
and tacking them to the wall.[68] Production is thus collaborative, as Kitano
will give up on an idea if his staff does not like it.[69] This interaction with
others continues on the set, where Kitano will alter his ideas depending on
events on the set and others' opinions. As the title of Shinozaki Makoto's
documentary on the making of *Kikujiro*, *Jam Session* (*Jamu sesshon: Kikujirō
no natsu no kōshiki kaizokuban*, 1999) emphasises, shooting resembles jazz
improvisation, where Kitano lets the film 'develop on its own'.[70] An actor
who was only planned for one scene, like Ōsugi Ren in *Sonatine*, can end up
appearing for the rest of the film. The script changes every day, something
that undermines the rationalisation of production, as sets and scenes prepared beforehand can be cut and never used. Actors cannot really prepare
their lines – which gives impetus to a reduction in dialogue and deadpan
acting – and sets are lit from all sides to accommodate sudden camera
changes.[71] Kitano often observes these events from a distance, using a
stand-in to test scenes in which he appears, and video assist to view what

has been shot. The production itself assumes a rhythm as Kitano shoots quickly, often using the first take, saying he can correct it in editing if it is not perfect. He thus rarely gives specific direction to his actors.

This mode of film-making appears to have been the norm in Kitano's films, the major exception being *Brother*. To the degree that production methods shape the text itself, Kitano's relatively consistent industrial strategy may be evidence undermining the claim that he continually 're-invents' his cinema. But it does not eliminate the issue of periodisation. With each film, subtle changes are reported in his shooting style, as scripts get more detailed and shots and takes more numerous.[72] A larger shift in his film-making will be addressed later in this section.

Cinema versus Explanation

Kitano's peculiar production mode was reported in the first articles about *Violent Cop*, but the surprise registered about this unique mode paled in comparison to that about the film itself. There was a vague sense of a significant difference emerging in Japanese cinema, even though it would take a number of years until critics could narrate this into a history. The major Japanese intellectual journal *Eureka* (*Yuriika*) did a special issue on Japanese cinema in October 1997 that was subtitled 'After Kitano', defining Kitano as the cornerstone of a new era. The film-makers covered in that issue – Kurosawa Kiyoshi, Aoyama Shinji, Tsukamoto Shin'ya, Zeze Takahisa, Miike Takashi, Kawase Naomi, Nakata Hideo, Koreeda Hirokazu, etc. – are now the familiar faces of 1990s' Japanese film. Kitano was thought to delineate this new generation.[73]

At the time of *Dolls*' release in 2002, the film magazine *Kinema junpō* surveyed eleven prominent film critics about when they first became conscious of Kitano and why. Ueno Kōshi cited 'a sinister brutality completely different from the representation of violence in Japanese cinema up until that point'; Watanabe Takenobu found that Kitano had 'decided to intentionally misdirect the techniques he learned from' film history; and Higuchi Naofumi said he focused on the pendulum swings between the 'cold-hearted' and the 'lyrical'. Terawaki Ken succinctly placed Kitano in context:

In the 1980s, as television dramas garnered widespread support from a young generation through a group of hit series called 'trendy dramas', Japanese cinema also had the tendency to follow TV's example in being easy to understand. A kind of cinema was in demand that, beyond preparing a clear story, used so much explanatory dialogue that the audience could understand the movie without much effort. . . .

At a time when easy-to-understand palatability was in demand – when one feared that the trend towards over-explanation was seriously constricting Japanese cinema – Kitano's brusque direction, refusing to cater to the audience, seemed fresh. He doesn't communicate this or that with dialogue, but expresses his ideas without words. The characters glare at each other, without relating their anger or resentment in words, and engage in sublime violence in silence.[74]

At the beginning then, Kitano was interpreted primarily in contrast to a certain cinematic context. He was an oppositional film-maker, but not necessarily in political terms; his enemy was another kind of film-making, one associated with two central terms: explanation (*setsumei*) and television.

Japanese cinema in the 1980s may have exuded the aura of postmodern pastiche, moving away from heavy politics to play with the classics of Japanese and Western cinema (Itami's *Tampopo* [1985] is a familiar example), but that surface lightness was often burdened with excess signification. This was less Peter Greenaway's flood of floating signifiers, than an even more redundant version of the redundancy of classical cinema, absolutely ensuring viewer comprehension by doubling narrative explanation. Not only did close-ups and editing analyse space for the audience, but dialogue repeated what the visuals had already said and music made sure nothing was lost. Yamada Yōji, the director of the Tora-san films, was probably the one most referenced in opposition to Kitano for his explanatory excess and do-good thematics. Yamada epitomised less the work of younger 1980s' directors, than the remnants of the old-left film-making of Imai Tadashi and Yamamoto Satsuo. Kitano himself said the Tora-san movies had 'degraded Japanese cinema',[75] and pointed out, in an interview with Hasumi Shigehiko, a difference between *A Scene at the Sea* and Yamada's *My Sons* (*Musuko*, 1991), films that both featured deaf characters:

HASUMI: You resist having everyone understand the film, don't you?

KITANO: That's right. There's something I hate about that. That's why I can't at all understand why anyone would shoot a movie like *My Sons* with that kind of title. . . . We lived through an age where we absolutely hated that kind of thing. You can see everything behind it. *A Scene at the Sea* is about the deaf, so if Yamada had shot it, he would have made such a wonderful tearjerker that I should have given the script to him (laughs). If he'd shot it right, it would've been a gentle movie that the PTA and their ilk would have been just thrilled with.[76]

Kitano's complaints resemble Beat Takeshi's skewering of postwar do-gooders, but they also express an aversion to a cinema that is transparent and obvious, wet and emotional. He was criticising movies that smugly knew right and wrong, curried favour with institutional elites, and then forced themselves on spectators through an overly redundant style.

Similar grievances were lodged against contemporary television. Abe Kashō focused on Japanese television in his conception of Kitano Takeshi battling Beat Takeshi. To Abe, Japanese television is a space where the answer for every question is prepared beforehand, pre-digested and easy to consume. Offering no real disagreements, television loses the distinction between subject and object and absorbs everything in a homogeneous identity. There is no alterity in this space, for television ultimately only refers to itself. Abe sees 'Beat Takeshi' as part and parcel of this system, his tendency to talk without really saying anything rendering him a 'light'(*kihaku*) semiotic existence. What saves Beat Takeshi, according to Abe, is the fact his body still presents itself in flashes, offering a material weight that Kitano Takeshi later utilises to combat the Beat Takeshi of television.[77]

Abe does not really cover the stylistic issues, but it is those that concerned Kitano the most. He once told a group of film students that

I think it's sufficient to have only two close-ups in a film. The NHK TV series *Aguri* just infuriates me. It's nothing but close-ups. I can't understand the sensibility that shows close-ups all the time even though human beings have individual sizes, from their head to their toes.[78]

His complaint was not only against the homogenisation of human differ-ence, but also against excess signification.

> If you look at a good *manzai* comedian, he doesn't say a single, unnecessary word. Even 'ah' or 'oh' are absolutely necessary lines. . . . But it really annoys me when I watch regular TV dramas. They have all this unnecessary dialogue. . . . even though they could just do it simply, just the essence. For example, even though there's only one person the character is talking to, they do things like, 'Hey, Tanaka!' But Tanaka is right there! Just 'Hey!' would suffice.[79]

Kitano pared down the dialogue of his own films, but not, as in the skits in *We're the Clown Tribe*, to ensure comprehension:

> With skits, you have to make the viewer completely understand. Making infer-ences is not enough. . . . So we always shot it carefully, but when I went into film, I was sick of the shooting style we did on TV. This time, I'd make the audience figure it out.[80]

This was essential to his aim of avoiding what he called 'kusai' (literally 'stinky') – what was hackneyed, over-emotional, conventional and fake. Eliminating excess explanation was thus aligned with Takeshi's honesty/*home*, but we shall see it had cinematic implicators too.

Hasumi and Kitano

Kitano's cinema, and that coming 'after Kitano', aimed to forbear expla-nation and combat TV's tendency to reduce all to a homogeneous identity. We have to understand why these issues were cinematically important, and what discursive contexts lent them priority. To do that, we must consider the influence of Hasumi Shigehiko, a man central in shaping both film crit-icism and film-making after the 1970s. Hasumi was a scholar of French literature at – and later president of – the University of Tokyo, as well as a film critic who, along with Yamane Sadao, fundamentally transformed the way films were talked about in Japan. Previous criticism was largely impres-sionist, as the critic spoke of what the film made her think about. In the

1960s, the common referents were politics and the other arts, but Hasumi and Yamane charged that this reduced films to political declarations or to the aesthetic standards of other media. They advocated criticism that treated cinema as cinema and bracketed out other considerations.

Crucial was their definition of the medium. Influenced by post-structuralist French theory, albeit in peculiar ways, Hasumi refused to offer a systematic film theory, or even pay much attention to unified narratives, preferring instead to focus on diverse moments in films, ranging from Godard to Hollywood B-movies, that offered a glimpse of cinema irreducible to words. Hasumi's most influential work was *Director Ozu Yasujirō (Kantoku Ozu Yasujirō)*,[81] which set the standard in Japan for looking not only at Ozu, but also at cinema itself. He rejects the notion that Ozu is a minimalist because it presumes that film is a plenitude that Ozu, in his perversity, has turned his back on. Cinema is instead pictured as an inherently limited medium that Ozu is one of the few to recognise in its true fullness. For example, Hasumi asserts it is impossible to show two sets of eyes looking at each other in a single shot. Editing can of course provide that impression, but to Hasumi that is an excess that conceals the true boundaries of film. The brilliance of Ozu, he argues, is his ability to both acknowledge that limitation by refusing proper eyeline matches, yet still create a rich drama of gazes. Here, as elsewhere, Hasumi valorises creations that achieve their results without relying on means external to the proper limits of film, that can in effect do what is impossible in cinema while only relying on cinema. For instance, Hasumi and his followers frequently assert that film is a medium concerned with the external inherently unable to portray psychology. They do not reject character psychology; what is valorised is the 'impossible' rendering of internal thoughts from without, not through tricks like close-ups and point-of-view shots. Hasumi's view of cinema was considered materialist in this regard, emphasising film-making rooted in film's materiality. It rejected idealism that tied films to social or political ideas; cinema ultimately signified only cinema, and nothing more. This can be seen as another reaction against the age of ideals, snubbing politics for a medium that offered no transcendental truths, only itself.

The influence of Hasumi and his view of Ozu was immense, extending beyond criticism into the realm of production. Students of his at Tokyo and Rikkyō universities, where he was an auxiliary teacher, who have become film directors include Kurosawa Kiyoshi, Suo Masayuki, Shinozaki Makoto, Aoyama Shinji, Shiota Akihiko, Nakata Hideo and Manda Kunitoshi. One could just as easily name the new period of Japanese film 'after Hasumi' as 'after Kitano'. And Hasumi was one of Kitano's most influential supporters. He interviewed the director numerous times, wrote about him in magazines and in the official pamphlets for his films, and even hosted the 'Takeshi Kitano International Symposium' at the 1996 Tokyo International Film Festival alongside Yamane. Hasumi, however, was always rather deferential towards Kitano, rarely imposing his own opinion in interviews or offering a concerted polemic about his films. That was left more to Yamane and Shinozaki. Shinozaki is arguably Kitano's best interviewer, a fact Kitano has probably recognised by hiring the young director to do the 'making of' documentary for *Kikujiro* and the TV movie adaptation of *Asakusa Kid*. While it would be hard to say that Hasumi directly influenced Kitano's initial films, he and his followers established the discursive context that both greeted his films and shaped their reception.

Shinozaki began his first interview article on Kitano, published in *Cahiers du cinema Japon* in the summer of 1991,[82] by declaring that the 'blood of cinema' flows through the director's veins. This rooted Kitano's body in the essence of cinema and his film-making in a non-conceptual, non-linguistic approach. With Hasumi also declaring that Takeshi's methodology is 'close to being completely unconscious',[83] such claims valorised Kitano as existing outside the established world of filmic learning, working like a primitive in ignorance of the excesses of cinematic civilisation, but therefore closer to its origin.[84] Kitano's primitiveness aligned him with what was considered the ineffability of cinema, its distance from the realm of language. An example of this was his tendency to excise the literary word (dialogue) and other forms of explanation. Shinozaki analysed the scene where Azuma checks his sister out of the hospital in *Violent Cop*, emphasising how Kitano 'completely cut explanatory dialogue' but still managed to suggest Akari's mental handicap by 'making manifest a cinematic space-time within extremely concrete images and sounds that transcend narrative'. It was the specific material elements of cinema, not what was external to it – words or narrative – that created meaning. Kitano's cinema was seen as a process of subtraction – not minimalism[85] – stripping away not only what was unnecessary, but also what might be too meaningful. Kitano's own example was Nitō's bare office in *Violent Cop*, from which he removed all the art department put in; many others have cited his creation of 'Kitano blue', an almost monochromatic scheme in which bright colours have been excised to leave a bluish tone dominating the screen.[86]

Kitano's films were pictured as divorced from conventional narrative. To Yamane, writing about *A Scene at the Sea*,

> He purposely removes all cinematic elements usually thought essential to establish the narrative. This film-making audaciously pursued with nothing hidden, succeeds marvellously. So what is the basis of its means of expression? The deep emotion ardently appeals to us only through the rhythm of the shots and the movement of the characters, and only that. It does not rely at all on linguistic explanation. Devoted to visual and character action, the purely cinematic elements of action and musicality end up founding the mode of expression here. In a sense, one can say that a sort of 'pure cinema' has been impressively realised.[87]

Other critics just noted a silent-film aesthetics, but Yamane stressed a cinema on the verge of breaking up: 'This methodless method would probably be impossible for an established film director. Of course the film (*A Scene at the Sea*) breaks down in a lot of sections, but even with that, it crystallises a fresh, cinematic fascination.'[88]

Shinozaki, Yamane and others would focus on techniques that undermined or caused the narrative to stagnate, such as long shots offering little factual information, long takes with dead time at the beginning and end of the shot, and still shots where characters stand, with blank faces, and do little. This first worked to strip characters of excess psychology. Shinozaki quoted Tenma Toshihiro, assistant director on three of Kitano's first four

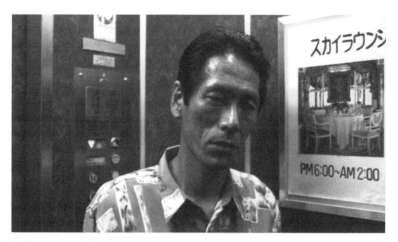

Deadpan acting in *Sonatine*

films: 'Normal film-making pursues the psychology of the characters, but
Kitano absolutely refuses to do that. In fact, when [psychology] emerges, he
rejects it.'[89] Also introducing Kitano's treatment of actors, especially his
tendency to cut away meaningful gestures, Shinozaki concluded that, 'The
actors, forbidden from acting, appear on screen as a bare existence. What
Kitano Takeshi demands of them is not so-called "fine performances", but
a corporeality that inscribes his (or her) existence into the image.'[89] This
explained the motionless, poker-faced acting, the poverty of character
interaction where bystanders do not react even if someone is shot before
their eyes. To Shinozaki, emotions are only presented through such external means as spatial configuration, blocking, gesture, etc. To some
observers, the blank, almost empty characters in Kitano's films evoke a
kind of existentialism, and that would be correct to the degree that they are
defined not by their essence but by their existence. The above view of
Kitano, however, would balk at ascribing existential angst to his characters
for the very reason that the psychologism such a portrayal requires is considered absent from his films.

What is supposedly rendered naked here is not just the characters, but
the film itself. Some commentators went to the clumsy extreme of arguing

that films like *A Scene at the Sea* lacked narratives, but Shinozaki and Yamane were more precise. Narration is stagnated through an 'idle time' (*muina jikan*), one manifested in the periods of play featured prominently in films like *Sonatine* and *Kikujiro*. Some may have tried to psychologise that as the calm before the storm, but Yamane, claiming that *Sonatine* lacked real drama, sharp editing, climactic scenes, or even a theme or a message, said that 'there is cinema and only cinema', a 'naked film' (*hadaka no eiga*), a 'zero point film' (*zero chiten no eiga*).[91] Shinozaki echoed that by citing Kitano's decision to avoid morally clear characters in *A Scene at the Sea*, precisely so that he could avert 'the entire movie becoming a lie . . . a social problem film'.

> Kitano's cinema is not so weak as to be absorbed into a single ideology. To begin with, it is completely divorced from the vulgar ambition to say something using cinema as a means. Kitano Takeshi is not trying to depict something using film, but rather aiming to manifest something that can only be represented in film.[92]

This discourse, while influential, also had problems. While trying to avoid reducing cinema to what is external to it, some of Hasumi's followers fall into reiterating tautologies of cinema=cinema. The aim is to prevent making film subservient to language, but then the language of criticism can descend into the masturbatory laudation of cinema. Very frequently, it lacks precision because it is still essentially impressionist criticism. Critics like Abe Kashō and Suzuki Hitoshi[93] have written lengthy works on Kitano that can be occasionally brilliant, but also descend into flights of fancy that stray from the text. More worrisome is the compulsion to divorce Kitano's cinema from TV. When Shinozaki claims you must forget Beat Takeshi in order to discuss Kitano,[94] the effect is to block a thorough investigation of the relation of not only Kitano's films, but recent Japanese cinema in general, to television. Such a stoppage can eventually construct cinema as a fetishistic object, hindering investigations of film's political economy and why criticism itself is clinging to cinema.

The Politics of Cinema

While the obsession with cinema sometimes functioned as an obfuscation device, there nonetheless was a politics behind this discourse and its appropriation of Kitano, an effort to criticise the status quo and change the motion pictures. First, it was a concerted effort to oppose a dominant conventional cinema. The nature of that cinema, and Kitano's difference from it, is ironically evident in a notorious essay by Kasahara Kazuo, a scriptwriter for many Tōei yakuza films, including some of Fukasaku Kinji's, that lambasted *A Scene at the Sea*. Kasahara outlined the ten 'fundamentals' (*koppō*) of storytelling that Kitano broke in the film, including failing to provide suspense, obstacles, villains, decisive moments, climaxes and a central theme.[95] Kasahara's complaints could constitute a scenarist's defence against someone who avoided a standard script,[96] but they also illuminate how *A Scene at the Sea* differs from the typical rendition of the same narrative. Kasahara offered several such versions himself. For instance, in describing how the film could better construct narrative obstacles, he proposed this narrative:

> Takako falls in love with Shigeru, who shares her disability. The people at work look down at Shigeru. Takako wants to provide him with strength and a dream, so when Shigeru picks up a broken surfboard, she suggests he try it. To respect her feelings for him, Shigeru reluctantly begins to ride the waves. He eventually conquers his disability and joins the ranks of skilled surfers. Seeing that Shigeru has gained strength, Takako wants to move Shigeru away from surfing because the sea, in the end, is a dangerous place for the disabled, and because her goal has been achieved. But unable to express themselves in words, the two cannot fully communicate their feelings. Shigeru tries to heighten his skill to further please Takako, and ventures out into a stormy sea. A tragedy occurs, their love shattered because they each tried to act out of regard for the other. Takako refuses to be separated from Shigeru and follows him into the depths of the sea.[97]

Kasahara does not necessary advocate this version as the best, but he utilises it to condemn *A Scene at the Sea* for not providing such narrative conflicts.

Other film critics appropriated these 'failures' as badges of honour, praising Kitano for his refusal to follow conventional cinema. Early writings on Kitano celebrate an almost violent difference from dominant film-making practices. What was wrong with the kind of film Kasahara represented? One could see objections coming from two political fronts: the reclaiming of the real and the recognition of the other. First, even though Shinozaki, in classic Hasumiesque fashion, rigorously avoids claiming realism in Kitano's work (because film cannot be subservient to any reality but its own), he nonetheless exhibits certain Bazinian affinities. Using Kitano as an example, he asserts that, 'What a film director needs is not intelligence or rich experience, but an animal-like sense of smell, the reflexes and appropriate powers of judgment to deal with the incidents and problems that occur on the set.' This again praised Kitano's primitiveness, but now through a point Hasumians often made: that films were made on the set or on location (*genba*). This assertion was not always true of Kitano, given his reliance on editing, but it echoes the traditions of European art cinema, influenced by the realism of André Bazin, that refused to determine a film either in the pre-production stage, or in the editing afterwards. To Shinozaki, 'filming is the encounter with something unknown',[98] and should emerge from dynamic interaction with the reality before the camera. Kitano was thus praised not only for his improvisation on the set, but also for downplaying the screenplay. Many film-makers in the 'after Kitano' generation also subscribed to the '*genba*' philosophy, especially directors like Aoyama, Kawase, Koreeda and Suwa Nobuhiro who had also worked in documentary. Suwa, for instance, did not use a script for his films *Duo* (1997) and *M/Other* (1999).

This is a discourse on realism that, while not forming the core of opinions on Kitano, crisscrosses it in crucial ways. Kitano often justified his work by contrasting it to the unreality of genres like the romance and the yakuza film.[99] His preference for changing styles was even justified by his fear that, if he continued with the same old violence, for instance, it would lose its reality.[100] This shows his strong aversion to falling into the clichéd mannerisms of pre-1990s' cinema, which were seen as no longer reflecting a changing reality. The desire for an alternative cinema was aligned with criticism of the superficiality of the bubble economy and the social and cultural bankruptcy of post-bubble Japan. Kitano was seen as offering *honne*/honesty, though again without the conventions of social realism, which were themselves seen as bogus. Suwa, for instance, distanced himself from such 'realism', while seeking out what he and many others called 'the real' (*riaru*).[101] While aware of Hasumi's dictate that film is ultimately film, many thought that radical, if not violent techniques like those of Kitano could, in Hasumian fashion, render possible an impossibility, like discovering emotion in a blank face, or a glimpse of the real in an artificial medium. Kitano was seen as offering a 'lack', a 'vacant space'[102] that expelled all meaning, undermining all forms of conventional knowledge and offering a hint of the real before meaning. The sudden intrusions of violence into the stillness, the narrative breaks and editing mismatches kept the spectator insecure and off guard, unable to rest assured about their knowledge of this film world.

Another problem with conventional cinema was its tendency to absorb and negate the other. Suwa once told my class, 'There is no other in the script', and by that he meant that the screenplay, by being an intellectual exercise often undertaken alone, never confronts a truly external, unknown existence but arises in a secluded world. Aversion to the script and celebration of the 'location/*genba*', both of which found an example in Kitano, were means of acknowledging an 'other' reality. Dominant film-making was criticised for absorbing or ignoring the other both through a self-circulating perpetuation of convention and the processes of explanation itself, which domesticate difference by knowing it. This absorption was politically volatile because it was a cinematic case of what Japanese national ideology, epitomised by the emperor system, was performing on the levels of culture and political economy. Myths of Japanese homogeneity have long obfuscated real internal divisions by eliding minorities like Ainu, Okinawans or ethnic Koreans, and by domesticating difference, including waves of globalisation, through stereotype, conventional knowledge, and reinforcement of an insular 'Japan' that has never changed.

Representing the other thus has political dimensions. Note that the word 'other' (*tasha*) here has different connotations from that in Western theory.

The sociologist Miyahara Kōjirō uses Kitano to make a distinction. The 'horizontal other', a term approximating Western theory's 'other', signifies groups marginal to normal society, but still on the same plane because they are 'known'; they are the others that dominant groups create to distinguish their own identity. To Miyahara, Kitano offers in scenes like the Russian roulette game in *Sonatine* the 'shock of the other' in a different sense, one he calls the 'vertical other'. This is an 'other' that exceeds the plane of dominant knowledge, 'an existentially alien substance' that resists identification because it is not like 'us' – because it possesses an 'absolute alterity'[103] not a difference easily explained. This other, which disturbs, not confirms constructions of identity, became the focus of many of the 'after Kitano' generation.

Aoyama Shinji, the director of such works as *Helpless* (1997) and *Eureka* (2000), was probably the film-maker who best theorised these issues in the 1990s. Distinguishing himself from the humanist film-making of the old left, Aoyama declared that his was a 'materialistic cinematic practice that runs counter to what is generally called "depicting humanity" or "depicting sympathy"'.[104] Far from assuming a shared humanity that can allow communication with the 'other', Aoyama asserted an impenetrability to the

Detached long shot in *Sonatine*

Zomahoun and the primitive black body

'other' as the basis of a different politics. Rejecting the political work of
1960s' Japanese New Wave directors such as Ōshima and Imamura, he
stated that a true new wave is 'nothing other than a discourse duelling over
the sole point of how to treat the other from a political perspective',[105] and
argued that such politics must recognise the unknowablity of the 'other'.

Such ideas lay at the foundation of what I term the 'detached style', a
mode of film-making that became prominent in 1990s' independent
Japanese cinema, defined by an aversion to devices that normally provide
knowledge of 'others' in film. These can include close-ups, point-of-view
shots and other subjective devices, analytical editing and similar means of
pre-digesting space for the spectator. While some could call this a post-
classical style, it is rooted in particular sociopolitical issues in contemporary Japan. When Aoyama once asked a panel at the 2000 Vienna Film
Festival to think about the relationship of the close-up and the emperor
system, he was challenging the way such devices can absorb others within
dominant systems of knowledge (recall Nibuya's 'violence of the camera').
Films in the detached style then detach the camera from their objects, using
long-shot long takes to respect the other in its alterity (which is why most
reject 'music video'-style editing as well). While elements of this style can

be seen in the work of a variety of 1990s' film-makers including Aoyama, Suwa, Kurosawa, Kawase, Koreeda, Zeze, Sono Shion, Takenaka Naoto and Shiota Akihiko, Kitano's early films served as one inspiration, if not model for this. Kitano's case, however, reminds us that few 'pure' examples of the detached style existed, since he could, for instance, combine long takes with close-up bursts of violence. The detached style was also essentially anti-aesthetic, since aestheticisation itself was a means of appropriating the other. Long takes, however, could sometimes fall into aestheticism, as is evident with Koreeda and the later Kitano.

Representing the Other: Empty Masculinity

Many 1990s' film-makers treated 'the other from a political perspective' through not just stylistic detachment, but also filming the ethnic and sexual others long suppressed in Japanese film. For example, Hashiguchi Ryōsuke explored gay life, Zeze, Miike and Yamamoto Masashi looked at Asian immigrants and Sai Yōichi took up both Okinawa and his own culture of resident Koreans. Kitano, stringently avoiding the social-message film, never made the problems of minorities the centre of his work, but minorities appear nonetheless. There are the physically disabled like the deaf couple in *A Scene at the Sea* and the paraplegic comedian in *Dolls*; the ethnic and racial minorities ranging from Denny in *Brother* to Zomahoun's characters in *Takeshis'*; and the many with homosexual tendencies, from Uehara in *Boiling Point* to the make-up artist in *Takeshis'*. Marginal spaces like Okinawa also figure prominently.

The question is how he has represented such figures. This is not an easy issue because in some cases his representations are disturbing. The black woman in *Boiling Point* appears to have no function other than to contrast with the white sand, and Zomahoun, although initially appearing in intelligent African dress, soon descends into the naked, primitive physicality Japanese culture has often imposed upon the black body.[106] Kitano's depiction of women is also problematic. While Kishimoto Kayoko has portrayed some strong women in *Kikujiro* and *Takeshis'*, the grand majority of Kitano's women are silent and docile, subserviently following their men. As in *Dolls*, some may be victims of male insensitivity, but such a narrative, as well as the women's reactions to it (e.g., insanity), is straight out of 1950s' melodrama. To the feminist critic Ishihara Ikuko, Takeshi's characters treat women in one of two ways: 'either coldly, not recognising their value from the start, or the opposite, giving them special treatment, as if they are heavenly. Neither case offers a normal relationship between a man and a woman.'[107] He thus treats women, according to Ishihara, like he does most of his characters, as things not human beings; those who are different are never offered as partners in sexual reproduction but are associated with death. Misogyny hovers in the background when films like *Kikujiro* and *Hana-Bi* portray women betraying men. It is thus disturbing that two of the most prominent expressions of male–female love in Kitano's work both involve Beat Takeshi's character shooting a woman. Kitano has earned a reputation for being unable to depict women and he himself confesses to being too embarrassed to portray sex. What emerges from this discomfort is sometimes violence, as rape figures in his early films. Love slides into violence and thus ultimately aligns with death. Such misogyny may fit with Beat Takeshi's subversive persona at home, but it is less palatable abroad, and so, argues Darrell Davis, Kitano conceals it with aesthetic views of the nation.[108]

Kitano's depictions of others, particularly gendered others, is disturbing, but we should not ignore the subtle complications. We could say, for instance, that Kitano's bold use of Okinawa as a liminal space undermining Japanese national identities takes on none of the realities Okinawans face as a minority culture in Japan, but they still circumvent conventional views of Okinawa.[109] On the question of masculinity, Isolde Standish argues that:

> Kitano (Beat) Takeshi's star persona is predicated on a spontaneous masculinity which draws on iconic meanings of stoicism and 'reflexive masculinity' institutionalized in the 1960s through the star persona of such heroes as Takakura Ken and the 1950s idol Ishihara Yūjirō.[110]

Mark Schilling also notes some of the parallels, but he rightly argues that Kitano's 'dirty heroes' 'are a far cry indeed from the noble stoics of 60s' icon Takakura Ken' and that the director 'rejected both the classically structured formulas of Shundō [producer of Tōei's 'chivalric' (*ninkyō*) yakuza series] and the chaotic semi-documentary realism of Fukasaku'.[111] Kitano's heroes do project masculinity, one that fans have found cool and attractive, but, at least in his early films, it is a scarred or warped masculinity. Uehara in *Boiling Point* reveals traits exactly opposite to Takakura, possessing none of the duty or 'gaman' (patient endurance) central to *ninkyō* heroes. Given how Nakamura Hideyuki defines the whole of Kitano's cinema as the 'picture of an external wound',[112] we must understand the duality of seemingly tough guys who are deeply-scarred, ranging from the blind Zatōichi to the guilt-ridden Nishi in *Hana-Bi*. Kitano's heroes are too lonely to be cool lone-wolf yakuza.

Wounded, if not castrated, masculinity was a central cultural issue in Japan after its defeat in World War II, a problem that Nikkatsu Action (with stars like Ishihara Yūjirō) and Tōei yakuza films attempted to solve by offering more perfect male bodies in fictional spaces. Seventies' cinema recognises the wound, featuring numerous depictions of scarred masculinity, like in the films of Hasegawa Kazuhiko (*The Youth Killer* [*Seishun no satsujinsha*, 1976]). Such problems would be concealed – or perhaps exacerbated – by the rise of a feminised girl/*shōjo* culture in the 1980s. Kitano represents a reconsideration of masculinity, but a masculinity that self-consciously borders on the empty. This is evident first in the childishness of Kitano's space of play – and thus the absence of full-scale adult sexual masculinity – but also in gender ambiguities that reduce male identity to zero. Unlike the violence of contemporary Hollywood action cinema (or that of Hong Kong), which, as Yvonne Tasker argues, attempts to reconstruct masculine vitality through a utopian fantasy of bodily control over others,[113] Kitano's violence heads towards self-annihilation. This is partially due to the lack of female sexuality in the early films. Kitano takes the homosocial space of the action film, which maintains a precarious balance between masculine camaraderie and the rejection of homosexuality, and pushes it to the extreme through characters like Uehara, who is just as willing to bugger his buddy as fuck his moll. Kitano's treatment of homosexuality seems ambivalent, demonising it in *Violent Cop*, normalising it in *Zatoichi* and rendering it the butt of jokes in *Takeshis'*, but he is more willing to foreground the homosexuality of homosociality than Hollywood action cinema.

What is important in Kitano is less the depiction of the homosexual other than the representation of a space that lacks the other. As Abe Kashō notes, Uehara basically exists before or outside of distinction, be it gender or subjective identity: he registers little difference between men and women just as he fails to distinguish between cutting off his own finger and that of his lieutenant. Not differentiating himself from others, he essentially is a self without an other. In a replication of Kitano's stylistic logic of subtraction, Uehara's group subtracts its others, starting with the black woman, then Masaki and Kazuo, and finally Uehara's moll. What remains, as one would expect of a self without an other, is an empty shell – an external wound. This could be the *reductio ad absurdum* of Japanese masculinity, showing the nothingness that results when cool men declare, as Tetsu does at the end of Suzuki Seijun's gangster flick *Tokyo Drifter* (Tokyo nagaremono, 1966), that 'I can't walk with women.' At the end of this path is death, so perhaps we can say the other Kitano's early cinema pursues is less a specific minority, than the otherness of otherlessness itself, the alterity of a space without established structures of difference that found meaning. His films can be quite ambivalent towards this space. On the one hand, they may criticise it as the deathly emptiness that must logically result from Japanese national ideology's effacement of others/minorities; on the other hand, they may desire it as a radical vacancy undermining the oppression of knowledge, a pleasurable though sometimes childish place of nothingness before difference, meaning and adult sexuality. The tension between these two informs much of his early work, and helps explain Kitano's ambivalent stance towards gender and sexuality.

The Reversal, Genre and Periodisation

Kitano's early cinema was thus produced and received at a particularly volatile point in Japanese film history, when the relationship of the image to national ideology was under question and an established cinema was being criticised for its unreality. While there are moments of tension and ambivalence in his work that make it difficult to call him the model for combating these political and cinematic norms, his early films served as both an inspiration and example to film-makers, even if it would be hard to find a director who copied him in style and stance (although some, from Takenaka to Aoyama, have been accused of borrowing too much). Kitano encouraged this oppositional image by calling himself the 'cancer' or 'virus' of Japanese cinema and its postwar culture.[114]

This image, and the stylistic elements that helped support it, such as long takes, deadpan acting, narrative stagnation and intrusions of sudden violence, continued to dominate accounts of Kitano's auteurist traits, even up until his recent films. But one could point to later films as evidence of Kitano backtracking on his earlier stances. The director who had declared 'I think it's sufficient to have only two close-ups in a film' ended up using far more than that in *Zatoichi*. Films from *Kids Return* on began to abandon the long-shot long-take style as the camera gets closer, the average shot length shorter and camera movement more deliberate and expressive. The jarring mismatches between shots receded as more classically edited scenes came to the fore. Breaks and interruptions continued to define Kitano's style, but these were now more motivated (especially through character psychology) and inserted within a larger continuity. At the time of *Sonatine*, Kitano had expressed his disinterest in facilitating audience understanding,[115] but lines such as Kikujirō's at the bus stop declaring that Masao is just like him, increasingly state the obvious. The images he uses, from the angel in *Kikujiro* to the colour symbolism in *Dolls*, can also border on the clichéd, giving visual evidence for his recent statements that he now sought to shape some films for all to understand.

A number of his supporters were vocal about their disappointment. Sono Shion, who directed some of the more extreme examples of the detached style such as *The Room* (Heya, 1992), drew a strong opposition between the cruel and unsentimental films of a 'real artist' (his examples are Kitano, Fukasaku and Kawashima Yōzō), and those that curry favour with the masses through emotion. He then fiercely criticised Kitano for making sentimental works like *A Scene at the Sea*.[116] Other directors like Aoyama published critiques of his work as the general opinion of his films declined in Japan after *Hana-Bi*, just as he was making a name for himself abroad.[117] In fact, a common complaint was that Kitano's later work abandoned radical experimentation to more consciously seek success, especially at foreign film festivals.[118] The film theorist Kimura Tatsuya, who found in *Hana-Bi* none of the shocking unpredictability of *Sonatine*, wrote this of the former: 'The only way to justify this state of affairs . . . would be to say capturing festival awards helps Kitano make more films.'[119]

To some, these shifts were registered on the level of genre and mode of narration. Although Kitano's work always touched on genre, especially the yakuza or the hard-boiled detective film, he was generally perceived, in Jean-Michel Frodon's words, as 'a director who has made a genre solely for himself'.[120] Kitano was seen to undermine convention through gaps and slippages that were unique to his film-making. One could argue that Kitano's primary form of narration in early works like *Boiling Point* was parametric, to borrow David Bordwell's term. There cinematic style creates its own order, motivated not by meaning or plot, but by the purely artistic concerns of film form.[121] This becomes less the case from *Kids Return* on, when art-cinema narrative takes precedence as film style becomes more motivated by psychology and artistic statement. Conventional genre also returns as a film like *Brother* valorises the elements of the yakuza film that *Sonatine* and *Boiling Point* had criticised. As a result of these shifts, a frustrated fan could write in reaction to *Dolls*, 'I hope Kitano doesn't succumb to his worst impulses and start turning out the kinds of movies he used to lampoon, or subvert, or do better.'[122]

The narrative of Kitano's constant change partially served as a response to these doubts. Complaining that Kitano had betrayed his principles missed the point because his more radical stance undermined all attempts to impose principles, challenging the spectator and pulling the rug out from under the film critical establishment. This can also be a critique of politics as a static set of principles and goals because one cannot expect a trickster to settle on a single stance. Perhaps Kitano was going even one step further than the detached style by rendering himself the ultimate other, one unknowable and indefinable. Kitano's early works exhibit tensions and ambivalences not found in less imaginative, detached-style cinema, complexities that make his work both challenging and fascinating. To reduce Kitano's cinema to a broader cinematic politics threatens to lose sight of its productive gaps and contradictions.

The danger, however, of using Kitano the trickster to explain these shifts is that it can cut off debate, de-legitimising attempts to generalise issues of style and context in his work. That resembles Hasumi's position, since it foregrounds the 'unexpected eruptions of . . . "extraordinary" instants' of cinema in his films,[123] over their stylistic, political or genre connections. Few have yet to truly theorise the political implications of Kitano's constant transformations, especially not to the level of Gilles Deleuze's notions of the rhizomatic or the body without organs, which it may resemble.[124] This lack of theorisation is a broader problem in postwar Japanese film culture that Abé Mark Nornes has discussed in relation to documentary,[125] but here it can exemplify the potential cynicism of this politics itself, which replaces concerted political action with destructive opposition for opposition's sake. Cutting off debate prevents us from seeing how Kitano's trickster image may be less guerrilla humour than an escape into equivocation, one that manifests the rise of apathetic conservatism in contemporary Japan. The case of Kitano ultimately raises practical questions about the political potentials of comedy, the efficacy of constant subversion or deferral, and the ideological role of theory in legitimising these practices.

One can argue that Kitano, far from being a trickster undermining categorisation, has in fact embraced such categories in his more conventional and genre-based recent work. It is here that the issue of periodisation arises: whether we can delineate distinct moments in Kitano's film-making career. The trickster argument is a denial of periodisation, as is its opposite, the assertion of total consistency from first film to last. But most commentators, including the director himself, have described periods in Kitano's work. The most prominent method has been to divide his career on or around *Kids Return* and *Hana-Bi*, but for different reasons. Many have used the bike accident to argue a thematic shift from a concern for death to a pursuit of life; others have cited the *Hana-Bi*'s award at Venice as separating a pure Kitano, free from outside concerns, from one sullied by success. Tony Rayns has seen a shift from the personal to less personal work in *Brother* and *Dolls*.[126] Bob Davis contrasts the early 'amateur' from the post-*Kids Return* 'auteur', the one who declares at Venice, 'I am the Master!'[127] Kitano's statements have sometimes been ambiguous about this, but in general he has narrated an evolution of skill, where his early films were simply 'bad' or reflected a lack of willingness to tackle cinematic issues.[128] His figure of the pendulum is another narrative, albeit one that is more cyclical.

Some have suggested more complex phases. Yamane Sadao has used the narrative structure 'kishōtenketsu' to argue for four-film groupings of his work, with *Sonatine* constituting the 'conclusion' of the first period.[129] Kitano has suggested three periods: the first up until the accident, the second a period of rehabilitation ending in *Brother*, and a third beginning with *Dolls*.[130] Picking up on that, Tsutsumi Ryuichiro has offered a strongly structuralist periodisation of Kitano's work, one which argues not only distinct themes in each period – or 'project', as he terms it – but that each concluding film must be the major statement on that period's theme (as he says *Brother* is on the theme of doubling).[131] Such formalised accounts of Kitano's career can provide productive hypotheses, but they also illustrate the problems of periodisation: that it obfuscates differences unsuitable to the structure (as Tsutsumi, for example, downplays figures of doubling in the first films) and prioritises internal structural imperatives over socioeconomic and other determinations. Any investigation of change in Kitano's work must balance internal and external determinants while not reducing the specificity of change to broad sociocultural generalisations.

Periodisation is so fraught with problems that some have simply conceived of different Kitano Takeshis existing simultaneously. Higuchi Naofumi has argued that there are two kinds of Kitano films. First, the comparatively popular 'evasive' ones (*hagurakasu eiga*) such as *A Scene at the Sea*, *Kids Return*, *Hana-Bi*, *Kikujiro*, *Brother* and *Zatoichi* that deceive us with 'a clear story based on psychological cause and effect'; and second, the less popular 'divergent' ones (*zureru eiga*), such as *Boiling Point*, *Getting Any?* and *Takeshis'* that focus on evasion itself at the expense of the narrative. Higuchi refuses to periodise these, treating both as rooted in Kitano's world, but differing in that the latter embodies that world's essence and the former 'evades' that through narrative.[132]

Analysis of the individual films, I believe, shows the difficulties of delineating periods, not because each film is completely different, but because each bears divisions and contradictions that cannot be reduced to unified periods. As argued above, one can assert broad transformations between his early and late films, but even recent works reveal elements resisting that general trend. Not to side with Higuchi's imprecise categorisation, but I see Kitano's theme of doubling applying not just to characters and narrative situations, but also to the level of film-making itself, as the same work can often reflect a split between reproducing dominant values and undermining them. The conflicting reception of each of his films often expresses those divisions. The question becomes whether these divided elements exist separately but equally – albeit in conflict – or whether they are contained within a frame that either establishes a hierarchy, or ideologically resolves their contradiction. My argument is that the former is truer of his early films, the latter of his recent ones.

Change and the Foreign Audience

There may be many factors behind this transformation in framing, but one of the most significant is shifts in the audience, with new viewers appearing in the latter half of his career bearing different expectations about Japan and Kitano Takeshi/Beat Takeshi than before. Kitano's concern for these foreign audiences was not wholly due to the sudden award at Venice, but was a necessity shaped by inherent contradictions in the Japanese film industry. Although the 1970s witnessed the decline of the major studios as production entities, those companies still maintained a near-monopoly on distribution and exhibition through block-booking contracts. Films released by the majors enjoyed national distribution, extensive advertising and in some cases guaranteed returns. Only production companies with strong business relations with the majors could enjoy such benefits.[133] Others, who actually produce the majority of films in Japan, are forced to compete for slots at the small number of theatres not controlled by the majors, which can lead to a delayed and often limited release with little advertising. While a major release involves 200 to 300 theatres nationwide, an independent one usually starts with one or two theatres in Tokyo, and then slowly moves around Japan a few screens at a time. Coupled with the weak position producers have in negotiating distribution contracts, this gap puts independent films at an immense disadvantage.

This situation explains why Japanese independent producers began in the mid-1990s to look to foreign film festivals as a means of survival. Even if a film did not secure foreign distribution, an award, or even a significant festival showing, became an important domestic publicity resource. When the magazine *Brutus* featured Kitano and Wong Kar-wai on its cover in October 1997, with the large caption, 'The only ones who don't watch Japanese films are Japanese', it was not only poking fun at a domestic market dominated by foreign product, but also attempting to convince Japanese to see home-grown movies because foreigners do. In the end, it was independents who first tried to globalise Japanese film in the 1990s. This gave impetus to the detached style since European festivals have long privileged long-take cinema.

These became strategies for Kitano's films as well, especially after Shōchiku dropped him with *Sonatine*'s failure. Office Kitano had to borrow the help of distribution companies like Nippon Herald or distribute films itself (starting with *Kids Return*). Even when *Hana-Bi* garnered loads of free publicity by winning at Venice, it still took four months for the film to open in Japan, and then it only showed in a handful of theatres at first. To Mori Masayuki, the problem was partially a lack of appreciation.

> Even though some film fans and critics highly praised his films, I don't think anyone on the level of the audience or, in fact, of the major distribution companies gave proper credit to the artist Kitano Takeshi. It so happened that there was an audience in London that did give proper credit . . . If we didn't get that as a starting point, we wouldn't have been applauded in Japan. I have a strong sense that foreign acclaim was imported back into Japan and became Japanese opinion.[134]

This became a strategy for Office Kitano.

> We don't have Kitano Takeshi speak directly about his films, but borrow the worlds (*sekai*) of other people, and have them speak about Kitano's realm from an objective position. We take the film abroad and say in Japan that we got this praise there. There's no other way to expand the audience for Kitano Takeshi's films.[135]

What foreign fans and critics thought of Kitano's films was thus translated and included in official publications, such as the handbill for *Getting Any?*, the first film after Kitano lost major studio backing, which extensively described the film's success in London. The foreign market also became crucial as *Hana-Bi*, for instance, opened in France and Italy before it did in Japan; Kitano's recent films can practically recoup their production costs solely through sales abroad. *Takeshis'* in fact collected about 30 per cent of its budget through foreign presales even before production began.[136]

Kitano's films began showing abroad just as foreign views about Japan were in transition. Foreign critics still use orientalist buzzwords like 'Zen' to explain his films, but as Japan abroad became more the country of anime and manga than geisha and samurai, Kitano became emblematic of the new 'Japan cool'. Hyperbolic appreciations of his work reveal the same operations of exoticism and desire as the old orientalism, only instead of fantasising a premodern other as a way of defining and dealing with modernity, fans were now desiring a more liberated postmodern other (one who was, for instance, constantly subversive) as a means of locating themselves within Western postmodernity. On the festival circuit, Kitano's films helped confirm visions of a universal post-classical cinema that was other to Hollywood, but which still confirmed contemporary American cinema's postmodern conflation of art and popular culture in new genres like the 'festival-gangster' genre[137] led by Scorsese and Tarantino.

Kitano repeatedly denies any interest in pandering to foreign taste and has criticised orientalist stereotypes. Part of his radical reputation at home stemmed from the view that he was an international director not beholden to 'representing Japan'.[138] Yet his own company was making foreign reception central to its marketing strategy. Pushed by this, it seems the discourse on and in Kitano's films has shifted away from the politics of Miyahara's 'vertical other' in early 1990s' Japan and towards a global economics of the 'horizontal other', where the opinions of foreign others provide understanding and identity to Kitano and his films, effacing some of the radical difference of his work.

Kitano attempted to trick his foreign audience as well, throwing them curveballs like *Kikujiro*. The problem was that it was harder to undermine audience expectations when the audience had expanded and differentiated: *Kikujiro*'s scenes of play may have confused foreigners hoping for yakuza bloodshed, but they looked all-too-familiar to Japanese used to Beat Takeshi. Confronted with multiple markets and audiences – and thus, one could say, with globalism – Kitano, I would argue, has tended to proceed as many Japanese have done in the last decade: latch onto the nation as an abstract but still serviceable frame for making sense of a globalised world. Takeshi has divided and directed his texts to different audiences. Darrell Davis speculates that 'as Kitano domesticates the national for export in his films, he could also be "savaging" it at home' in television shows like *This Is Strange, Japanese* (Koko ga hen da yo, Nihonjin).[139] But mixed messages at home sometimes become mixed-up signals abroad, as Kitano has offered both orientalist aesthetics in *Dolls* and a manga-like world in *Takeshis'*.[140] While Takeshi has often criticised the Japanese nation-state, the nation as a more abstract entity has surfaced as an amorphous frame for accommodating his contradictory texts and divided markets. With the debates still continuing over whether Kitano's author image is defined by continuity or discontinuity, his self-definition as 'Japanese' has become one of the stronger continuities. Let us look for such framing continuities as we now review the 'differences' of his individual films.

Part Two

Another Kitano Takeshi: The Films

Violent Cop

If later Kitano films foreground their difference from previous works in his oeuvre, his first directorial feature, *Violent Cop* is a film in between, both citing and distinguishing itself from an earlier 'Beat Takeshi'. The Japanese title cites intertextuality, the relationship of one text to another ('sono otoko, kyōbo ni tsuki' is literally 'that man is equipped with violence'). 'That man' already takes us beyond *Violent Cop* to other works: while narratively it refers to Azuma Ryōsuke, the film's brutal police detective who uses even more questionable techniques than Dirty Harry, most people in Japan in 1989 would have also initially connected the title to another character outside the film, Beat Takeshi. That association was not just the result of advertising design, which centred on his full-length figure, nor of star discourse, which always exceeds the limits of the character and the film text. The title audaciously called upon the common impression that the television personality Beat Takeshi was a violent man. This perception derived in part from the violent aspects of his humour, as well as from the roles he tended to play as an actor, ranging from the mass murderer Ōkubo Kiyoshi to another brutal killer in *Comic Magazine* (*Komikku zasshi nanka iranai!*, Takita Yōjirō, 1986). Yet such impressions were most forcefully based on the incident that took place on 9 December 1986, in which Takeshi, infuriated by the aggressive reporting of his extra-marital affairs by the tabloid weekly *Friday*, led members of his Army to the publisher Kōdansha's offices and assaulted five members of the editorial staff. Takeshi was arrested for inflicting bodily injury and the incident created both a public furore and a crisis in his career, as he was forced to withdraw for nearly seven months from the six regular television programmes he was involved in at the time.[1]

Maverick Shōchiku producer Okuyama Kazuyoshi, who would later produce *Boiling Point* and *Sonatine*, came up with the title and presented it, along with the script, to Takeshi during his period of atonement. Expectations over the violence in the film multiplied when Kitano took up the megaphone after the withdrawal of Fukasaku Kinji, the maker of such yakuza genre hits as *Battles Without Honor and Humanity* (Jingi naki tatakai, 1973) and *Graveyard of Honor* (Jingi no hakaba, 1975).[2] These feelings are exemplified by the first sentences of an article in the major film magazine, *Kinema junpō*.

> Just hearing that Beat Takeshi will star in a violent picture, plus try his hand at directing, is enough to pique one's interest. Knowing that Beat Takeshi doesn't just normally reveal an independent opinion about 'violence', but shows it with his behaviour, one has to wonder what kind of 'violent movie' he will make.[3]

Shōchiku took advantage of such interest and, in the words of Okuyama himself, 'developed an ad campaign that bordered on the underhanded in exploiting the image of the *tarento* Beat Takeshi to the fullest'.[4] The official pamphlet sold at the theatre contrasted Beat Takeshi to other 'extreme' performers who had softened down with success, calling him still 'dangerous' and quoting him as joking, 'Where did I study reality? I practiced on Kōdansha.' In the end, the studio earned ¥780 million on a film that only cost ¥460 million to make.[5]

Violent Cop in part lived up to these expectations by delivering characters, such as Azuma and Kiyohiro, whose violent means exceed what is reasonable for their ends and thus verge on the insane. From the first scene, where Azuma beats up a high-school punk, his methods seem questionable and earn the frowns of the new station chief. When a drug dealer is found dead, Azuma begins to investigate with a greenhorn detective named Kikuchi, but finds out his best friend in the force, Iwaki, is on the payroll of the drug boss Nitō. Iwaki is soon found dead and Azuma breaks all regulations in going after Kiyohiro, Nitō's violent henchman, only to lose his job. The bloodshed escalates as Azuma guns down Nitō and Kiyohiro kidnaps

Akari, Azuma's mentally handicapped sister. The crazed violence culminates in a shootout that leaves both men dead.

Violence was the focus of many contemporary reviews, which either justified it as an accurate depiction of an increasingly violent Japan, or condemned the fact that audiences could not identify with such cold-blooded figures.[6] What underlined *Violent Cop*'s difference was first the notion that its violence was unlike that of other films. The film's official pamphlet promoted this: 'In an age when simply showing extreme façades – spectacular car chases, fireball explosions across the screen, heavily armed detectives confronting a formidable crime syndicate – suffices for expressing violence, Beat Takeshi aims for something different.'

Kitano is quoted as declaring that 'Truly scary violence is not battling away with guns. It should be internal to the everyday.' While publicity statements rarely function as good analysis, it is true that violence in *Violent Cop* is intermeshed with normal life. From the kids beating up the homeless man to Azuma chasing his prey in a car, violence is merely an extension of everyday activities, often rendered ordinary through humour or play (but without offering strong approbation or even cynical parody). Some characters react to violence as if it is common and extra-diegetic figures such as music or sound effects are reduced to a minimum or operate, such as when Shiota, a fleeing suspect, clubs the young detective Honma with a bat accompanied by lyrical music, to nullify the extraordinariness of violence.

As part of a general strategy of eliminating excess that I will discuss later, *Violent Cop* strips much of its violence of bravado and spectacle, if not of narrative or semiotic embedding. One example is when a bystander is accidentally shot as Kiyohiro attempts to gun down Azuma. While the scream of the woman's friend marks it as a shocking event, the editing neither amplifies the significance of it (for instance, by providing close-ups of the friend to underline the tragedy), nor accentuates the violent act through such devices as manipulation of sound (instead, there is no music and the sound of the gun is itself muffled). *Violent Cop* has been subject to hyperbolic rhetoric regarding its violence, but one of its interesting paradoxes is that despite being called 'one of the most visceral, bloody and sadistic thrillers ever made',[7] there is actually very little garish on-screen bloodshed. One

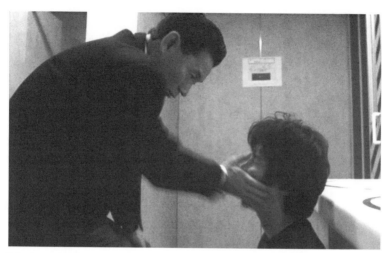

Takeshi's real violence

reason violence does not stand out is because the everyday is so cruel and violent. The film offers a litany of examples of the corrupt or unfeeling, from the kids throwing cans at a boat captain to Kikuchi, Azuma's partner, practising his golf swing outside Iwaki's funeral, so commonplace they rarely occupy the centre of the frame. Lacking difference, violence infects everything and thus threatens to become mundane.

Azuma and Kiyohiro stand out in contrast to the banality of bureaucratic violence, like the cover-up of Iwaki's murder, but what is disturbing about *Violent Cop* is less the content of their acts than how the film views them. Consider the scene when Azuma continually slaps the drug dealer in the toilet to extract a confession. To many observers, that is the prime example of the film's realism, of presenting violence without fictional frills (Takeshi is *really* repeatedly slapping the face of the actor). Yet what renders this scene so violent – what presents violence not as outside but inside the ordinary – is the long take that posits an observer coolly refusing to lessen this violence, even by utilising ellipsis through editing. To Yamane Sadao, the film as a whole offers 'a camera that stares at its subject with utter coldness, cutting so sharp it chops things apart, rhythm born of the bold exchange of close-ups and long shots, and the contrast between heartless character actions and an inhuman urban landscape'.[8] *Violent Cop* less depicts a violent world, or even comments upon it, than embodies the violence itself, violence deeply imbricated with the camera gaze.

This attitude towards violence and observation was demarcated through another set of distinctions readily apparent to viewers at the time: that between Fukasaku and Kitano, and between Nozawa Hisashi's script and Kitano's reworking of it. Fukasaku Kinji was another film-maker well-known for depictions of violence, even up to his last works, *Battle Royale* (2000, which featured Beat Takeshi) and *Battle Royale II* (2003). His yakuza films in the early 1970s were particularly significant for their move away from the stylised, utopian violence of Tōei's 1960s' yakuza fare, which provided a cathartic epiphany over any form of moral ambiguity. Fukasaku's heroes were more anarchic, refusing institutional versions of morality and knowledge, while remaining painfully aware of the barrenness of cathartic violence. Yet they were never nihilistic, not even Ishikawa Rikio in *Graveyard of Honor*, whose seeming amorality never overshadowed his strong sense of individual freedom, born in the immediate postwar period but trampled on by the institutionalisation of later postwar Japanese society. His violence is then never purposeless or unsympathetic.

By his own account, Nozawa's script was written with Fukasaku's previous films in mind. 'As one could figure from his past oeuvre, Fukasaku's real aim was to present the angry outburst, the indefatigable instinct for struggle of a protagonist who, in an extremely realistic situation, smells of actual life.' While the film was to be neither a 'social realist drama' nor a 'critique of power', but rather an 'astounding action film',[9] a sense of social criticism permeates Nozawa's script. The scenario describes the visuals which were to appear behind the opening titles: the 'pollution-filled streets' hidden behind the façade of an advanced culture, the prostitutes, drug addicts, drunks and brawling punks that could serve to justify Azuma's violence. Azuma is a loose cannon, but Nozawa provides more emotional justifications for his actions. The tragedies of Honma and Iwaki are described in sentimental detail, and several scenes of Azuma's past with Akari imbue the film with nostalgia for a better time. Given how the police cover-up of

Stripping the image of explanation

Iwaki's murder is drawn out over several pages, Azuma's conflict with his superiors becomes one between the tough, but not always clean beat cops (who appear much more professional than in the film) and their media-concerned elite superiors. Nozawa's Azuma is much closer to Don Siegel's Dirty Harry: a dirty cop, but one who must stoop to that in a world where the authorities are just as corrupt as the criminals.

This alternative 'Violent Cop' was not behind-the-scenes trivia, but was published in the September 1989 issue of the screenwriting magazine *Shinario* (*Scenario*). A complete transcript of Kitano's film was available for comparison in the 15 August *Kinema junpō* (both would have hit newsstands right before the film's 12 August release).[10] Kitano was widely quoted about his decision to drastically alter Nozawa's script. What Kitano excised was not only those aspects of the movie that made it a Fukasaku film – the narratives of nostalgia and sympathy that justify the excessive use of frustrated violence – but many of the regimes of narrative explanation itself. The most obvious case of this is when the dialogue from Azuma's confrontation with Iwaki is literally stripped from the image, leaving only a long shot from outside a café, without the sound of their conversation. This is in deep contrast to the emotional gravity of Nozawa's version, which is centred on the fact that Iwaki had lent Azuma money – probably dirty money – for Akari's hospital bills. Shinozaki Makoto noted how long shots and other devices eliminate much of the explanation when the sister is introduced,[11] thus eliding the original script's detailed descriptions through doctor explanations and flashbacks of her condition and the relationship between the siblings. In this sense, *Violent Cop* utilises more of the conventions of art cinema such as ellipsis, de-dramatisation and understatement than would be found in Japanese action films like Fukasaku's.

Violent Cop is sometimes confoundingly persistent in its pursuit of the logic of subtraction. This act of removal can prove jarring when, for instance, the station chief, surrounded by his lieutenants, demands Azuma's resignation. This shot is followed by one of Azuma, unmoving; then a close-up of the chief also motionless; a close-up of Azuma's badge; and then a full shot of the two all alone in the room in the same positions. The sequence is jarring, first because it is hard to see the shot of the badge as an action occurring at that moment given Azuma's immobility. Even if we imagine there has been an ellipsis, the exact same blocking of actors in the following shot – but with the surrounding characters now gone – renders it a very harsh temporal ellipsis, one that makes us wonder whether a scene is missing. In fact, a total of nine scenes from Nozawa's script have been chopped from between the shots of the captain and the badge, a considerable portion of the plot. This gives the impression that the ellipsis is calling attention to its own violent act of cutting.[12] The transformation of the original script turned *Violent Cop* from being a film about violence into being a film embodying violence in its very form.

Information about character psychology is considerably lessened by this brutal slashing. The main event occurring in these nine scenes is Kiyohiro's first encounter with Akari, where he takes advantage of her tendency to mistake friendly men as marriage partners and makes her a willing girlfriend, a fact revealed to Azuma by Nitō. This renders their conflict personal and provides the reason for the seasoned cop to quit the force. The film excises all of this, however, obscuring not only the personal motivations for Azuma's resignation, but also the emotional processes that could create empathy for his actions. Azuma is structured as a largely exter-

The violent ellipsis: the chief's office

The violent ellipsis: Azuma

nalised character, one whose presence is felt more from what he does than what he thinks.

One can say that the object of the cinematic violence is the body, especially that of Beat Takeshi. His body not only inflicts violence, it is the one most obstinately represented in the film, particularly through the act of walking. In a film that eliminates excess, one action that remains excessive is walking. Not a few commentators complained of the time devoted to characters marching, apparently without narrative motivation, but such walking underlines the replacement of the mental with the physical. This is most evi-

The violent ellipsis: the chief

The violent ellipsis: after the badge, a different time

dent when Azuma, after visiting a potential informant, walks past Kiyohiro, and even keeps on walking for some time before 'realising' that it was his rival. No close-ups are given to psychologise his late recognition of Kiyohiro, so in a film where the labour of detection is often elided (such as how Azuma found Kiyohiro's hideout), excess walking in effect substitutes for mental action. Abe Kashō sees the walking as central to the film's reworking of the Beat Takeshi image. To him, Takeshi's acquired way of walking, where a swaying of the body almost literally pounds the pavement, is part of a strategy to strip Beat Takeshi of his televisual identity and return him to the

Beat Takeshi's walking, thinking body

physical body that is not allowed in television's constant act of reducing the body (what is external to TV) to images (what fits television's codes).[13]

Violent Cop plays with and works against the known text 'Beat Takeshi'. The film first utilises familiarity with Beat Takeshi, often reinforcing knowledge of him. It, for instance, offers gags typical of the comedian, such as when Azuma finagles money out of Kikuchi or Honma. Yet Azuma also differs in crucial ways from this public persona. If there was something surprising to Japanese viewers about the film, it was less the fact that a comedian was acting violently (this was already known), than that he had become silent. Beat Takeshi, more than anything, was a loquacious star. Azuma, in contrast, like many of the characters Beat Takeshi plays in Kitano's films, is basically taciturn.

There are several potential motivations for this character definition. One is generic. From the stars of *jidaigeki* period films to the Tsuruta Kōji or Takekura Ken gangsters of Tōei yakuza films, the hero of Japanese action cinema has often been defined by his taciturn nature, as someone whose actions not only speak louder than words, but also epitomise the '*gaman*' (patient endurance) central to the mentality of the 'hard school' (*kōha*) hero, who endures injustice after injustice until he must strike out in the cathartic finale. In contrast, loquaciousness is often the mark of the weak male of melodrama (the *nimaime*) or of the young samurai or gangster who has yet to steel his nerves. Azuma is a *kōha* hero in that he does not complain or express his emotions, yet by violently lashing out from the very first scene, he is far from exhibiting *gaman*. Also by refusing to follow the codes of duty or to proffer the kind of detached, but still deep-rooted concern Hirono shows for his community in *Battles without Honor and Humanity*, Azuma fundamentally deviates from the hero of gangster or samurai cinema. Not being a fundamentally psychological character, Azuma's lack of words is associated with the film's general strategy of stripping off excess, eliminating his trappings just as all of Nitō's furniture is removed from his office.

The lack of words also helps strip Azuma of the connotations associated with 'Beat Takeshi'. *Violent Cop* is one attempt to undermine the 'necessity' of laughing at the body of the actor Beat Takeshi. This involves violence against both audience expectations, as well as against the body itself and its accumulated meanings. What remains after the stripping off of words and star persona is a character who basically 'expresses' with his body; such bodily movements may substitute for psychology, but they do not necessarily become equivalent in signifying power. They denote less mental or emotional states – excepting, perhaps, the bad mood (*fukigen*) that Shinozaki reads in Azuma[14] – than the violent reduction of meaning to the material.

Many read *Violent Cop* as the first of Kitano's films to express his death wish, and so the violent stripping of meaning from the body can be metaphorically aligned with the wilful self-annihilation of its two most violent protagonists. Note how this may relate to motifs of circularity and stillness. *Violent Cop*, like *Boiling Point*, *Kids Return*, *Dolls* and *Takeshis'*, is framed by circular structures. This is evident first in its narrative circularity, which begins with doublings such as that between Azuma and Kiyohiro (whose similarities have sparked some to claim an almost homosocial relationship between them)[15] and concludes with the plot device of Kikuchi assuming the roles of both Azuma, taking over his job, suit and even gait, and Iwaki, receiving bribes from Nitō's successor. But it is also apparent in the framing device of freeze frames. The freeze frame of the secretary at the end doubles the shot of the homeless man at the beginning. While his shot cannot easily be read as a freeze frame (since there was no action beforehand to establish its motionlessness), its stillness is emphasised by the violence that occurs afterwards. Such stillness is repeated throughout the film and is a marker of Kitano's style, especially as expressed in the deadpan faces of many of his characters. Such moments of stillness, precisely because they last for some time, help de-dramatise the moment, providing an excessive void as a substitute for the excised excess. The stillness can also emphasise through contrast the violence that sometimes follows, just as the extended shot of Azuma and Kikuchi in the car renders Shiota's subsequent breaking of the windshield all the more shocking. This stagnant immobility, however, never morphs into the idle play of *Boiling Point* or *Sonatine*, thus rendering *Violent Cop*'s stillness bleaker and unavoidable. Circularity threatens both to reinforce fate and reduce all to a zero broadly drawn.

Stillness emphasises violence, and vice versa, yet these textual relations are, like other intertextual moments in the film, ones less of mutual support than conflict. While *Violent Cop* cites the violent Beat Takeshi, even augmenting that in its advertising, it simultaneously freezes the mobile Beat body in multiple moments of stillness that continue, in a frame that shifts from stillness to movement to stillness, until that body moves no more. 'Beat Takeshi' is then reduced to non-movement in a medium that is supposedly defined by movement, an ironically cinematic means of erasing meaning. Yet at the same time, we should not forget that the film also shows another, interweaving trajectory, from movement (Azuma walking on the bridge), to stillness (Azuma's death), to movement again (Kikuchi resuming Azuma's march), reviving in a different form the body that had been reduced to mere body. The film, one can say, is on the borderline between these two, between severing and resuscitating intertextual relationships, between a frame that closes and a frame that opens up – between creating distance from the identity of Beat Takeshi and reviving that in the new identity of Kitano Takeshi.

Boiling Point

Many cite *Boiling Point* as the starting point of an authorial identity. To one critic, 'Given that not only the script but also the staff [for *Violent Cop*] were decided beforehand, it is *Boiling Point*, featuring a screenplay penned by Takeshi himself . . . that can be termed the real début film of the Kitano crew.'[1] This auteurist discourse, however, is often complexly intertwined with another that provisionally separates this film from the rest of Kitano's work, either as a lesser 'practice' work (*shūsaku*[2]), or as a uniquely superlative piece. Much popular criticism and average viewer responses found *Boiling Point* 'uneven',[3] 'choppy', his 'oddest' film that is 'not as good' as *Sonatine* or *Hana-Bi*,[4] a failure that contributed to the narrative that Kitano was an amateur director who got better with later films, a story the director himself sometimes gave in later years. Yet it is precisely its unusualness, its perceived unconventionality, that prompted some to laud it as Kitano's best because it was the least bound to the rules of motion pictures, exhibiting a 'youthful' play with cinema that was lost when Kitano stopped treating film-making as a hobby and began to see it more professionally.[5] We shall see that *Boiling Point* is possibly Kitano's most experimental film, challenging spectator interpretations of character, narrative and genre.

On the auteurist front, the film is often depicted as containing, perhaps in underdeveloped form, many of the themes Kitano would pursue in later films, such as the will to die, a circular and repetitive temporality, aphasia and a silent-cinema aesthetics, utopian moments of childlike play, and still, stone-faced moments interrupted by sudden intrusions of comedy and violence. Motifs such as flowers, the beach, Okinawa, yakuza and sports that would figure prominently in subsequent works are already visible. The film can be viewed as a precursor to *Sonatine* (the trip to Okinawa) or *Kids Return* (the pair of futureless kids). Also produced by Okuyama Kazuyoshi at Shōchiku, *Boiling Point* was subject to an advertising strategy that tied it to both *Violent Cop* and the persona of Beat Takeshi. The pamphlet and poster design resembled that of *Violent Cop* in focusing on a single object, this time a bat that recalled the beating in the first film. The catchline, 'Virus intrusion. Destroying your frontal lobes', echoed *Violent Cop*'s own stance as a damaging attack on the audience. Advertising relied on Beat Takeshi's popularity by crediting the direction to him and not Kitano Takeshi (as is actually written in the credits). Moreover, some ads used the phrase, 'The Gundan let loose!' to give the impression that, with many of the Takeshi Army/*Gundan* members appearing, this was a comedy in the line of *Super Jockey*, a variety show featuring Beat Takeshi comically torturing his followers.

On many levels, however, *Boiling Point* worked against these and other expectations. Its story, about members of a sandlot baseball team who try to obtain guns to help their coach, an ex-yakuza named Iguchi in trouble with the mob, may sound like a continuation of Kitano's violent narratives, but the film is oddly vacant. The hero Masaki may throw the punch at a gangster that gets his gas station in trouble and spurs Iguchi's unwise intervention against his former gang, but he lacks both Azuma's energy and bodily presence. Masaki and his buddy Kazuo head off to Okinawa and get mixed up with a crazy gangster named Uehara (Beat Takeshi's only appearance in the film), but the guns they get are ineffective and Iguchi never reappears in the film. Even Masaki's romance with a beautiful waitress named Sayaka seems pointless as they finally drive a gas lorry into the rival mob's office – or so we think. Those who anticipated the antics of Beat Takeshi and his Army were given a film that, while humourous in parts, sported few of their classic gags, had a slow tempo and 'ended' tragically. While Guadalcanal Taka (Iguchi Takahito, who plays Iguchi) was probably closest to his *Gundan* personality, others like Ide Rakkyo (Ide Hiroshi) are barely recognisable. As if contradicting its own advertising, the official pamphlet stated that Kitano had the Army members appear using their real, not stage names, precisely in order to eliminate the sense that this was a '*Gundan* movie'.

Differences can also be noted with *Violent Cop*. The critic Sera Toshikazu has argued that Kitano, by 'purposely bringing in a hero who in terms of character is opposite to that of the previous film, blocks spectator identification and ceaselessly refuses to allow the film to stabilise itself narratively'.[6] Although both Iguchi and Uehara share character traits with Azuma, the clearer narrative framework in *Violent Cop* allows for greater audience empathy with and a more stable understanding of Azuma. Iguchi also comes off as compulsively childish, and Uehara as a wholly unpredictable yet still fascinating perpetrator of mad violence.

It is on the level of narration that distinctions are often noted. Yomota Inuhiko argues that while the 'chain reaction' of events in *Violent Cop* renders it 'centripetal', the repeated digressions of *Boiling Point* make it a 'centrifugal' film.[7] Abe Kashō similarly defines *Violent Cop* as maintaining 'continuity' (in the sense of endurance [*jizoku*] exemplified by Azuma's walking), but describes *Boiling Point* using words like 'diffusion' (*kakusan*), 'explosion' (*bakuhatsu*) and 'dispersion' (*bunsan*).[8] Although the sluggish Masaki gets the narrative started with his punch, he is more reactive than active, letting Iguchi and Uehara take the narrative lead in crucial sections. It is thus difficult to select a central protagonist in the film. Moreover, the location of action is also diffused, as the story wanders off to Okinawa with little preparation. As Abe explains, the narrative exhibits crucial moments of sudden explosion – the truck detonation, Uehara's machine gun going off accidentally, even Masaki's slugging the gangster – but these are often unexpected, without clear motivation or narrative preparation. Many have noted how illogical the story is. Why spend so much time travelling to a location to acquire a gun that will never be used for its intended purpose? Why would Uehara have to cut off his lieutenant Tamaki's finger in atonement if he intended to kill the boss that ordered it anyway? The ultimate dispersion of narrative energies is certainly the ending itself, which returns after the explosion to Masaki sitting on a toilet – a repeat of the first image in the film that intimates that all of what we have seen is just the reverie of a slacker sitting on the crapper. Some narrative turns are simply never explained. Kazuo meets Masaki at a café with the express purpose of complaining about travelling to Okinawa; he leaves money and insists he will not go. This is presented in one medium long shot, with Kazuo exiting screen left, leaving Masaki alone within the frame. The film then cuts to an extreme long shot of Masaki alone on a beach. One assumes this is Okinawa and that he is there by himself. There is then a reverse shot of Kazuo standing up in the bushes behind Masaki, apparently after defecating in the grass (continuing the motif of bodily excretion). No explanation is ever given as to why Kazuo is there.

To some, *Boiling Point* represents Kitano Takeshi's purest expression of a cinema without explanation, one that impacts directly without narrative or even linguistic mediation. Without even a musical score to help the viewer, the film proves difficult to read, a complication that begins with the original title, which the majority of Japanese would not be able to pronounce without help.[9] Add on an ending that seems to undermine the very existence of its own narrative and *Boiling Point* would seem to border on the meaningless.

This narrative unconventionality is paralleled by deviations from classical stylistic norms. While a strategic use of ellipses conceals important narrative information, the film simultaneously extends many shots beyond the conclusion of narrative action, or starts them before the action begins. Such dead time contributes to the sense of stagnation that Shinozaki Makoto and others have emphasised about the film.[10] The film often cuts to other spaces with little apparent reason, such as the brief shot of Kazuo in front of his green grocer's inserted during Masaki and Sayaka's trip to the ocean. It lacks motivation, showing a space that will never figure narratively. Most narrative ellipses are elucidated post facto, so the film is not incomprehensible. Yet visual narration is still discordant. After showing Masaki and Kazuo walking on the Okinawan beach, for example, there is a cut to a long shot of the Okinawan gang facing the camera. The motivation for this sudden shift to a new space and characters will become apparent later, but it is jarring at first. The editing is particularly disturbing because it begins not with an establishing shot, but with an apparent point-of-view shot, with Ozawa and his lieutenants looking at the camera and verbally berating the (unknown) person they are looking at (which could just as well be the audience). Only after inserting a medium shot of Ozawa and Minamizaka does the film finally show who they are rebuking: Uehara and Tamaki.

Much of what is distinctive about the film's style revolves around such spatial constructions, especially the unstable framing of off-screen space and structuring of point of view. Framing can be unconventional, often failing to centre narratively important characters, leaving empty space above their heads. Just as editing elides some narrative events, so framing keeps many off screen. The first instance of this is when Kazuo is tagged out at third base, an event that is only intimated through off-screen sound. Characters will talk to figures off screen who have not been introduced, or conversely, we will hear a character out of frame who has not yet been shown (as when Mutō, the enemy gang's underboss, visits the gas station). Edits will elide shifts in off-screen space, such as when Sumiyo, Uehara's moll, comes up to bat during the beach stickball game: although Masaki is pitching when she comes to hit, it is only the shot after her at-bat – and thus after she gets hit several times with the ball – that reveals Uehara is now throwing. In most cases, the film will eventually reveal off-screen space, confirming what the audience already suspects, but one scene foregrounds the mistakes viewers can make. When Masaki contemplates asking Sayaka out at her café, a medium-long shot of her approaching him in the foreground cuts to a close-up of him asking when the place closes. The assumption of course is that Sayaka is hearing this question, but a different voice proves this wrong – there is a waiter out of frame we did not know about. Off-screen space in *Boiling Point* can be unstable, creating an uncertainty that helps associate space out of the frame, often suggested through off-screen sound, with the unknown and the dangerous.

Point-of-view structures, and the accompanying delineation of space and spectator positioning, can be ambiguous in *Boiling Point*. This is par-

Peculiar framing and empty space

ticularly the case when Masaki 'sees' Uehara and Tamaki slain at the airport. The first shot of Tamaki returning to the parking lot and the last one
of him getting shot are framed by views of Masaki looking. Reading what
comes in between as his subjective vision is problematised, however, by the
lack of an establishing shot connecting Masaki and the parking lot, the
complete absence of sound in the images of the gangsters, and Masaki's
failure to react to the shooting. The multiple camera placements, including
a return to Masaki and a (also suspicious) subjective shot from Uehara's
perspective, also complicate that point-of-view structure. The editing and
framing in *Boiling Point* thus create instabilities and ambiguities in space,
which themselves complicate the 'suturing' of the spectator into the film.
Echoing his own comments about *Violent Cop*, Yamane Sadao argues, 'This
is not the representation of violence, it is the violence of representation
itself.'[11]

Narrative illogicality and spatial instability do not mean that *Boiling Point*
fails to pursue consistent narrative structures. There are two it utilises in
particular, comedy and the youth picture, though in a fashion that simultaneously complicates them. With regard to comedy, Jerry Palmer has
observed that the absurd operates through a combination of logic and a narrative surprise that disturbs that logic. That shock, which he calls peripeteia,
becomes comic, and not another narrative of shock, such as horror, precisely because the implausibility of the situation is combined with another
logic that explains it. That combination both insulates the comic – making
it painless – and offers the spectator the pleasure of both experiencing the
flash of tension between these logics and recognising the solution.[12] Many
of the gags in *Boiling Point* work through peripeteia. Take, for instance, the
hilarious moment when Masaki, having hit his home run, passes Kazuo on
the bases. That action is not plausible/allowable in the rules/logic of baseball, but it is explicable through another logic: that Masaki does not understand the rules of baseball, and is too excited to notice the warnings of
others. Kitano's use of slow motion for this moment, a clichéd device for
dramatic moments in sport, amplifies the conflict between these two logics
by adding a parodic touch. One could say that the central gag of the film –
that it is nothing but Masaki's *rêve de toilette* – operates similarly, taking the

absurdities in narrative logic in the film and 'explaining' them through the alternative logic of the dream.

It is important to note, however, how the narrative structure of the gag in *Boiling Point* is homologous to that of violence in the film. Many of the gags work by surprise reversal: we thought Kazuo was not going to Okinawa, but there he is; we saw Sayaka agree to go motorcycling with Masaki, but they are pushing a car in the next shot. Yet the surprise can often be doubled with violence. This is certainly the case with the punk who immediately crashes his motorcycle upon receiving it. A dose of humour can also temper the violence such as when Uehara kills the American soldier: the fact that this takes place in broad daylight, in front of an American military base, renders the moment absurd, something further augmented by Masaki and Kazuo's befuddled attempt to run off with the guns without even hiding them.

The combination of the gag and violence can be disturbing, however. This is most evident with the killing of Uehara. Tamaki catches up with Masaki in the airport, and hands him a bag with some cash and a present. Masaki takes out the present. Then there is a cut to a silent shot of Uehara sitting in the car, beginning to look, followed by a supposed point-of-view low-angle shot of Tamaki surrounded by two gangsters. The editing returns us to Masaki who, also in low angle, begins to open the present. Just at that instant, the film cuts to a shot of Uehara, finally with sound, being shot. The present is 'butterfly eggs', a novelty gag; when opened, they make a cracking sound and out spring fake butterflies (the spray of blood on Uehara seems to approximate this action). This kind of surprise gag is perfectly at home in this film, but here it is directly interconnected with another shocker: a gangland slaying (a connection foreshadowed by the first shot in the club of the Okinawan gang, who sit in front of a window decorated with butterflies).

This combination of the gag and violence can be humourous, but the alternative logic/frame explaining these absurdities can sometimes be so disconcerting that it undermines the comic effect. Consider the moment when Uehara's gun, hidden in the bouquet of bird-of-paradise flowers, accidentally goes off in the gang office. That can raise a laugh in the audience, especially given Uehara's nonchalant reaction to it, but the response of the characters is more disturbing. Reacting neither with excess fear (like Tamaki did to having his finger cut off – which could render the scene comic) nor with prudent defence (immediately drawing their guns or hiding – a more 'realistic' response), they instead barely move. Ozawa slowly stands up, as if to provide a better target. This has its own absurd implausibility, but instead of being solved by an alternative logic that renders the scene funny, it suggests more disturbing implications: that these characters somehow wish to die.

One can say that by exploring various interrelations between violence and comedy, Kitano in *Boiling Point* is not simply exposing the inherent violence of comedy, but self-consciously questioning its borders. His unusual spatial framing is echoed by a strategy to complicate the frames that define the comedic and render it safe, not horrific. *Boiling Point* utilises many of the structures of comic narrative, but it fails to provide a consistent, stable and alternative logic conducive to safe laughter. Its most powerful frame is that of Masaki's dream, but that as much betrays expectations as offers solutions to the absurd. It could be called a comedy, one whose dispersive and illogical narrative structures resemble those of vaudeville, which refuses to be comic.

By challenging the line between comedy and horror, the film has to face its own monster, Uehara. On the one hand, he is the epitome of the trickster whose logic, trying to use Tamaki's finger for his own, or blaming Sumiyo for engaging in sex that was ultimately under his own orders, defies rationality and challenges order. On the other, he is a misogynistic homicidal maniac who is sexually aroused by violence and is almost gleefully bent on self-destruction. He, more than anyone else, is the virus mentioned in the advertising, preaching the illogical pleasure of self-annihilation (the frontal lobes being the site of analytic reasoning) and perhaps infecting Masaki, who proceeds to destroy himself.

This threatening instability also has the potential of undermining the other structuring form in the film: the coming-of-age narrative of the youth film. *Boiling Point* traverses several genres, including the yakuza movie and comedy, but the one it specifically cites is the youth sport story. This citation comes when Akira, another team member, tells Masaki, 'If you don't swing, nothing will start' (*furanakya hajimannai*). It is a problem the film itself is facing: unless our sluggish protagonist does something, the film's story itself cannot commence. The phrase would remind any Japanese spectator of the 'spo-kon' (*supōtsu konjō* – sporting spirit) movies and manga from the 1960s and 1970s in which heroes like Hoshi Hyūma (of *Star of the Giants* [*Kyojin no hoshi*], penned by Kajiwara Ikki and Kawasaki Noboru) exhibited a gutsy, fighting spirit in undertaking superhuman practice regimens until they became sporting heroes. Akira cites this democratic spirit: if you try hard enough, even you can be the narrative hero. This model influences the subsequent action as Masaki now begins to act, first literally taking a swing at the gangster, then making a play for Sayaka, then really swinging the bat in the game, then volunteering to go Okinawa to get the gun, and, finally, plunging the truck into the Ōtomo office. Without these actions, there would not be much of a story. The prominence of this narrative has led some to consider it the message of the film, with Tony Rayns, for instance, enunciating the film's 'moral' as 'it takes decisive action plus irrationality to really shake things up'.[13] The narrative of the underdog rising to claim victory is foretold in the Japanese title (as explained in the official pamphlet): the '3-4x' is one way of denoting a victory snatched from the jaws of defeat at the last bat; 'jūgatsu' is October, the time of the final pennant race in the Japanese baseball season.

Masaki does get things shaken up, but focusing solely on that ignores how the film undermines this narrative, by for instance first, having his dramatic home run end in failure, and second, making it clear that few of Masaki's actions are 'decisive'.[14] Pummelling the yakuza, as Iguchi points out, plays precisely into the gang's hands; Masaki did not strike up a conversation with Sayaka, she did; going to Okinawa was Iguchi's idea (and, once there, Uehara and Tamaki did all the work); and committing suicide for a cause mostly over and done with, with a girl you want to marry, right after telling your boss you're coming in to work the next day, is far from 'decisive'. Masaki moreover is at the beck and call of cinematic enunciation. We never see Masaki deciding to punch Kanai: the film only offers a shot of Kanai reacting to something off screen, after which the punch comes. In a film in which many characters do not reveal their inner side, Masaki's 'decision' only fills an off-screen absence. More obvious is how his approach to Sayaka is structured. It is Akira who prompts him to find a girl during a shot of Masaki in which Sayaka just happens to appear for the first

Masaki follows the framing

time in the background. It as if the dialogue and the framing conjure her up, with perfect timing, and press Masaki into making a play for her.

His almost puppet-like status is peculiar given how this, after all, is his dream. If a daydream is a narrative of wish-fulfilment, *Boiling Point* fulfils somewhat deranged wishes with its repeatedly unsuccessful plot actions. Certainly there is an element of fantasy in an idler like Masaki successfully scoring a girl played by Ishida Yuriko (already a famous starlet at the time), but to promptly commit suicide with her – for little reason – indicates a fundamental undermining of the youth-film narrative. Aspects of the youth film do remain, especially in episodes of male camaraderie epitomised by the popsicle scene between Kazuo and Masaki. But if the youth film is fundamentally a linear coming-of-age story, *Boiling Point* encloses a space of childish play with a temporality of repetition and circularity. Not only can scenes internally repeat their mini-narratives as in the karaoke episode, as Uehara and Tamaki repeatedly punch the same gangsters, but circularity seems to enable the kind of prescience of Uehara in the car, foreseeing his own death in a flurry of shots, but doing nothing to change it. The ending not only undermines any sense of coming of age, it returns us to the beginning. That has prompted not just one critic to consider *Boiling Point* one of

Kitano's bleakest films, one in which 'continuing to live a banal everyday life is more of a hell than dying in a blaze of glory'.[15]

What could be the motivation for making such a distinctly peculiar film that complicates generic narratives, if not narrative motivation itself? Some critics in Japan try to see its lack of explanation as an embodiment of cinema itself,[16] while those abroad attempt to find some social critique (usually pitting the individual against Japanese 'group society').[17] Perhaps impressed by the differences from the classical style, some have also attempted to term the film realistic,[18] despite the fact the film is purportedly an irrational dream. We have already seen there is evidence for portraying the film as a kind of alternative cinema, rejecting elements of classical narrative and the clichéd stories of youth film. It is hard to claim an overarching narrative of critique or resistance, however, when the framing narrative – the dream – fits the structure of the gag, possibly declaring, to quote Iguchi's girlfriend watching the sandlot ballgame, that 'we the spectators are the real fools'.

The ending has infuriated a number of observers, making *Boiling Point*, in some ways, a litmus test for how to represent Kitano: as an auteur honing his form, as a social rebel, as an artist engaging in pure self-creation, as a bungling amateur, or as a joker mocking the critics and the masses. But it also fundamentally challenges how we frame this text, especially how we connect cinematic elements into an interpretation. With the ending seemingly undermining such interrelations, what remains are disconnected, perhaps lyrical moments: Uehara in the field of flowers, the pink ball flying through the blue sky, the group licking popsicles as folk music plays on the radio. Perhaps the ending works to clear the field for such special moments, making them the film's centre. And yet it still may be a youth film, albeit a diminutive one. For the film is not completely circular: the Masaki who exits the toilet the second time is different from the first, running instead of walking. Maybe his dream did have an effect, though one that is small and uncertain. Perhaps *Boiling Point* is cinema before narratives begin, without the certainty that they will begin; the pre-narratives that may or may not frame stories of young people and auteurs coming of age.

A Scene at the Sea

If *Boiling Point* offered film critics a second Kitano film useful for construct-ing auteurist readings, some found him throwing 'an unexpected curveball' with *A Scene at the Sea*.[1] It was this work that introduced debates over what kind of auteur Kitano was – a consistent one, or one who continually re-invents himself – and embodied some of the contradictions of his cin-ema that would later come to the fore. These debates illustrate not only the critical camps that would form over his work, but also how his multifaceted film-making explored ways to straddle variant positions, such as from the coldly detached to the emotionally nostalgic. We will see how different con-ceptions of performance would foreground competing ideas of the relations between the seeing and the seen, between acknowledging gaps and using frames so as to conceal them.

The director whose previous works had been typified as violent, elliptical, de-dramatised, minimal and narratively eccentric had suddenly produced a sentimental love story about a young deaf man, Shigeru, who finds a broken surfboard when working as a garbage collector, and tries to master the waves as his deaf girlfriend Takako looks on. There's a tale of success, as Shigeru gets good enough to win a prize at a surfing competition; one of romantic tribulations, as Takako gets jealous of the increased atten-tion he gets from a surfing girl; and even of tragedy, as Shigeru dies at sea at the end. From an auteurist standpoint, some would isolate this film as a work 'with the least of himself in it'.[2] Others would still find continuity with previous movies, connecting *A Scene at the Sea* with *Boiling Point* in terms of the beach as a liminal space of play,[3] or Shigeru with Azuma and Masaki in their silence.[4] The fact that Kitano was credited for editing and planning (*kikaku*) for the first time also increased his aura as the artist in charge. But others would argue that Kitano resists auteurist readings themselves. The critic Sasaki Atsushi, who lauded the film for coming closest to the ideal of 'showing' and 'telling nothing', audaciously wrote that as long as he had this movie, 'I don't need another Kitano Takeshi film . . . in fact, I don't even need the film director Kitano Takeshi himself.'[5] The uniqueness of this (and other texts) meant that the 'auteur theory almost goes straight out the window as far as Takeshi Kitano is concerned'.[6]

In interviews, Kitano seemed to align himself with both sides of the issue. He stressed that continuing with the same kind of violent cinema would not only become 'boring' to him, but threatened to anaesthetise audiences to its effects, turning 'fake' and forcing him to concentrate only on upping the ante.[7] He therefore felt he had to 'throw away that style for the time being'.[8] Asked why he chose a topic so far from his previous work, he responded, 'It would probably be because it was something no one would ever think I'd film. If I said I'm making a pure love story, everyone would be bowled over. That's also fun.' Kitano thus emphasised the differences from *Boiling Point*. 'It couldn't be a rude film like the previous one, so I decided to add music. *Boiling Point* had the desire to irritate the audience and make them mad, but *A Scene at the Sea* doesn't.'[9] He summarised that 'this time it's a movie that everyone can understand'.[10] Nevertheless, he admitted to a continuity in his cinema that could be called authorial: 'Although I planned to change things entirely, in the end something like my touch still came through.'[11]

A Scene at the Sea's status as a love story raised questions about the film's conventionality for many commentators. The seeming contradiction of an unconventional film-maker making a work 'everyone can understand' was mirrored in dual reactions to the film. Some praised the movie's emotional effect: the critic Yamane Sadao wrote of it as a 'heart-warming, emotional love story',[12] the director Wakamatsu Kōji emphasised how much he cried,[13] and many Japanese spectator reviews spoke of its 'kindness', 'sadness' and quiet emotionality.[14] However, other reviews asserted that the film 'detests sentiment and sweet emotions',[15] that its 'story of youthful love in the summer, with only small ups and downs, is quietly presented largely without heightening the emotions'.[16] Not a few observers felt this 'kind' film was in fact extremely cruel (*zankoku*),[17] a judgment Kitano did not disagree with.[18] Even an advertisement for the film combined these 'wet' and 'dry' qualities, speaking (presumably from Takako's perspective) of wanting 'to cry until my body was wrung dry, but not one tear was spilled'. More than a few crit-

ics made it their project to explain how such an unemotional film could be
so emotional.

   In some ways, it was easier to explain why *A Scene at the Sea* is so cold,
than why it is emotional, when looking at issues of narrative, scriptwriting,
genre, character, acting, camerawork and location. A common refrain is
that the film lacks much of a narrative. While *Boiling Point* at least offered
narrative conflict between the Ōtomo gang and Masaki and his friends,
A Scene at the Sea had few such tensions. There was Shigeru's struggle with
the sea, the small disagreements with Takako, and possibly the divisions
between the deaf and the non-deaf, but these are largely minimised in the
film. Without presenting clear goals to achieve, the film refuses to render
Shigeru's developing skills a matter of narrative suspense.[19] The romance
with Takako is somewhat bumpy, primarily because of Shigeru's almost
self-consuming pursuit of surfing and Takako's sometimes mistaken jeal-
ousy, but it starts mid-stream (we do not see the budding of their relationship) and fails to achieve any identifiable goal (such as marriage). Major
conflicts that were originally planned, such as Takako's parents' attempt to
force her into an arranged marriage, were cut during production. Finally,
while some misunderstandings arise between the deaf and the non-deaf,
most felt these did not transform Shigeru's condition into a social issue.
Kitano himself stressed differences between the film and other Japanese
works treating the physically impaired, such as *Faraway Koshien* (*Haruka
naru Kōshien*, Ōsawa Yutaka, 1991) or Yamada Yōji's *My Sons* (1991) that portray them as victims struggling to overcome social obstacles.[20] While
Sasaki's argument that the film borders on 'narrating nothing' lacks support
in narrative theory, the film's deviation from conventional narratives was
annoyingly evident to a screenwriter like Kasahara Kazuo, as we noted in
Part I. Some found it to be a film less about transformation than about a
state of being.

   Other formal elements were thought to diminish the film's emotional
impact. Kitano's choice of the Yoshihama beach on Shōnan Bay, with its
concrete walls and highway overhead, is far removed from the beauty of his
Okinawan beaches. The assistant director, Kitahama Masahiro, reported
that camera distance was even greater than on previous films.[21] Kitano

expressed this as a way of both avoiding the 'warmth' of the youth film and a means of creating a detached, almost clinical observer.[22]

> I wondered if it couldn't just be a story of a guy who hated humanity dying at sea, so I made sure the camera did not get emotionally close to the characters. If emotion enters the picture, then you have to do a whole bunch of things, so I thought it was best to do it like filming animals, like viewing animals in a safari park.[23]

As if confirming their animal-like nature, the director confessed that he had little attachment to the two lovers and thought Shigeru, if anyone, was the bad guy.[24] Extending this, Abe Kashō argues that Shigeru's failure to treat either Takako or his garbageman partner Tamukai very well is formally aligned with the fact that he has few point-of-view shots. While she looks at him repeatedly, he rarely returns the favour. This lack, he adds, renders Shigeru into a 'sort of thing' defined by brutishness (*jūsei*).[25] It was argued that the characters, rendered in such a camera style, resist easy emotional identification.

Such arguments portray the film as distinctly unkind, yet they don't account for the testimonials of empathetic attachment to the film and its characters. Despite the cool, objective cruelty of the camera, many have noted that no one in the film is depicted with the kind of amorality Uehara is. In order to avoid the stereotypical film about the victimised disabled, the other characters are made neither villainous nor entirely good. This is particularly the case with Nakajima, the surfstore owner, who helps Shigeru considerably, but also initially overcharges him for the board.

Other strategies work more clearly to create emotional identification in spectators. Some praised these devices, but others would cite them as the film's faults, marring either the uniqueness of *A Scene at the Sea* or deviating from a perceived authorial norm. Hisaishi Jō's score was subject to the most criticism, especially after *Boiling Point*'s lack of non-diegetic music.[26] Hisaishi would become Kitano's regular composer, but this was his first pairing with Kitano, after coming to prominence with his lyrical scores for the animation director Miyazaki Hayao. Feeling the film would be unbearable without a score,[27] Kitano first wanted to use music in a fashion contrary to convention, inserting it when it was not needed, and not inserting it when it was required. He eventually settled on 'neutral' music that 'made you cry but also didn't make you cry'.[28] But many felt the electronic-voiced 'Sayonara' over the image of Takako pushing Shigeru's surfboard out to sea at the end too clearly directed the audience's emotional response. To Horike Yoshitsugu, this was evidence Hisaishi did not understand Kitano's intentions.[29]

The second object of debate were the memorial images appended after the makeshift funeral scene. The film was originally supposed to end with Shigeru's death, but Kitano, responding to opinions that the film was too unfeeling, added something 'extra' (*omake*) to 'service' viewers who might have been upset.[30] He felt they were also necessary from the standpoint of realism, offering images of the good times Shigeru and Takako had that were not shown in the poker-faced film.[31] Some critics such as Abe Kashō found the images justified: not only did they continue the motif of commemorative photos established with the second surfing competition, but they also elaborated on the theme of death. The director Aoyama Shinji was not the only one to use Hasumi Shigehiko to interpret the film.[32] Hasumi's famous statement that commemorative photos in Ozu Yasujirō's films are markers of death because they threaten to stop cinematic motion[33] is equally applicable to *A Scene at the Sea*: Shigeru's death occurs immediately after the photos are taken and one put on display. Abe, for one, reads the entire film, despite the absence of the actor Beat Takeshi, as being the images after Beat Takeshi's death, with the broken surfboard serving as his gravestone.

Yet the final images also imbue the movie with nostalgia. The Japanese title, which literally means 'The Quietest Sea that Summer', already refers to a past event, summer at the beach, that has often founded nostalgic narratives of youth in postwar Japan. The pamphlet emphasises this emotional story by quoting Kitano in large type: 'This film is replete with unfilled dreams of my youth.' Abe reads Shigeru as an embodiment of Takeshi's youth, but a more direct link exists in the film: Koiso Katsuya, who appears here as the plumper of the two soccer youths, played Takeshi as a boy in the 1985 television adaptation of *Yes, Takeshi!*. Seeing him, astute viewers could not only relive the series' nostalgia for 1950s' Japan, but also their own enjoyment six years before. Just as nostalgia can only have as its object what is lost, or never existed, so the film depicts a youth Kitano never had (his mother would not even let him learn how to swim) as well as 'memories' in the last shots that we never saw.

The narrative itself was sometimes accused of being old-fashioned. The director Negishi Kichitarō, for instance, pressed Kitano in a roundtable discussion on why Shigeru had to die at the end; if the film was truly attempting to deviate from the norms of the Hollywood love story, in which death has become a clichéd device, it would have been more radical to leave Shigeru alive.[34] The relationship between Shigeru and Takako was also seen as anachronistic.[35] This referred not only to their poverty (this was Japan during the economic bubble), but also to the image of a couple achieving mutual understanding without words (the two barely even use sign language). This kind of relationship, expressed by such terms as *isshin dōtai* ('being of one heart and mind'), may be a long-held Japanese ideal, but it always threatens to obfuscate the difficulties of communication, especially between genders. The feminist critic Niizawa Hiroko criticised *A Scene at the Sea* for representing an outdated, middle-aged Japanese man's standard for male–female relationships: the man does what he wants while the woman patiently looks on, folding his clothes.[36] The film's nostalgia results in part from the depiction of such archaic social forms.

Also crucial in the evocation of loss, memory and nostalgia is the positioning of the spectator in relation to the narrative. Although much has been said about the camera's objective detachment, if not cruel indifference, certain formal strategies encourage empathy and identification, the primary of which is point-of-view structures. *Boiling Point*'s strategy of complicating point of view is repeated in *A Scene at the Sea* with the first few shots, in which a silent image of the sea is followed by a two-shot of Shigeru and Tamukai, and then a close-up of Shigeru.[37] The initial shot could be from either Shigeru's or Tamukai's perspective, with the lack of sound giving only partial evidence that it is Shigeru's. Takako's subjective shots predominate and are comparatively easy to read. Overall, the spectator is most often situated with Takako's position. This is evident through camera movement, which, while largely motivated by character action (although it will often commence late or stop early to manufacture dead time at the beginning and end of shots), often follows Takako's lead, not Shigeru's. In emotionally important moments such as the bus scene, the camera stays with her. In such scenes, Takako's psychology is not abstruse, her feelings being obvious when, for instance, she sees Shigeru with the tangerine woman. In terms of narrative, *A Scene at the Sea* is a considerably more comprehensible and logically motivated film than *Boiling Point*.[38]

There is a lot of hyperbolic discourse about Kitano's film, but the fact remains that *A Scene at the Sea* has been read as offering both anti-narrative coldness and readable structures of identification and narration. We must try to account for both trends within the film. One way is to consider *A Scene at the Sea*'s attempt to find alternative means of constructing empathetic understanding that, while succeeding in communicating emotion, seem colder than standard formulae precisely because of the way they restructure the relationship between the image and the viewer.

This is partially what the critic Yoshimi Takashi searches for in his analysis of two of the more ambiguous scenes in the film: the bus scene and the lovers' witnessing a man fall into the ocean. To him, 'Kitano Takeshi vigorously avoids spectator identification by shooting from a distance, but he involves the spectator using methods other than identification.'[39] The bus scene is coloured by two narrative ambiguities: why Takako stays on the bus after Shigeru is refused entry, and why she decides to get off when she does. The scene with the accident is particularly important narratively – it comes right after Takako has returned the engagement ring – but while it suggests the two remain a couple, it does not say why. Certainly the audience can speculate on answers to these questions – for example, Takako probably boards the bus because she resents Shigeru ignoring her – but the film does not guide us to these interpretations. Yoshimi suggests that what makes us accept these sudden narrative shifts is Kitano's editing, which, he argues, creates connections between spectator and character not based on simple forms of identification. In the bus scene, he explains, we are initially caught in Takako's psychological drama; again camera movement and position have aligned us with her character. Yoshimi focuses on the initial insert of the old lady in the bus. Although it becomes apparent that her sole narrative role will be to urge Takako to sit down (Takako's refusal indicates her mental anguish), to Yoshimi the first insert is the 'face of an other' that disrupts the psychological narrative. The initial confusion the viewer experiences at the intrusion of an 'other' into this closed drama is, to Yoshimi, homologous to Takako being disturbed from her reverie by the lady's interruption. To him this creates a tenuous connection between viewer and character based not on identity or knowledge, but rather through sharing lack of knowledge, creating not identity but 'overlapping' (*kasanariai*).

Yoshimi sees a similar operation occurring in the bicycle accident scene, but this deserves more attention. In the shot from behind the lovers, the bicycle is so far in the distance, it is barely perceivable, and thus seems an unlikely candidate for changing their fates. The emphasis on their backs, as well as the camera distance in frontal shots, downplays the emotional resonance of the scene. The mishap itself seems almost absurd, a chance event that seems to suggest their change of heart is similarly accidental. Yoshimi argues that it is precisely because cause and effect has been suspended that an alternative logic can take effect where spatial integrity

Chance accidents and chance reunions

(the fact that the foreground and background are both in focus) creates relational necessity.

This homology between formal structures and narrative relations is intriguing, but it raises the issue of the function of looking in the film. Yoshimi argues that editing tenuously connects the viewer and the largely unrelated groups on the beach through a shared, largely meaningless gaze at surfing. What he fails to pursue is the possible significance of this relaxed staring. One crucial aspect of this spectatorship is its theatricality, one based in scopic inequality. In both Shōnan and Chiba, where the surfing competitions take place, the basic spatial construction between seer (sand) and seen (sea) is the same: those looking are on the beach and shot from the sea, those seen are shot from the shore. There are no shots from past the water's edge of those surfing, those riding the waves never have a subjective shot, and hardly any shots clearly include both the looker and those at sea.[40] While there are instances, such as when the photographs are taken, of those on the beach looking at others on the sand (although rarely through a true point-of-view structure[41]), the film consistently constructs a spatial division between beach=seer and surfer=seen. This is a theatrical geography,

Surfer=seen

Beach=seer

one that is reiterated both by the structure of the surfing tournaments themselves, and by the reminder of a judge to one of the surfers: 'You are at sea, we are on land watching your performance.' The shot combining seer and seen that Yoshimi identifies with the bike accident is thus an exception to the film's norm and cannot provide a model for how the spectator is 'ten- uously' connected to the beach scenes. It is also a gendered division as only men perform and women remain on shore to watch. This may seem to reverse the gendering of the gaze in classical cinema, rendering men 'to- be-looked-at'. Yet this remains ambivalent in the film: men gain privileged access to a realm of play always valorised in Kitano, but at the cost of tempt- ing death.

What bridges the fundamental separation of seer and seen is montage, particularly in the Kuleshovian sense. On the set, Kitano spoke admiringly of the power of montage to make, for instance, even a happy dog seem sad. While some reviews lauded the acting of the principals, Kitano staunchly refused to 'let the actors act'.[42] This was a strategy to avoid forcing meaning on the viewer, but it also amplified the importance of montage. The actor's expression is essentially blank even in dramatic scenes like when Takako discovers Shigeru's surfboard, it being the duty of montage – and the spectator's reading of such shot combinations – to bridge spatial and narrative divisions and create meaning. In Kitano's first film as editor, it is editing more than *mise en scène* that produces narrative meaning. This creation of meaning beyond the pro-filmic event at times puts editing at odds with a narrative strategy that consistently works to eliminate the *'kusai'* or artificial elements of the story.

In a complicated analysis, Aoyama Shinji attempts to read this montage of looks in light of Japanese ideology. He first notes the punctuation in the Japanese title, the combination of both a comma and a full stop. The comma echoes the comma in *Violent Cop*'s Japanese title and the 'x' in the title of Kitano's second film; to Aoyama these signify the strategies of hesitation and narrative rupture that typify Kitano's early film-making. The full stop, however, connotes closure, and foreshadows the general disappearance of narrative hesitation in favour of closure in the later work. *A Scene at the Sea*, to Aoyama, is a peculiar work embodying both tendencies. On the side of rupture, Aoyama argues, noting some of the same imbalances of viewing cited above, that while Takako may look at Shigeru, and thus at her love, a living person, his perspective, in part because it is not shown, is metaphorically tied to an unseen point (what he calls the 'vanishing point') and thus to death. Aoyama notes how reversals operate at certain moments to stave off the threat of death (his examples include Takako exiting the bus and turning back towards Shigeru, and Shigeru reversing directions to meet Takako in front of her house). The editing on the beach, however, maintains this threat through a structure that fails to complete the reversal. In a normal film, he argues, the reversal of looks between two people works to enclose the spectator within their internal drama. When one of the two, however, fails to return the gaze like Shigeru does, the processes of closure and internalisation are betrayed.

Aoyama argues, however, that the final, memorial images undermine the rupture enabled by this construction of looks. The film still fails to provide the return look, but neither does it give any point-of-view shots (except, perhaps, from the perspective of a camera taking the photos). No one is looking out at an other, or at a vanishing point, because everyone, including the spectators, is brought into an internalised space of memory. To Aoyama, the happy, comic moments masking Shigeru's death don't only typify how the Japanese mass media tend to ideologically mask threatening ruptures, but they also construct a problematic closure to the film. Shigeru's death creates one disturbing closure for the text, but the memorial images add another closure that, while not eliminating the fact Shigeru died, converts an exteriority (death) into a more pleasing interiority (memory). Aoyama asserts that this internalisation of the external, this closure of the ruptured gap, is typical of how Japanese national ideology has tended to absorb the other into closed and safe narratives.[43]

Aoyama's argument is not without its complications, but it does remind us of the issue of performance broached earlier. For what is formally distinct about these last images on the beach is that they have eliminated the difference between the space of performance and the space of spectatorship. Most of what is seen is performed for the camera, or is a kind of play that itself seems enacted for the look. Those who were viewers – especially Takako – now take part in the performance. This may seem to undermine the binaries established before, but this all takes place on the sand. Takako can ride the board, but only when it is resting on the beach. Dividing spectators on the beach from the spectacle of performance was one way Kitano literalised the distance between film and spectator. When the cinematic spectacle, as with the surfing in the film, fails to be that dramatic, the performance becomes detached from the audience. The effort to identify and empathise with characters must cross this gap, an abyss shadowed by the spectre of death, through montage structures that refuse to readily fold the spectator into a set of mutual gazes. As a whole, identification is only tenuous, and largely based on the homology between spectatorship in the film and in the film's viewer.

The final, memorial images, however, close this gap. Performance is reduced to play closed off from the external world. The spectator may not be inserted into the narrative through shot/reverse shot structures of mutual looks, but as the sole addressee of this performative enunciation (there are no other lookers in these shots), the viewer becomes the privileged lord over these proceedings, which are framed for consumption. Identification with the camera's gaze then reconfirms the power of the spectator.

Both cold and emotional, featuring two endings and containing two different constructions of performative space, *A Scene at the Sea* is a fundamentally divided work. At its best, it re-emphasises these gaps and challenges viewers to create alternative, tenuous and sometimes dangerous connections across these known chasms; at its most problematic, it too easily closes those gaps through conventional framing ideologies that eliminate divisions and enclose everything in a bordered space of performance for the self. *A Scene at the Sea* prefigures the gaps evident in Kitano's career as a whole, but in a way that is raw and still lacks the frames that would aesthetically structure these divisions in later works.

Sonatine

Given its story, *Sonatine* is variously termed Kitano's return to home ground after *A Scene at the Sea*, the culmination of his previous work, the conclusion of a trilogy including *Violent Cop* and *Boiling Point*, a sequel to his début film, and to some, the director's best work. The head of the Kitajima gang orders Murakawa (Beat Takeshi), a skilled but world-weary yakuza, to Okinawa to help settle a war involving the friendly Nakamatsu family, but the situation smells fishy from the start. Fighting had mostly stopped, so the arrival of Murakawa's troops only incites the rival Anan gang into more attacks. Murakawa, Katagiri, Ken, Uechi and Ryōji hide out at a beach house and bide their time with games in the sand as Murakawa makes friends with a woman named Miyuki. When a hitman kills Ken, however, it soon becomes apparent that this was all a scheme by Katagiri and his lieutenant Takahashi to take over Murakawa's territory. The surviving members then plot revenge.

Shōchiku's advertising stressed the continuity with previous work, playing up the reunion of Kitano with producer Okuyama Kazuyoshi and using the tag line 'Sono otoko, koko ni nemuru' (literally 'That man sleeps here') to reference the Japanese title of *Violent Cop*. Such marketing failed, however, as *Sonatine*, released on 4 June 1993, became a box-office disappointment, earning back only ¥60 million in rentals from a budget of ¥500 million. That inevitably forced changes in Kitano's directorial career. Okuyama, who lost his position at Shōchiku in part because of this ignominy, parted ways with Kitano and the director, upset with the studio's handling of his films, used his own company, Office Kitano, to manage his subsequent work.

Amid this financial disarray, discourses about the film were confused if not contradictory. One saw an opposition similar to that with *A Scene at the Sea*, with some praising *Sonatine* as a film without narrative or characters, while others insisted it was his most conventional work to date. How to label the film became an issue as it was placed in such categories as 'gang-

ster film', 'private film', 'art cinema', or even 'student film.' Even the
pressbook seemed at a loss, stating in language largely unthinkable for
press materials from a major studio, 'One has to get used to Takeshi's films
. . . before trying to understand them.' Kitano also offered varying images
of the movie. In interviews intended to sell the film, he seemed apologetic
and quipped that it would fail financially. He was more confident in other
interviews, asserting his artistic command over what he also called a 'private film'. In still other places he said *Sonatine* was the easiest of his works
to understand.

Discussions about *A Scene at the Sea* shared similar divisions, but
whereas that film mirrored those ruptures through challenging the spectator to bridge the gaps, I argue that *Sonatine* frames these divisions in a
seductive reiteration of differences that borders on the utopian, but only by
dangerously treading the line between identity and emptiness, nation and
nothingness, life and death. Empty looks and incomplete suture outline a
void that is pleasurable, yet also disturbing because it reminds one of death
lurking outside the frame.

To clarify the uniqueness of *Sonatine*, it might be helpful first to introduce what its critics said. Perhaps the most pointed critique was offered by
Tamura Tsutomu, a central figure in the Shōchiku Nouvelle Vague, the
movement that helped found an alternative, political cinema in the 1960s.[1]
His critique illuminates not only *Sonatine*, but also how it diverges from that
legacy. He argued that *Sonatine* was no different from what he called a student film: too centred on its author, based on an uneven mix of the scripted
and the improvised, depending too heavily on in-group interpretation, and
lacking a unified style. There was much that he praised about the film, particularly the temporality and the rough but still effective use of ellipses. But
he essentially faulted *Sonatine* for being inconsistent in its attack on dominant cinema. He found this most evident in the ending. If Kitano was truly
offering a version of 'smiling nihilism', he should have concluded the film
not with the attack on Katagiri in the hotel and Murakawa committing suicide afterwards, but rather with a more ironic twist, with Ryōji, for instance,
being unable to turn off the hotel lights, and the two having to return to the
beach to wait some more. This conclusion, by avoiding the nationalist ideol-

ogies implicated in suicide (*à la* Mishima Yukio), would be more nihilistic. The current ending, Tamura argued, owes too much to yakuza genre conventions of betrayal and revenge and engages in overt narcissism, giving only the film-maker's character the choice of his own death – with the beautiful Miyuki waiting to boot. He concludes: 'I don't think there's anything that is expressed in the film that goes beyond just slightly overturning commercial film conventions.'[2]

From these criticisms, one can extrapolate a position on alternative cinema that Tamura utilises to criticise *Sonatine*. It asks for an overturning of commercial cinema conventions through formal experimentation, based on a unified stance that is embodied in the text and is essentially extroverted, extending into the realm of social meaning. 'I wanted him to have enough discernment to cut out the narcissism and render the death ultimately farcical. It would've been better to spoil our pleasure by stating that the situation won't change with just one person wanting to die.'[3] As Tamura argues for a more consistent nihilism, he also establishes standards for character and narrative. He calls *Sonatine* a 'short film' because its narrative doesn't exhibit significant changes: 'it's just . . . the death of a guy who wants to die.'[4] A feature-length narrative to him would have to involve, for instance, Murakawa changing his mind. But *Sonatine* rarely narrates such mental processes.

> If you think of the person killing as an active subject, [Kitano] cheats by not showing the active person acting – he just immediately shows his trump card. . . . The subjectivity [*shutai*] of each killer is different, but here the same card is abruptly played and blood splatters.[5]

Tamura's vision of narrative, while challenging ideologies of closure and the power of the individual, nonetheless relates narrative change to the creation of social meaning, and centres that meaning in the subjectivity of the protagonist. A number of Tamura's films, from his sole directorial work, *Voluntary Villain* (*Akunin shigan*, 1960) to scripted works for Ōshima Nagisa such as *Violence at Noon* (*Hakuchū no tōrima*, 1966) and *Japanese Summer: Double Suicide* (*Muri shinjū: Nihon no natsu*, 1967), feature characters who desire death, but who are subject to both accidental and external forces, their death or survival marking turning points, albeit sometimes ironic ones, in narratives of social repression.

One can disagree with both Tamura's assessment of *Sonatine* and the standards he uses, but his words illuminate *Sonatine*'s difference from Nouvelle Vague predecessors. As we have already seen with the reception of Kitano's previous films, it was precisely the empty characters and meaningless narratives that attracted many film critics and viewers to this director. Analysing the discussions on *Sonatine*, one can discern at least two discursive frameworks countering Tamura's critique.

The first is the rejection of psychological characterisation, if not subjectivity itself. Murakawa begins the film by confessing how tired he is, a statement that could align *Sonatine* with a number of narratives featuring tired gangsters or gunslingers. Many observers, however, did not discern a psychological presence to Murakawa, calling him instead the 'empty centre' of the film.[6] This was perceived as a difference from previous yakuza cinema. As Abe Kashō argued, while Uehara in *Boiling Point* shares the destructiveness of Ishikawa Rikio in Fukasaku's *Graveyard of Honor*, a figure as attractive in his anarchic freedom as he is repulsive in his morals, Murakawa is too close to death even to evince such vitality. The fact that Murakawa's feet are barely shown at the beginning renders him, to Abe, not only a floating entity, but also, given that Japanese spirits traditionally do not have feet, a ghostly one. Murakawa does not rush towards death as Azuma does, evincing evidence of life before death, but is already dead. *Sonatine* is then but a tale of the dead confirming their demise. Although some have tried to equate Murakawa with the stoic yakuza hero, stalwartly suppressing his emotions and overcoming his fear of death – 'a new version of gangster cool'[7] – critics such as Abe don't find that. The Russian roulette scene in particular contrasts Murakawa's unwavering smile with the relatively realistic reactions of Ken and Ryōji. His expression is explained post facto by the joke that there are no bullets, but until then the smile is unreal, if not monstrous. It is a sign of his alterity that resonates well after this scene. The characters are again seen as indefinable things, to some, 'bodies with nothing (*nanimo nai shintai*)'.[8]

One finds the absence if not repudiation of the kind of subjectivity found in Tamura's alternative cinema. The term 'subjectivity' (*shutai, shutaisei*) has a complicated history in postwar Japanese intellectual thought, beginning with the *shutaisei* debates after the war and continuing with the radical politics of the 1960s and 1970s.[9] Confronting a wartime ideological structure that subsumed individual subjects to the state, postwar thinkers asked how responsible subjects could be formed to bear the individual or collective agency for radical democracy and social change. Debates in the film world continued in the late 1950s and 1960s about the representation of 'modern subjects', with Ōshima in particular depicting those agents of desire who go against the social flow. *Sonatine*'s empty characters may possess a critical valence: to Abe, Murakawa's 'alienation from the earth' and lack of destructivity (unlike Uehara) render him a 'modern person', suffering from such ailments as alienation and a lightness of being.[10] Yet the film does not necessarily condemn these conditions, since Murakawa is never the object of concerted critique. If he embodies modern ills, it is in an ambivalent age that can just as equally enjoy such ailments, that can utilise Murakawa as a critical fulcrum against both pretensions of a fullness of being and, perhaps, the ideal of a subjective agency for social change as well.

Tamura may have preferred Murakawa to signify the difficulty of individual action in changing the world, but another discursive framework resisted the ascription of such social or political meaning. As with *Boiling Point* or *A Scene at the Sea*, *Sonatine* was seen as a film whose narrative was essentially meaningless. Yamane Sadao said that 'in this film there is no plot resembling a plot. There is little dialogue and almost no dramatic drama.'[11] The yakuza story was considered largely irrelevant. The purported meaninglessness of the story was due not to the illogicality of the plot, as in *Boiling Point*, nor to a lack of narrative conflict, as in *A Scene at the Sea*. *Sonatine* was thought to be governed by the unchanging temporality of death. As Abe Kashō noted, time in the Okinawan section is figured by three shots of the full moon, presented on different days, but showing no shift in phase. Slight differences may appear in such a changeless frame, but they are ultimately enclosed in the timelessness of death. In Abe's coinage, this is death-only-ism (*yuishishugi*).[12]

On a more basic level, *Sonatine* was depicted as repeatedly delaying or refusing meaning. The critic Ueno Kōshi, for instance, describes the editing in terms of how a slight deviation (*zure*) – a mismatch or a narrative jump – produces a 'strange suspension of meaning' because 'our understanding of what is going on always occurs a moment late'.[13] He says that Kitano pursues a condition in which 'everyday gestures are in a state undifferentiated from the body, just before or just after their meaning is formed as an action'. 'Because that is stripped of meaning and shifted away from narrative, . . . it always strikes the viewer as a surprise.'[14] Devoid of significance, the image cannot also be beautiful. Although many commentators did marvel at the film's aesthetic moments, such as when the hitman throws the red flowers, many resolutely maintained that Kitano consciously avoided aestheticising his subject.[15] If the film was seen as beautiful, it was under standards distinct from usual cinematic aestheticisation.[16]

This envisions *Sonatine* peeling away the layers of meaning that have accumulated on the world, reducing it, as close as possible, to zero so that the 'thing' underneath is laid bare. If *Sonatine* is political, it constitutes to Abe a radical rejection of modern media society, wherein the effort to 'sincerely kill' Beat Takeshi becomes nothing other than the 'mournful rejection' of 'all of televisual modernity'.[17] This supposes that signification can be removed to reveal what is true underneath and partially accounts for claims about the realistic effect of the film.[18] To many film critics, what is ultimately exposed here is cinema itself. Ueno chastises another critic for attempting to reduce the film to various conceptual meanings. 'Viewing a film is to have your existence in some way threatened', he asserts. Ascribing meaning to a film is to him a self-defence mechanism, one that not only avoids the work, but also, by implication, the assault that Kitano launches. This aversion to meaning is also a reaction to the political metanarratives of Tamura and others that focus not on the material text itself but on the allegorical meanings it points to. Its radical rejection of certain forms of interpretation may itself constitute a politics, but only to the degree political meaning in the traditional sense has been rebuffed.

Accounts of *Sonatine* are influenced by these desires for a pure cinema and a naked material reality. Such desires may obfuscate other aspects of the text, however. For instance, commentators such as Tamura already noted the conventional aspects of the yakuza narrative. Others, such as the screenwriter Arai Haruhiko, argued that *Sonatine* revealed that Kitano was becoming more 'normal' or professional in his film-making, for instance adding a melodramatic touch in cutting between Murakawa and Miyuki at the end, or by confirming for the audience the theme of the film through Murakawa's statement, 'When you get too scared of death, you start wanting to die.'[19] The film director Koreeda Hirokazu, while stressing *Sonatine*'s resistance to interpretation, nonetheless called it a 'very orthodox' film in its use of nonverbal action to narrate the story.[20]

Psychology was the bone of contention. While many like Koreeda could claim that Kitano 'doesn't enter into character psychology',[21] Kitano himself stressed the importance of character mentality to the film, at the expense of the story.[22] *Sonatine* uses a number of devices, from a dream sequence to subjective shots, to offer information on inner thoughts and interests. This may be one aspect that signalled to some Kitano's shift from action to art cinema. Abe sees this as a crucial difference from *Violent Cop*, but he focuses primarily on the literal shift from cinema centred on physical energy to a lack of such energy. David Bordwell defines art-cinema narrative as operating through three interlocking procedural schemata: objective realism, expressive or subjective realism and narrative commentary. In particular, he argues that the art film functions through ambiguity, especially an ambiguity over whether a specific device such as an unusual insert should be read as character psychology (subjective realism) or as an authorial device (an intrusive, overt form of narration).[23] Perhaps the divisions in *Sonatine* between minimalistic external narration and psychological depiction are themselves a sign of art-cinema narration. An analysis of subjective narrative structures initially seems to support this.

Most of the point-of-view shots in the film are Murakawa's and serve to orient the viewer, within limits, through his perspective. The most obvious example is the film's sole dream sequence. On the night after playing Russian roulette on the beach, there is a cut from a shot of Murakawa sleeping to a subjective view of Ryōji and Ken looking into the camera, presumably trying to stop Murakawa from shooting himself. A viewer could initially read this as a memory of that day's incident, but the different geography (Murakawa now has his back to the sea) and the fact he now shoots himself indicate this is a dream. The scene communicates Murakawa's disturbed mental state and his death wish, but as is typical of art-cinema narration, that psychologisation is not without its complications. First, the sound accompanying these subjective images – a rising 'whooshing' sound – matches that of the previously objective Russian roulette scene, thereby disturbing the 'objective/subjective' division. Second, in what could be considered another of Kitano's 'impossible' subjective shots, we are given a second subjective shot *after* Murakawa shoots himself. This is the point of view of a dead man.

In other scenes, subjective camerawork can be narratively ambiguous if not deceptive. At the start of the film, Murakawa and Ken visit a mah-jongg parlour to press the owner, Kanemoto, to pay up. The first shot begins with a medium close-up of one of Kanemoto's employees, the camera moving back as Murakawa and Ken enter. A look to the left by the employee at the end of the shot, combined with a subsequent shot of Ken looking right creates the impression that Ken and the man are looking at each other. Ken

Reverse fields . . .

. . . with little in common

then shifts his gaze to the left, after which there is a cut to a medium shot of
Murakawa. Since this shot is followed by one of Kanemoto, it may not be
from Ken's subjective perspective, but it does encourage viewers to assume
that he is looking at the two men talking, a supposition seemingly confirmed
by a return to a medium shot of Ken again looking screen left. That reading,
however, is undermined by the next shot, which shows for the first time a
group playing mah-jongg. Is this what Ken has been looking at? The off-
screen voices of Kanemoto and Murakawa appear to indicate that they are in
the same room as Ken and the parlour game, but even that proves incorrect,
as a later shot finally reveals Murakawa exiting the office, outside of which
Ken has been standing. The lack of an establishing shot at the beginning of
the scene, which constitutes a pattern in the film, both symbolises the spatial ambiguity that invades the work (and prompts mistaken readings of
space) and complicates the reading of character psychology through point-
of-view editing.

Let us examine the editing more closely. As we noted in the last section, *A
Scene at the Sea* creates a fundamental gap between those looking and those
being looked at, those spectating and those performing. The gap is homologous to the one that the spectator must bridge in connecting shots, different

spaces, and even empathy and cruelty, the two faces of the film. *Sonatine* shares a structure of looking and being looked at, but the gap is different. Kitano will frequently do 180-degree reverses between frontal shots of characters or groups of characters, such as in the bus scene or the first visit to the Okinawa office. In many cases, there are few common elements between these shots to confirm their spatial contiguity; only narrative continuity (e.g., a conversation) and sound space (Kitano will often keep the person talking off screen) confirm the spatial unity. In extreme cases, only editing maintains tenuous links between characters . An example is the scene when Murakawa's crew introduce themselves in the office. It begins with a medium close-up of Kitajima looking at the camera and is followed by a broader shot of Murakawa, Takahashi, Ken and Katagiri. The presumption is that this is Kitajima's point of view, but a subsequent shot of him does not appear until the end of the scene, undermining that supposition. No single shot places Kitajima in the same frame with any other character, and again only sound establishes his spatial contiguity (and only in the second shot of him). Still, his exact location in the room is unclear (there is a chance, as with mah-jongg parlour scene, that he is not even in the room). These medium close-ups establish a look that

An impossible space

Matched gazes with the same background

is tenuously linked to other characters through montage, but which is isolated unlike in *A Scene at the Sea*, as if it is not looking at anything. In other cases, montage can work to create a look that is spatially impossible. This is the case with the dream sequence that offers two shots, one of Murakawa, one of Ken and Ryōji, each with the sea in the background even though they are supposedly looking at each other. Only montage and the supposition of a subjective camera create this special relation.

These are again gaps that the spectator will have to work to cross. Yet the structure here is not as strict as in *A Scene at the Sea*. There is no division between those who only look and those who are only looked at – both sides look. As if to mirror that, the camera will not infrequently leave its position between these two sides to shoot from behind one or the other. Murakawa is the character with by far the greatest number of subjective shots. This serves to define him as a spectator, and one who frequently looks at performances. These can range from the killing of Kanemoto to the dance that Uechi choreographs. Miyuki's husband[24] problematises his position as a spectator by charging him with voyeurism (*nozoki*), the perverse pleasure of looking. The accusation seems groundless: Murakawa is too empty a character to exhibit such specular pleasure, an impression confirmed by his lack of sexual reaction to Miyuki's exposed breasts. But it does raise two issues: the role of the spectator in the performance and the pleasure of the look if it is not necessarily sexual.

Murakawa's reaction to the husband's charge – head butting and then shooting him – indicates the degree to which Murakawa directly intervenes in what he is looking at. While he stays a spectator in some instances, such as the dance sequences, in many others, such as when he first sees Ken and Ryōji playing on the beach, he crosses over the line dividing the seer and the seen and becomes involved in the performance. Murakawa, however, is involved more as a director, setting his traps and manipulating his sumō dolls. It is significant that other characters like Uechi and Ryōji are given point-of-view shots precisely when they help stage performances themselves (Uechi with Ken and Ryōji's dance, Ryōji with the massacre at the hotel). It is tempting to read this as a cinematic metaphor, since Kitano also sets his traps (deceiving the viewer about who might be the rival gang in the bar shootout) and manoeuvres his blank-faced actors. But becoming a performer in one's own performances can be debilitating. Just as Beat Takeshi enters into performances Kitano has staged to undermine his persona, Murakawa also occasionally becomes the performer, but narratively at the price of his death. Murakawa is rarely the subject of others' point-of-view shots, a fact that underlines the power differences between director and actor. However, the killing of Ken, the film's first spectator who is completely transformed into a performer in Okinawa, proves to be a traumatic event: Murakawa, the audience to Ken and Ryōji's antics, is virtually paralysed (unlike Ryōji, who immediately flees). In the next scene, Murakawa finally becomes the sole object of the other characters' gaze, as Katagiri, Ryōji, Uechi and Miyuki watch him play Frisbee alone on the beach. While Murakawa remains an important actor, it is in some ways Ryōji who becomes more the director towards the end, dealing the final blow against Takahashi and managing the lights for the final attack. He, significantly, also gets the film's last true point-of-view shot: of the flashing lights in the hotel, *Sonatine*'s final cinematic metaphor (Murakawa's machine gun, especially when firing at the camera, strongly resembling the light of the projector in the theatre).

Following this metaphor, we can say that Kitano is emphasising the violence of the look and the camera, a perspective further pursued in *Brother* and *Zatoichi*. Not only does Murakawa the looker attack who he was looking at, but in many of the killings in the film, the deadly bullets emerge from behind the camera. Nakamatsu, Uechi's boss, is filmed frontally when he and his lieutenants are gunned down, and the film never offers a reverse shot of the shooter, as if leaving the camera the only suspect on the scene. But if Yomota Inuhiko finds the representation of violence in *Sonatine* lessened, as if it is 'in quotation marks',[25] it is partially because the power of the look is in check, framed by emptiness. This is especially evident with human gazes. The threat behind the looker paralyses, gluing her to her seat. What expresses this disempowered gaze is the vacant stare.

Kitano's films are dotted with characters gazing off into space with no indication of the object of their glance. Their absent stares are hard to psychologise and the lack of action renders them moments of narrative stasis. *Sonatine* reformulates these empty stares. With a frontal cinematography that often captures characters with their shoulders square to the camera, *Sonatine* often features characters looking at the lens. Generally forbidden in classical cinema, except in comedic moments like in Chaplin's *The*

The empty look

Pawnshop (1916), these looks at the camera have reminded some of Ozu Yasujirō. While, as David Bordwell iterates, Ozu's characters do not actually stare into the camera but rather above it,[26] Kitano's work seems to share that look at a time when many directors, from Suo Masayuki to Takenaka Naoto, were emulating Ozuesque touches. What distinguished *Sonatine* is the fact that the look at the camera is not always tied to a look at a person, or otherwise framed within a point-of-view structure as later Kitano works would often do. Certainly there are instances, such as the William Tell game between Ken and Ryōji, where the look at the camera is reciprocated by a reverse shot of the looked-at character staring back. From the very first scene, however, *Sonatine* signals the presence of a different look at the camera. Right after the shots of Ken staring at the mah-jongg players, the film returns to Ken, seemingly confirming the subjective structure. However, camera angle and distance are slightly different and now, unlike the first shot, he is looking at the camera. The shifts in angle and his gaze are not clearly motivated: this might be the point of view of the woman at the edge of the frame at the mah-jongg table who turns towards the camera at the end of the previous shot, but there is no subsequent shot of her and she never reappears in the film. Up until near the end, further looks at the camera will mostly be justified by other characters' gazes, but one particular scene denotes a problem which will be pursued later. This is a short insert of Uechi and Katagiri inside some club, staring off screen right. We can hear a fight occurring off screen, but the film never shows us what is going on (the script explains that two Murakawa soldiers are beating up some Anan men). This frustrating framing and editing, denying us what we desire to see or what is seemingly important narratively, will meld with later looks at the camera.

The most significant shift occurs after Ken is shot. Murakawa and Miyuki are initially shown looking at Ken's fallen body. There is then a shot of the assassin looking at the camera. A previous shot of him from the same angle and framing was read as Ken's point-of-view shot, but now the subjective source of this shot is dead. This again retroactively questions the previous point-of-view shot, while also repeating the motif of the 'look of the dead'. But the killer's gaze at the camera helps establish a shift that will be developed in the subsequent shot: the look at the camera becoming an ultimately empty stare. While narratively the killer's glance can be explained as a residual of his previous look at Ken, the next shot of Murakawa staring at the lens is more disturbing because it has no such justification. There are scenes in the film where the editing more closely performs the operation of suture, stitching the spectator into the film with more clarity than previous work and offering an identity of position that is often aligned with the primary figure of Murakawa. However, the editing of empty stares and the look of the dead, coupled with framing that sometimes fails to provide the visual command of space that suture promises through reverse shots, all contribute to a more nebulous, if not vacuous subject construction.

The construction is not unpleasant and can align with the stagnant, unproductive, yet pleasurable play on the beach. The space of play formed in Okinawa is utopian partially because it offers powerful identities like Murakawa the director, but also because such identities are rendered free of time and responsibility by being empty. To Hase Masato, *Sonatine* represents a shift from repetition as an excessive attachment to life in *Violent Cop* to repetition as an almost pleasurable acceptance of death.[27] In a sense, it is the pleasure of a second childhood – almost a return to the pre-Oedipal stage before the institution of divisions in time and space – and of emptiness and liminality. Yomota sees the rather good mood of Murakawa's playful men, their obliviousness to violence, as stemming in part from the fact that 'the concept of the other itself is on the verge of extinction within them'.[28] The bright Okinawan beach is not a 'natural' offering of freedom in contrast to the darkly blue, claustrophobic and artificial Tokyo, but rather, as Hasumi Shigehiko argues, a space unrelated to such binary divisions and thus all the more free and utopian.[29] It is a liminal space between such poles as life (represented by the flower at the end) and death, performer and spectator, viewer and viewed. One can also see it as a site of narrative liminality, as the conflicting genre definitions – art film, gangster film, student film – merge and collide, sending off sparks like the fireworks on the beach. The spectator can enjoy this textual space, which touches on the borders of various genres or narrational forms, without ever committing herself to them. This liminality also relates to the nation to the degree that Okinawa, and especially Miyako Island, where *Sonatine* was filmed, are on the very edge of Japan, possessing a unique climate and culture that colours the film through dancing and musical rhythms. There is the danger of exoticising Okinawa for Japanese eyes, but Kitano never makes it the paradise that such directors as Nakae Yūji or Shiina Makoto have, particularly through nostalgically emphasising communion between a *Gemeinschaft* society and the beauty of nature.[30] At worst his Okinawa becomes a fantastic space freeing us of binary oppositions, one that is always tempered by the fact that this Okinawa is defined less by Japanese national consciousness than by a non- or *inter*-nationality.

If this is what makes *Sonatine* pleasurably utopian, what renders it powerfully disturbing is the impossibility of the gaze beyond this borderline space. First, as we noted, the look is progressively disempowered within the film, in part by the realisation that what is behind the look – the killer, the camera, the cinema, the auteur, even the nation – may be more violent and controlling than at first thought. Processes of framing and editing direct and restrict the gaze, undermining the ability to see what one wants. Borders are re-imposed, confirming what was already evident in the geography. Although *Sonatine* does not feature the simple spatial divisions of *A Scene at the Sea*, and thus appears more spatially free, no character actually enters the sea like in that film and *Boiling Point* before it. Again, there is no camera shot from the water, nor any character movement into the sea or towards the water's edge. Just as the look is restricted, so is character movement, making *Sonatine* one of a number of Japanese films that narrate efforts to escape Japan, fleeing to the beach or other such border, only to face boundaries that prove more impenetrable than thought.[31] The best that *Sonatine* can offer is the look beyond the border, the empty look off screen or into the camera, looking beyond the frame not only within the diegesis, but figuratively even outside of it. That, however, cannot be shown in the film, because that both exceeds the cinema and the nation in which the characters are trapped. It is a space *Sonatine* connects with death.

Getting Any?

Getting Any? is not a film by Kitano Takeshi, at least not according to the advertisements. It was billed as the 'début film of Beat Takeshi', and most discussions of the movie began with such words as 'complete change'[1] 'surprise' and 'sudden reverse'.[2] If some saw *Sonatine* as the culmination of a four-part period of Kitano's career, *Getting Any?* was the beginning of a new stage, one that involved not only a reappraisal of fixed ideas about Kitano's cinema, but also implicitly a critique of auteurist discourses themselves. Even more than *A Scene at the Sea*, this film helped establish the opinion that Kitano always 'slips by when you try to get a hold of him'.[3] *Getting Any?* was considered Kitano's intentional attempt 'to overturn the various discourses and fixed ideas that had come to accumulate around his work up until then'.[4] Kitano encouraged these ideas in a foreword to the printed version of the script:

> The people who have supported my four films up until now will probably fall out of their chairs upon seeing this, my fifth movie. They'll probably ask, 'Is this by the same director?' That's because it's completely veered off course. [5]

Getting Any? could be called the *tsukkomi* (straight man) of Kitano's oeuvre, taking a jab at both his previous works and those who thought they had understood him, making them *boke*/clowns. The film can thus serve as our test case for considering the relation between Kitano's comedy and his film-making, not just in the kinds of gags offered, but in his general attitude towards his cinematic career. The crucial issue will be what the *tsukkomi* of *Getting Any?* can mean given the weakening of *tsukkomi* discussed in Part I.

Considering it an attack on auteurist generalisations served as one justification for the film, but some observers were hard pressed to find others. *Getting Any?* was one of Kitano's least successful works critically, finishing 39th in the illustrious *Kinema junpō* critics poll, the lowest result for a Kitano film. Critics said it was unfunny, pointless, without a plot, without meaning, trashy (*kudaranai*) and the 'graveyard' of Japanese comedy.[6] It is ostensibly about Asao, a not-too-young schlep who tries various stupid ways of getting laid, starting with buying a car and – since all his plans naturally fail – continuing with flying first class on a plane (for which he needs to rob a bank for the money) or becoming an actor. Even this rather goal-oriented narrative soon falls apart as Asao is mistaken for a gangster or suddenly decides he wants to turn invisible so that he can peep on naked women. It so happens that a mad scientist (played by Beat Takeshi) fulfils his wish, but when Asao tries to renew the invisibility effect, he turns into a huge fly and is attacked by forces familiar from Japanese monster movies. The narrative is quite a mess (though to some, a delicious mess), and in a curious fashion the film's producers seemed to acknowledge its faults. After the success of *Sonatine* and *Violent Cop* at festivals in the United Kingdom, *Getting Any?* was premièred at the London Film Festival in December 1994, but in a version some thirty-four minutes shorter than the Japanese release print. In Japan, press screenings were not offered before the opening, and even the pamphlet for the DVD contains a somewhat critical essay.[7]

Yet as was the case with *Boiling Point* and *A Scene at the Sea*, faults to some were pluses to others. *Getting Any?* represented a 'challenge to the audience',[8] one that 'shook the foundations of established ideas of what cinema is'.[9] Kitano himself declared that, 'this is something that has never existed before'.[10] Against those who found the film pointless, Inagawa Hōjin declared that it 'repeats empty proliferation – it is made of the wreckage of zeroes bred over and over again with each other. One can even dare say that viewing these ruined zeroes is one of the adventures of this film.'[11] This adventure extended to challenging the sensibility and hierarchies of culture. To Sera Toshikazu,

> *Getting Any?* is from start to finish a truly trashy film. The ideas are vulgar, the gags unfunny; letting everything slide until it all collects in a pile of shit at the end is utterly reprehensible. But that is what Kitano 'dared' to aim for in this

film. He was in no way striving to create a hilarious, knee-slapping comedy. He gave that up by casting Dankan in the lead role. The purpose is not to make us laugh, but to make us thoroughly disgusted and blurt out 'What trash!' Without a doubt this film director, who emerged from a rundown entertainment district, tried to make history's worst and grossest film in order to confirm his origins.[12]

Some critics were able to connect this lowest of films into Kitano's thematics of death. Especially in light of his motorcycle accident on 2 August 1994, a mere three days after finishing editing *Getting Any?*, a few commentators interpreted the mishap as the death wish of films like *Sonatine*, and saw *Getting Any?* as Takeshi's 'suicide note'.[13] Sera argued that if *Sonatine* was the complete rejection of Beat Takeshi by Kitano Takeshi, this next film was Beat's 'counterattack' or, in a more extreme expression, Takeshi's 'attempt to commit suicide as a film director'.[14] To Yomota Inuhiko, it was a 'radical experiment in which self-criticism becomes self-destruction'.[15]

Foreign critics, many of who were unsure about the film, attempted to at least justify it as a glimpse of Japanese culture or as an accurate view of what Kitano, as Beat Takeshi, was like as a television comedian.[16] However, most Japanese critics, echoing Sera's comments, underlined the differences between *Getting Any?* and Beat Takeshi's televisual comedy. To some, it was simply a matter of different financial and censorship conditions, as Kitano could spend more money and offer more adult humour in cinema than on the small screen. Yet the dominant impression that *Getting Any?* was not only unfunny, but that it might have been intentionally so, bolstered the interpretation that Kitano was distancing himself from his televisual humour. In retrospect, Kitano spoke about the conflict between expectations that he do a comedy and his desire to deviate from that humour.

I was very conscious of being a comedic talent at the time, but it really turned me off when comedians filmed comedy without any changes. It was just a given that it would make people laugh. So I thought I'd be adventuresome and attempt a different kind of humour. I thought it had to be a film where I'd break up the

straight humour a bit and have them laugh at the system of humour itself. So I
purposely made it clunky. And then the entire film became clunky.[17]

To Kitano, *Getting Any?*, which he once called his *magnum opus*, was supposed to be 'a film that makes fun of comedy itself'.[18] The film thus
demands to be analysed not simply in relation to Kitano's other films, but
also to Beat Takeshi's television work and trends in comedy in contemporary Japan. These issues were outlined in Part I, but here we should first reiterate Kitano's historical relation to the *tsukkomi/boke* issue before
proceeding to an analysis of the manifestations of these structures in *Getting
Any?*.

We have already noted the Two Beats's important position in the weakening of *tsukkomi* versus the *boke* (the fool) in *manzai* comedy. Yet while
Takeshi could act the *boke* on stage, his 'poisonous' gags still functioned like
social commentary, taking a *tsukkomi* jab at social hypocrisy, postwar
humanism, knee-jerk leftists and the mass mentality. But he never gave up
his own status as *boke*, making a fool of himself for the audience. In that
stance, one could read his devotion to the culture of old-style entertainers
(*geinin*), a commitment that is evident both in his occasionally old-school
comedy (in the use of silly make-up, slapstick and standard gags) and vocal
respect for Fukami Senzaburō and other erstwhile entertainers. Even that
was double-sided, however, as his devotion was always tinged with a cool
distance. Such a stance was visible in the way he both enabled the playful
space of friends/*nakama* on shows like *The Genius Takeshi's Enlivening TV*
and stood outside it, never directing forceful *tsukkomi* at the amateur participants, yet shrugging his shoulders at their antics. To Ōta Shōichi, this
mixed reaction could signal both the end of *tsukkomi* as a transcendent
entity, able to stand outside and above these foolish amateurs and criticise
them, as well as Beat Takeshi's limited attempt to comment on the incipient
space of 'friends' from within.[19]

It would be rash to apply this reading of Kitano's comedic background to
Getting Any? as is. First, there is the problem of transposing a variety format
to a narrative-based fiction film. Henry Jenkins has described the tense
relationship in the early years of sound cinema between the vaudeville for-

mat, with its loose narration, anything-for-a-laugh spirit and self-reflexivity, and the classical style, which valorised transparent linear narration.[20] It is additionally tough to reproduce on film a TV variety format that depends on a mixture of audience distance and participation and a porous boundary between reality and TV, real time and TV time, the space of the spectators and the space of the programme.

Yet *Getting Any?* can nonetheless be considered a rather bold attempt to import this very different format into a medium that, as one can see with the fate of Hollywood's vaudeville stars in the 1930s, was ultimately averse to such an alternative. The film shares much with variety television in terms of both the space of friends and narrative structure. With multiple voices reading the Japanese title, which includes the word 'minna' (everyone), *Getting Any?* is from the start a space of group play, one lorded over by the director Kitano and populated by many familiar figures from Takeshi's Army, including Dankan, Guadalcanal Taka (the Cessna pilot) and Sonomanma Higashi (the drug tester) in larger roles, with Yanagi Yūrei, Suidōbashi Hakase, Rassha Itamae, Tsumami Edamame and others playing smaller ones. The narrative itself privileges the structure of skit comedy. The first half may be unified by Asao's attempt to attract girls, but that often functions as a mere excuse to string together a set of skits that sometimes detour so much, they essentially interrupt the narrative. The second half tends to have longer narratives, albeit less unified by a set goal, as if the basic structure has shifted from short skits to extended parodies.

In many cases, the narrative exhibits illogicality, lack of motivation, discontinuity, dead ends and simple contradiction. At times, it resembles a Road Runner cartoon, as Asao formulates his plans and his traps, only to get caught in them, sometimes at the cost of his own life – but returns in the next shot as if nothing happened. The gangster don can get Asao to volunteer to kill the enemy boss in one scene – thus giving Asao his chance to do a Takakura Ken imitation – only to in the next introduce Asao to the target through a photograph, leaving us wondering how he knew the target in the first scene. A writer like film director Yamaguchi Takayoshi has been tempted to read the entire film, *à la Boiling Point*, as a dream in order to account for these inconsistencies.[21] Kitano's careful insertion of Asao's fan-

tasy scenes in the film, as well as the fact that the narrative shifts significantly away from Asao towards the end, discourages this reading however. To
use Steve Neale and Frank Krutnik's definitions of the terms, we could say
the film is actually a thorough privileging of the comic over the comedic, of
momentary laughs over narrative-grounded comedy.[22] In taking this radical
step, the film approximates the kind of self-reflexivity of variety programming, a task augmented by the proliferation of movie and TV citations.

Yet the persistent criticism is that the film is not very funny. Yamaguchi,
for instance, concludes his essay with the following:

> This inconsistent attitude – Does it want to make us laugh? Does it not want to
> make us laugh? Or is laughter just irrelevant? – is in no way pleasurable for the
> audience and can only be called a fault of the film.[23]

Some complain that the film is sloppy. The screenwriter Tanaka Yōzō complained that many jokes lacked sufficient build up.[24] Kitano's decision to
keep his camera back in many scenes – to film comedy with the same
detachment as he does many of his serious films – seems to communicate a
lack of support for these gags, a decision that can leave some jokes,
especially the older, more familiar ones, naked and humourless.

Instead of concluding that this is a fault of the film, one could argue it
constitutes Kitano's critique of comedy or the space of 'friends'. Simply put,
the film refuses to render *tsukkomi* as a hidden assumption enabling a space
of group play free of criticism. The film is not without *tsukkomi* – its cruel
treatment of Asao is in fact classic Beat Takeshi *tsukkomi* – but many comic
scenes, such as the Cessna pilot's on-board service show, are simply presented as is, with little discernable *tsukkomi* except for the passengers'
faces, which are actually rather ambiguous. On variety television, such weak
tsukkomi is augmented by various devices: first, *tsukkomi* provided by the
audience; second, weak *tsukkomi* supplied by visual devices such as camerawork, editing and subtitles on screen; and third, a *nori* or communal
enthusiasm that raises the level of fun. In *Getting Any?*, however, these
elements are unstable, if not entirely absent. Audience expectations could
provide the necessary viewer *tsukkomi*, and certainly billing the film as Beat

Multiple Takeshis in *Takeshis'*

Subtracting furniture and colour (*Violent Cop*)

More than homosocial (*Boiling Point*)

Gag editing . . .

. . . and violence (*Boiling Point*)

Everyday cruelty: golf at a funeral (*Violent Cop*)

A Scene at Sea: commemoration covering death

Sonatine: the violence of the camera

Hana-Bi: framing Nishi and colour

Beauty framing beauty and violence

Kitano Takeshi, the angel (*Hana-Bi*)

Impossible POVs: the dragonfly's perspective (*Kikujiro*)

Brother: attacking the lens

Sawako and Matsumoto, unrealistic beggars (*Dolls*)

The violence of cinema and comedy (*Takeshis'*)

Takeshi's directorial début was aimed at this, but the resulting picture is a
curious *mélange* that is neither the Kitano Takeshi of *Sonatine*, nor the comedy of *We Are the Clown Tribe*. The camerawork is often inconsistent in
encouraging audience *tsukkomi* or providing it itself. Most importantly,
Getting Any? lacks *nori*. This is evident just by comparing it to the last sections of *Kikujiro* in which Takeshi, working with Army members Great
Gidayū and Ide Rakkyō, creates the kind of warm space of fun similar to that
of much TV comedy. *Getting Any?* is too cruel, too cold and too inconsistent
to build up such momentum. With its repeated stressing of performance as
performance, the film also fails to break down the walls between performer
and audience that in TV comedy expand the humourous space of friends
beyond the proscenium and into the audience.

It is possible, following Ōta, to consider the filmic style of *Getting Any?* as
the cinematic equivalent of Takeshi's silent, unenthusiastic, if not cold
reaction to the world of 'friends' that had come to dominate Japanese TV. It
is his identity as an entertainer, emphasised later in *Zatoichi*, that may provide the ground for this wordless critique. *Getting Any?* not only mobilises
dozens of *geinin*, but often pays respect to them. Arguably the film's most

Geinin performing

enjoyable scene is when Kitano simply lets the Chanbara Trio reunite to do the kind of performance (Yamane Shinsuke slicing everything from a fly to an atom!) that made them famous on the Osaka comedy stage. The direction, which constructs this precisely as a performance (played for the camera, which is often looked at), uses this space both as a respectful refuge and as a professional realm critical of a humour based on amateurs just being stupid.

Yet as Ōta says, even Kitano's scowl cannot find the proper words of criticism. The film's inconsistencies communicate a larger ambivalence towards its subjects. While Kitano can add a few cinematic inserts to the Chanbara Trio scene to augment and amplify its humour, many of the film's vaudeville-like performances, like the *taiko* drummers at the end, are not favoured with such cinematic *tsukkomi*. Kitano also refuses to parody these *geinin* entertainers.[25] The fast motion reaction to Asao's screeching violin or the Mickey Mousing with the salesman hitting the boy can function as *tsukkomi*, but they are less jibes than slight twists on the situation. This is often the case with the use of music. For instance, while the first song played as Asao looks for a car-sex companion, 'What to Do?' ('Komatchau na', a 1960s' tune popularised by Yamamoto Rinda), does spin the situation by contrasting the situation with the voice of an innocent girl asked out on a date for the first time, most of the songs, as some complained, do not comment on the scene, but rather trace it,[26] simply repeating what is in the image. This is the case with 'The Apple Song' ('Ringo no uta', a famous postwar tune) during the William Tell scene or 'Midsummer Event' ('Manatsu no dekigoto', a song about a riding in a car) when Asao steals the yellow vehicle. Other songs, such as Baishō Chieko's 'Downtown Sun' ('Shitamachi no taiyō') or Takakura Ken's 'Karajishi botan', rather redundantly reinforce the references (the former helping the Kawaguchi factory scene cite 1960s' youth films like *Kupora, Where the Furnaces Glow* [*Kyūpora no aru machi*, 1962]; the latter citing yakuza films starring Takakura). The movie quotes numerous films and television shows, from *Mothra* to *Zatoichi*, from *The Guardman* (a TV action show) to Nikkatsu Roman Porno (through Roman Porno actress Ezawa Moeko's sex scene in the Kawaguchi sequence). It also alludes to many postwar incidents (the 1948 Imperial Bank poisoning case

[*Teigin jiken*], or the still unsolved 1968 ¥300 million armoured car robbery [*Sanoku-en jiken*]) and personages (having the real Miyaji Toshio, famous for never putting his money in the bank, play himself as a businessman with cash in his attaché case). These allusions are often presented as is, with little sense of parodic jabbing.[27] The casting of Kobayashi Akiji as the squadron chief managing the fly man crisis is telling. Kobayashi played that role in the *Ultraman* television programmes yet, apart from one shot in which Kitano has him wear a dog costume, he is largely playing his role as he did nearly thirty years before. It is hard to distinguish these citations from the kind of imitative tracing that, by allowing TV viewers to recognise a quotation, encourages the formation of another space of 'friends' sharing popular cultural knowledge. The general weakness of *tsukkomi* in the film threatens to turn its comic performances into neutral ground themselves. Humour, as with much variety programming, is then largely based on inside jokes or a community of viewers who laugh, not because it's funny, but because that community's shared knowledge constructs it as humourous.

One could argue that the fact that *Getting Any?* is a film and not television, is its primary form of *tsukkomi*. In this case, it is the very presentation of variety TV in cinema, a medium lacking television's community of viewers and performers, that is sufficient to lend a critical edge to its depiction. This may explain why cinema is so important to this film – how, in Abe Kashō's words, it can be a 'metaconsciousness' of cinema[28] – as it both cites numerous films and shows the production process itself. This could again revive the opposition between Beat Takeshi the TV performer and Kitano Takeshi the film director. But contextual factors render this opposition unstable. Not only was the film advertised as a Beat Takeshi film, but in this age of videos and DVDs, the film was probably most watched at home.[29] Moreover, the philosopher Nibuya Takashi argues that Kitano fails to pursue the violence of his medium in the film. If it aims to present the violence of humour, such as when Asao swats the fly, it forgets the cool violence of the camera itself. In the end, Kitano just renders violence violently, with the laughter lost somewhere along the way.[30]

Perhaps Kitano's inability to commit himself to a strong *tsukkomi* indicates that he has not escaped the ambiguous mixture between spectators and viewers that Ōta identifies as central to the contemporary 'friendly' space of comedy. The shift from an audience divided from the performers by the stage to viewers allowed through television into the intimate space of the comedy is crucial to the creation of the pseudo space of 'friends', but Ōta stresses that viewer participation is always tinged with the divisions of performance. His book begins with an analysis of contemporary patterns of speech, particularly the recent use of the verb *ukeru*. What once was a backstage term for describing whether a gag worked or not, has now come into common parlance as means of describing something funny. There is a curious duality about its use, however: while on the one hand, 'Kore ga ukeru' describes the user's own involvement in the laughter (e.g., 'I think this is funny'), it also simultaneously introduces a cold, objective evaluation to the statement ('I judge that others would think this is funny'). To Ōta this illustrates how contemporary Japanese both insert themselves into the humourous space of 'friends' as well as separate themselves from it. This evinces the encoded nature of participation in this social sphere (that one is not simply being funny, but acting out codes of humour), as well as the lack of commitment to either participation or critical observation. Kitano Takeshi, one can recall, has repeatedly spoken of his relation to himself in similar terms: a division between himself and another, coolly observant self viewing from above. Takeshi can thus be said to embody this characteristic of the age, but we must also ask ourselves how much his films, if not also his directorial career, are similarly shaped by a society where *tsukkomi* is so weak, it cannot even criticise itself, where ubiquitous self-observation (self-*tsukkomi*) has rendered the line between the critical subject and the object criticised so ambiguous, that it has lost its critical edge. The frame of *tsukkomi* has weakly but pervasively enveloped everything without allowing for a truly external other. The question is whether Kitano, in challenging television, Beat Takeshi or even auteurist definitions of Kitano Takeshi, is really able to land a hard blow against his targets, or whether he only offers a soft twist precisely because such self-abuse is already accommodated within the system.

The danger is that this view allows for no alternative. I do believe Kitano's early cinema sought out means for escaping a world in which self-critique differs little from self-congratulation, precisely by critiquing *manzai*. Bob Davis has attempted to find an equivalent to *manzai* in Kitano's style, seeing a repartee occurring between what he terms Kitano's 'default style', a static, quiet, de-dramatised and flat cinematography working like the 'straight man', and the sudden explosions of violence that act like the *boke*.[31] The suggestion is intriguing, but where I think Kitano's cinema may find an alternative to the self-observant space of friends is not through a stylistic approximation of *manzai*, but through a non-*manzai*, one which avoids the ideological space of contemporary *manzai* through self-consciously emptying *tsukkomi* of substance. This strategy results in Kitano's default style, which works to avoid the communal construction of weak *tsukkomi* by violently asserting its emptiness. It is this in-your-face emptiness that paradoxically creates a critical *tsukkomi* through rejecting substantive *tsukkomi*, through breaking the frame not by pummelling on it from without, but by creating an utter vacuum from within. We could then say that the violence in Kitano's films resides less in the difference between a neutral style and the moments of violence or comedy, than in the violence or absurdity of the default style itself, which defines all other moments in the film. This ideal of an empty *tsukkomi*, however, may have only been realised in some of Kitano's early works, such as *Boiling Point* and *Sonatine*. *Getting Any?* remains a curiously borderline work, recalling the radically empty *tsukkomi* of previous films, but ambivalently looking forward to the conventionally weak *tsukkomi* of movies like *Kikujiro*.

Kids Return

Kids Return is often discussed in terms of autobiography. The film tells in flashback the story of two delinquent high-school friends, Shinji and Masaru. Although Masaru uses violence and pranks to upset the teachers and extort money from classmates, he is felled one day by a student's boxer bodyguard and decides to join a gym. It is Shinji, however, just tagging along, who proves to be the born pugilist, so as he develops into a potential champion, Masaru disappears to join the ranks of a local yakuza family. Neither enjoys success as an older boxer named Hayashi tempts Shinji into using destructive techniques and Masaru is maimed when he speaks out against mob superiors after his boss is assassinated. Even Hiroshi, their classmate, suffers failure in the workaday world after succeeding in marrying Sachiko, a pretty café waitress. It seems the only ones who do well are a pair of students aspiring to be *manzai* comedians.

Kitano stated that the teenagers in the film were partially based on characters from school, and that their experiences are culled from his own life. He also joined a boxing gym in his teens, and as an adult, worked for a time as a taxi driver, a scales salesman and of course a *manzai* performer (the *manzai* performances were filmed at the Suehirotei, an old Two Beats haunt). Lines such as the taxi passenger's about the cushiness of a cab driver's job come word for word from Takeshi's memory.[1] The connection most often made between the film and Takeshi, however, centres on the scooter accident that occurred on 2 August 1994. *Kids Return* was the first film Kitano made after the accident and many attempted to read it through that. The title, actually taken from Beat Takeshi's first collection of poems published in 1986,[2] was interpreted as announcing Kitano's return to the director's chair. The director himself joked that he picked this more conventional story, which he had first conceived some five years before, for his return film because if he had done something wild like *Boiling Point*, people would have thought he had suffered brain damage in the accident. Time and time again, Kitano stressed that *Kids Return* was his 'rehabilitation film' after the disasters of the accident and *Getting Any?*[3]

If the doubts Shinji expresses to Masaru at the end – 'We aren't finished, are we?' – were taken to express the qualms Takeshi himself experienced after the accident, Masaru's response – 'We haven't even begun!' – was Kitano's ultimate answer.[4] Most considered this a positive ending, a sense reinforced by the fact that the heroes were alive for the first time at the end of a Kitano picture. A news weekly gave the standard account:

> The heroes of *Kids Return* don't die. Rather, they strongly and stubbornly try to keep on living. The theme of death has been replaced by one of life. Anyone would connect this change of heart to the bike accident, which, for a time, many truly thought to be a failed suicide attempt. Without a doubt, that accident was the experience of confronting death, of staring it directly in the eyes. If that's the case, it wouldn't be strange if Kitano began to lose his reason for continuing to cling to death.[5]

To some, *Kids Return* was the beginning of a new cycle of Kitano cinema, one coming after the first (ending with *Sonatine* or perhaps *Getting Any?*), and ultimately continuing with positive films like *Kikujiro*.

Kitano was somewhat ambivalent about this interpretation. When persistently pressed by an interviewer insisting on the film's turn towards the positive, Kitano responded that it was little different from his previous work, ending he said on a minus note.[6] A number of critics agreed, calling *Kids Return* Kitano's cruellest film to date, one that presented young Japanese trapped in a circular temporal existence with no future.[7] The film thus focuses attention on a crucial issue: the meaning and function of repetition and circularity in Kitano's work, if not also his career. We will see that *Kids Return* is an ambivalent consideration of the possibility of return, of the conflict between hopeful change and fateful repetition, both for Kitano and his characters.

Conflicting interpretations of the film often revolved around the ending. It is Kitano's first film to be narrated through a flashback structure (which would become more prominent in his subsequent films): it begins with Shinji and Masaru apparently reuniting for the first time in a few years, pro-

What Shinji does in practice . . .

. . . he repeats in the match

ceeds with a narration of their past, and then concludes in the present with
them returning to their old schoolyard. The beginning of the final scene
echoes the first scene of the flashback, almost down to the same shots. The
crucial issue is whether anything has changed, and is even raised by Shinji
as they still ride their bikes in circles. The potential lack of progress, and a
fundamental circularity potentially undermining any hope of future change,
places a cloud over this reunion. Yet to some, the final dialogue nonetheless
offers hope that a narrative of change can begin. The film possibly accentuates this reading by concluding with Masaru's statement and punctuating it

with the start of Hisaishi Jō's kinetic music.[8] This exemplifies the kind of visceral thrill that Yamane Sadao connects with the film's prominent use of motion, manifested in both cycling and camera movement.[9]

Our interpretation depends on the definition of change in a film fundamentally structured through repetition. Recurrences abound in *Kids Return*. Many have noted how the temporality itself appears ambiguous: not only do Shinji and Masaru seem not to age, making the span of time between their failures and their reunion difficult to calculate (the teacher's grey hair at the end is the only indication time has passed), but the era is also unclear. While there are iconographic indications of present-day Japan (the cars, women's fashions, etc.), the grey industrial urban landscape, the rundown school, if not also some of the story situations (e.g., sneaking into a porn theatre – not renting an adult video) suggest a period one or two decades ago. This ambiguity can be partially explained through the cyclicality. Other lives seen at the end, such as those of Sachiko (asked out to a movie by a man sitting in the same seat as Hiroshi), the teacher and the students (still staring out the window), and even those at the gym (spitting out boxers who follow the same path of promise and self-destruction), are repetitive too. Certain locations and actions, such as riding over the pedestrian bridge, are seen over and over. Masaru and Shinji are particular sites of repetition, pursuing lives defined by the recurrences of play (at school) and training (at the gym), and often doubling each other. The two repeat word for word the *manzai* act of the comedy pair, and much of the narrative centres on characters imitating and being influenced by others, particularly Shinji. Even Shinji's successes are simple recurrences. Kitano offers us a montage of his winning bouts, but always combining an image of him in practice with a shot of him in the actual match repeating the same moves.

The novelist Abe Kazushige, in investigating the function of repetition in *Sonatine* and *Kids Return*, argues that repetitions in the former are placed concentrically around a main circle: Murakawa heading towards death. Murakawa, according to Abe, is fundamentally trapped in repetition, unable to master one of the primary circular motifs in the film, the Frisbee. The circles in *Kids Return*, however, are decentred, with peripheral characters proliferating in multiple directions. Abe sees their first ride in the school-

Circularity versus change (the beginning)

Circularity versus change (the end)

yard as the epitome of a closed form of circularity: they move, but with Shinji facing backwards and Masaru forwards on the bike, they are essentially going nowhere. The ending is different, he argues: now they are both facing forwards. Abe takes this change to indicate the film's ultimate rejection of repetition, its final assertion of 'no return'.[10]

Others have offered conflicting interpretations of this scene. Reading *Kids Return* through Deleuze's notion of *l'image-souvenir* (recollection image) Horike Yoshitsugu sees the speed of the bicycle as not only the instigator of the central flashback, but also the figure of the circulation between past and present from which Shinji and Masaru can never escape. This motion from past to present and present to past is symbolised by the first bicycle scene, where, especially with the two facing in opposite directions, the track of the front wheel can represent both the past as well as the present. To Horike, the final scene only offers a possibility that Shinji and Masaru can escape the shared nature of this closed system (focusing on the fact that Masaru is really facing sideways, he speculates about them entering their own times).[11] If Horike argues that repetition is trapped in an inescapable circle, Abe Kashō contends the circle is eventually reduced to a zero. Repetition in *Kids Return*, he argues, is not homogeneous as in *Boiling Point*, but involves some character changes. What stays the same is the oppressively grey landscape. This indicates to Abe that the film's cruelty has less to do with the fates of Shinji, Masaru or Hiroshi than with the fact that they, in a temporally ambiguous world, cannot grow up even though they are forced to enter an adult world.[12] Abe even argues that temporality is so undermined by this cruelty that the film is not properly cyclical – for that involves a broad circular sweep of time the story does not have – but rather a singular, empty zero.

Kids Return is then a return to the narrative problem of *Boiling Point*: how to describe a narrative when many of the story shifts are negated through repetition and circularity. What distinguishes the former from the latter is possibly a remaining sense of irreversible, linear time. Ueno Kōshi points to numerous small, but significant changes that reveal the cruel advance of time.[13] Perhaps the most prominent of such irreversible temporal changes is the fall of Shinji and Masaru, a dramatic vector that is not to be found in *Boiling Point*. Masaru is left scarred, unable to use his right arm, and Shinji is reduced to working a dead-end job. To Yomota Inuhiko, *Kids Return* then is repetition that 'cannot escape a decline in value'.[14] Our question is why these two experience their declines in fortune and how this is significant to the narrative.

There are various reasons for their fall. Some see the two as social rebels, refusing to accept Japanese conformism or the stifling rat race, who are in the end punished for their transgressions.[15] At the very least they are pictured as pegs that, either consciously or unconsciously, do not fit in the holes provided by society, starting as failures and only fulfilling that destiny[16] or becoming victim to social hierarchies.[17] On an individual level, Masaru is faulted for being unable to reconcile his vision of himself with his social reality, and Shinji for lacking the individual agency to cease slavishly following the dictates of others.[18] One cannot escape the sense that they also remain Kitano heroes, falling as a result of their own self-destructive urges.[19]

Let us consider Shinji's case more carefully. His fall is often blamed on Hayashi, the older boxer who teaches him illegal moves, prompts him to ignore his diet regimen and gives him the weight-loss pills. In a popular youth film from the 1960s like those starring Wada Kōji, he would be the villain threatening the success that the audience, siding with the hero, strongly desires. *Kids Return*, however, lacks the moral clarity of such conventional narratives. While Hayashi may be the first to teach Shinji an illegal punch, the film had already revealed that the gym regularly teaches such moves. Furthermore, although Shinji follows Hayashi's lead, his reliance on others is not the sole reason for that. One could imagine Shinji as a slave to authority figures, doing what he is told both at school and at the gym. But he is not, first because of a rather special, if not somewhat homosocial attachment to Masaru. Hayashi in no way substitutes for Masaru, so his attractiveness to Shinji must stem from the way of life he offers. Hayashi, for instance, is the first character – including even Masaru – to tell Shinji to act on what he thinks best, not to be 'a toy' of the gym owner. Certainly this may serve to lure Shinji into his grasp, but his advice, when directed at a figure we know follows others, raises the possibility that Shinji's decline is the result less of his dependency on Hayashi, than of his first freely chosen decision. This remains ambiguous, but the prominent critic Kawamoto Saburō reminds us that, if the film's cruelty stems from the characters' inability to escape oppressive social hierarchies, Hayashi is the sole figure free of such relations. To Kawamoto, this is the film's central irony: 'If one wishes to be free in today's society, it may be necessary to become a skunk like Hayashi. Hayashi thus maintains a strange allure because he alone is a *warped* free man.'[20]

This freedom is significantly related to the issue of play. Hayashi calls the gym owner old-fashioned because a regimen of no drink and no play is to him unrealistic in modern Japan. Hayashi is thus a proponent of play, especially unproductive play: he eats and drinks but without letting his body absorb any of those elements. That may be a cheap form of irresponsibility, but play in Kitano's films has often been irresponsible and unproductive. Shinji's decision to begin drinking may be both an expression of his free will and a determined effort, similar to Beat Takeshi's, not to abandon the playful world of his adolescence.

Sera Toshikazu finds a duality in Kids Return's vision of play and circularity: 'This circularity probably has two meanings. In one, it is, as Kawamoto Saburō has noted, the stifling pressure of a space from which there is no escape; in the other, it is the comfort of a moratorium on adulthood.'[21] The film qualifies this dangerous comfort by rendering play differently than in Kitano's previous work. Kitakōji Takashi has identified Okinawa as Kitano's model for the space of play, a spot for idleness without purpose in which one practically loses one's sense of self. He also finds this Okinawa in Kids Return in the form of the schoolyard, which is always empty whenever Shinji and Masaru play there, as if offering them a never-ending alternative space apart from others.[22] The schoolyard exhibits crucial differences from the Okinawan beach, however, because it lacks the brilliant sun, the colours white and blue, the close connection with death and the wide-open horizon. While one might agree with Kawamoto that the circular motion of the bicycle in the yard offers at least the dream of a space free of hierarchical relations, this is still a claustrophobic site, one surrounded by that maze of grey roads. One reason that Kids Return feels oppressive compared to Boiling Point or Sonatine is because it lacks the liminal space of idleness, that almost surreal escape from reality.

This shift in representation might constitute Kitano's self-critique of the space of play. The pressbook and official pamphlet of the film declared the film an exploration of the kind of freedom Shinji and Masaru enjoy. 'Against a freedom without risk, Kitano Takeshi prepares a response invoking cruel damage. He investigates the meaning of what we call "freedom" through the two who suffer this damage and the people that surround them.'[23] Although Kids Return does not oppose the space of play with the noble responsibility of adulthood, it is more ambivalent about the consequences of this idleness than previous films. It does not condemn play, but renders it in greyer tones, underscoring that idleness is not paid for through the lightness of death, but through the weight of living on.

The changed attitude towards play is evident in *Kids Return*'s construction of performance. Spaces of play in *A Scene at the Sea* and *Sonatine* are often performance sites accompanied by divisions between spectators and actors. Such spaces also exist in *Kids Return*. Their cycling in the schoolyard is viewed by a student and the teacher. Shinji and Masaru's pranks are also theatrical, such as when they dangle a 'puppet' into the proscenium of the classroom window. They even put on performances themselves, dressing up as businessmen to view a porn film and copying the *manzai* act of the comic pair. But the situation changes after they graduate, especially for Shinji. The gym's hope, 'Eagle', puts on a show for his girlfriend, but Shinji never does that, probably because his likely intended audience, Masaru, never comes to watch. Masaru may have his moments of bravado as a gangster, but his crime, in the end, seems to be in speaking out when he was supposed to be a spectator, in proclaiming he will act even if no one will watch him. Hiroshi definitely has someone he wishes to perform for, but not only does he lack the talent to put on that show, but the film effectively deprives him of his audience, never showing Sachiko once outside the café. The narrative thus consciously undermines the structure of performance. This is in contrast with the *manzai* pair, who slowly build their audience in the theatre. Their space of play is clearly framed (by the proscenium), as well as permitted (it was recommended to Shinji and Masaru by their teachers). Boxing, however, at least in the case of Shinji, is a framed space of performance without the playful interaction between spectator and audience. That is perhaps another reason he and Masaru return to the schoolyard stage, but too late, for they are now actors without the qualifications to be there.

This change in the space of play/performance is aligned with a debilitation of the look. If *A Scene at the Sea* and *Sonatine* depended crucially on point-of-view structures of looking and being looked at, the hollowness of boxing in *Kids Return* is exemplified by the fact that there are no point-of-view shots of Shinji's matches, as if he performs without an audience.

Subjective shots have not been eliminated from the film, but they have largely moved from the space of performance into the more conventional realm of shaping character relations and prompting spectator identification (particularly with Shinji). What is missing from *Kids Return* are the long glances at the camera, the gazes into space that defined such films as *Boiling Point* and *Sonatine*. It is as if that far-distant horizon, the liminal space just off screen, is obscured by the frame and the grey cityscape. What reigns over the film is the gaze of the narrator that structures these lives. The film offers the powerful trick of rendering the falls of Shinji, Masaru and Hiroshi simultaneous through parallel editing. Abe Kashō, for one, found *Kids Return* to be 'the film of a scriptwriter', with multiple characters and perspectives interwoven in a far more complex manner than in previous films. This master perspective is still rather cold. Despite those who found his gaze in the film compassionate, Kitano said he again aimed to present these characters from a detached perspective, as if they were animals.[24]

This film, which presented more rigid frames for play and performance, was itself more conventionally framed. Most critics and Kitano himself considered *Kids Return* his most orthodox film to date. To Sera,

> With his début film, Kitano discovered his own gift by breaking through the cinematic frames that he had been given as much as possible. But here, as if trying to test his own hand, he purposely builds up existing cinematic frames. He picked an easy-to-understand plot, created expressions for the actors, and represented the pains and nostalgia of adolescence by discovering his own shadow in the group of high-school students that includes Hiroshi and the *manzai* duo.[25]

Kitano explained he had to use a more conventional, more explanatory style in order to accommodate Andō Masanobu and Kaneko Ken, the two relatively inexperienced actors playing Shinji and Masaru.[26] Abe Kazushige saw Kitano abandoning his sense of timing (*ma*) – especially the frequent use of blank time at the beginnings and ends of shots – in order to convey this more complex plot and increase the pace of the film.

The text of *Kids Return* then mirrors the world it depicts, embodying a more rigid cinematic frame that itself allows Kitano less room for filmic play. Although Kitano seemed more willing to accept the 'kusai' (mawkish) aspects of narratives he would have rejected before, the film still avoids many of the conventions of popular youth films (the prominent presence of sex and girls, here reduced to Sachiko in a side role; or the place of the family, which is never shown) or of school dramas on TV. Marking Kitano's return to box-office success after Office Kitano took over distribution of the films, *Kids Return* repeats and reproduces certain cinematic conventions while also offering a version – a double, one could say – that varies from the norm.

Kids Return is a film structured around pairs. This is not simply a factor of the doubles and repetitions in the film. Somewhat ironically, *Kids Return* has its own double in the form of a short story 'sequel' published a year and a half after the film's release.[27] Simply entitled 'Kids Return 2', it takes up Shinji and Masaru three years after their fall (though it is not clear how long after the last scene in the film). This even more orthodox narrative can illustrate much about the film. It extends the cyclical nature of Shinji and Masaru's lives as they again become boxers and yakuza, but this time with clear aims. Masaru joins another mob to take revenge when his former gang destroys his only chance of going straight. Shinji returns to the ring when he learns that his girlfriend Manami is being pressed by her parents to accept an arranged marriage, a development he cannot stop if he remains a part-time rice delivery boy. Here the characters act on their own decisions in ways the novel clearly states are more adult. They also perform in spaces with a specified audience, with both Masaru and Manami being motivational presences at Shinji's bouts. Finally, the story allows them both a certain degree of success: Shinji a boxing title and Masaru his revenge (in exchange for being led away by the police). It even promises a continued narrative: against Masaru's assertion that they are now over, Shinji insists on their continued friendship.

Although one could explain the differences between the film and its sequel through their different media (the story, for instance, allows for internal dialogue that Kitano shuns in the film), the latter can still be said to be an extension of the positive aspects already cited by some in the former. It is the return of one version of a film that, in its proliferation of repetitions and doublings, already created various versions. The short story's more satisfactory narrative can help us understand the degree to which *Kids Return* may use conventional genre frames only to consciously trap its characters in the circularity of narrative. Still, the pleasures of those frames remain, and Kitano, far from denying them altogether, develops them in another medium. Perhaps we can say Kitano is trapped in his own repetitions, unable to escape the urge to try again. Or perhaps he is, as Abe Kazushige argues, proliferating the circles themselves, ambivalently offering various stances to be played out and repeated in his films and their interpretations. In the end, I believe *Kids Return* is his deepest introspection on the pleasures and dangers of that repetitive play.

Hana-Bi

Kids Return had foregrounded the issues of repetition and change in Kitano's career, especially the question of what kind of return the director had made after his accident. *Hana-Bi* (released as *Fireworks* in some countries) would repeat the problem of return, as Kitano's own narrative of discovering life after the accident would be doubled by aspects of the film's story, in which doubled characters came to the fore to explore different outcomes of Kitano's return. What would be added to the equation was a new frame: triumph abroad and the prospect of a foreign audience. Kitano had enjoyed some success in Europe, especially in the United Kingdom with some of his first films, and at Cannes with *Kids Return* in 1996, which earned critical acclaim but no awards. *Hana-Bi* grabbed the Golden Lion for best film at the Venice Film Festival, repeating the accomplishment of Kurosawa Akira's *Rashomon* in 1951 and Inagaki Hiroshi's *The Rickshaw Man* (*Muhōmatsu no isshō*) in 1958. The feat helped secure foreign distribution contracts as *Hana-Bi* became Kitano's first work to open in the United States. Even in Japan, the victory at Venice helped *Hana-Bi* become a small box-office success.

The question was whether this new international frame altered Kitano's work. To many commentators, *Hana-Bi* was a compilation (*shūtaisei*) of the best elements of his earlier films. The situation of a detective (Nishi, played by Beat Takeshi) caring for a sick family member while battling a cruel yakuza killer performed by Hakuryū was shared with *Violent Cop*; the loving couple who remain mostly silent (Nishi and his wife) was found in *A Scene at the Sea*; and two men following different fates shown through parallel montage (Nishi and his partner Horibe) was developed in *Kids Return*. Kitano himself spoke of initially intending *Hana-Bi* as an 'upgraded' version of *Sonatine*,[1] and as being 'composed of the best things I picked up' from previous films.[2] Shinozaki Makoto tried to clarify Kitano's comment by arguing he did not mean 'reproducing condensed versions' or 'simply refining' what had been done before. Kitano, he stressed, is the 'greatest critic of [his] own films', 'constantly rejecting [his] previous film while making the next one'.[3] *Hana-Bi*, he argued, was fundamentally different in its use of depth, colour, landscapes and *mise en scène*. Abe Kashō agreed, declaring that the use of the term 'compilation' in appraisals of *Hana-bi* was 'crude' (*sozatsu*). Abe offered a list of *Hana-Bi*'s cinematic techniques that were relatively new to Kitano's oeuvre, including flashbacks, dissolves and camera movements that establish the location of scenes.[4]

The duality of authorial continuity/discontinuity found its analogue in *Hana-Bi* in two characters who, as some said, 'appear to be cinematic self-portraits of the director at different moments in his life'.[5] Horibe is a police detective paralysed in a shooting incident who loses the will to live until he takes up painting; his former partner Nishi, who feels responsible for the shooting because he left the scene to visit his hospitalised wife, commits a bank robbery to help Horibe and the widow of Tanaka, a detective killed in a subway shooting by the same criminal who shot Horibe. With the remaining money, he goes on a last trip with his own terminally ill spouse, chased by the yakuza and his former police colleagues. We must consider how the film shapes these two avatars of Takeshi, as well as how the foreign shapes this split. As noted by Shinozaki Makoto, Darrell Davis and myself on separate occasions,[6] *Hana-Bi* features more symbols of the nation, such as Mount Fuji and cherry blossoms, than any of his previous work. Even as it propelled Kitano to global fame, we shall see that *Hana-Bi* was deeply entwined in discourses about frames, borders and the nation, exploring different Takeshis in order to enshrine the newly international 'Takeshi Kitano' as a 'Japanese' film director.

Hana-Bi was possibly an even more autobiographical work than *Kids Return* because it bore the traces of Takeshi's 1994 motorbike accident. Confined to the hospital for several months, he began painting like Horibe does in the film. The works that Takeshi produced found their way into the movie, becoming one of two visual traces of the accident on celluloid, the other being Beat Takeshi's scarred and partially paralysed face. Especially since Kitano frequently spoke of the film as curiously arising from the

The transcendental POV?

paintings he had done (most were completed before the film was fully conceived, including even the crucial 'suicide' canvas), it was as if these painted
scars of the accident shaped this more colourful work.

Horibe was often interpreted as a representation of Takeshi after the
crash, someone who had actually confronted death and decided to accept
life, discovering colours in the process. Horibe thus illustrated '[i]n
Takeshi's worldview' the conclusion that 'there is only one path to redemption — to face impending loss with a welcoming and tractable outlook',[7] a
lesson lost on Nishi, who 'has adopted such an inflexible and uncompro-
mised attitude toward the world that it will . . . sooner or later destroy him'.[8]
Although Horibe does not figure in the film as a master painter, one of the
roles of this artist was to narrate. Given Kitano's statements about the paintings shaping the story, their creator in the diegesis, Horibe, comes to function as a surrogate narrator. Indeed, some of his later paintings, especially
the one of suicide, appear to foreshadow, if not prompt Nishi's fateful
story.[9] Nishi, in contrast, represents Kitano before the accident. Like
Murakawa and Uehara before, this violent character was an excessive
element in a world that could no longer allow him to live; unable to fully
master it, he set out on a road towards death. Nishi in this sense is more

narrated than narrating, a character doomed to erasure as the ultimate narrator, Kitano himself, changed his outlook on life.

Kitano's own statements, however, complicate this simple division. While he acknowledged elements of himself in Horibe and Nishi,[10] he challenged the view that valorised Horibe's choice of life over Nishi's selection of death.

[T]o me, by dying, Nishi and his wife take a step forward to the next life, while Horibe, by not killing himself, will not be able to live a fruitful life. By choosing to live he chooses to die slowly, a slow suicide.[11]

Hana-Bi's difference lay less in its view of life than in its approach to death.

I feel that the meaning of death in *Hana-Bi* is different from that in *Sonatine* and *Boiling Point*. In the latter two films, there's a sense the characters try to solve problems through death – death is a way to escape those issues. In this film, the hero does not escape into death, but actively approaches death on his own.[12]

This asserts that Nishi is not a character entirely subject to fate. Narratively, the relationship between Nishi and Horibe is one of reversal. If Nishi is initially the silent man with a broken family, he regains speech and familial bonds as the voluble Horibe loses his family and, for all intents and purposes, verbal language. The contrast is most apparent in the latter part of *Hana-Bi*, as Kitano uses parallel montage to connect the two men. Both pursue painting – Nishi painting the car – but in terms of plot order Nishi begins before Horibe does. His 'artwork' is both more proactive and practical. He is less a narrator foreshadowing events than a director, preparing his own script, props and costume, and ultimately appearing in front of the camera (the surveillance setup at the bank). Compared to his relative inactivity in the first half, Nishi in the second functions as the central protagonist, pushing other characters towards action and orchestrating events, from the bank robbery to the trip, that fundamentally shape the narrative.

Against this, Horibe seems a more reactive, if not repetitive character. He is the first one to mention painting, but just to immediately dismiss it. He can only act on his desires when prompted by outside forces. His paintings operate similarly. While the flower-shop scene offers a conventionally romantic narrative of the artist inspired by nature, it is interesting that some of the paintings Horibe envisions, such as the lion with a sunflower head, are actually shown two scenes earlier when Horibe is moving along the road, frustrated after his initial attempts at drawing. Such inserts accord with the non-linear narrative that dominates the first half of the film, but they call into question the status of the paintings. Although they are psychologised in the flower shop, that is less the case on their first appearance. Given their spatio-temporal ambiguity, the inserts cannot be rearranged into a proper temporal order like most of the inserts in the first half can (of the subway shooting, etc.). Their presence is obtrusive, asserting their existence before Horibe 'imagines' them. This partially undermines the narrative of romantic artistic inspiration. In terms of plot order, Horibe only repeats what the audience has already seen. This impression is only reinforced by the existence throughout the diegesis of Kitano's paintings, starting with the first hospital scene. Usually singled out by camera movements or lighting, they are also obtrusive inserts without clear narrative motivation, yet their similarity to Horibe's work reduces his creations to repetitions, now of Kitano's *mise en scène*.

Abe Kazushige argues that Nishi escapes the repetition entrapping Murakawa in *Sonatine* and achieves a perspective, represented by the extreme high-angle shot of his partners getting shot in the subway, like the angels in Wim Wenders's *Wings of Desire* (*Der Himmel über Berlin*, 1987). He thus argues that Nishi is the angel who, starting with the first drawing in *Kids Return*, increasingly becomes a motif in Kitano's work. In *Hana-Bi*, paintings of angels have an almost transcendent status, appearing both non-diegetically, under the credits, and diegetically, in the landing of the hospital staircase. To Abe, Nishi is outside the circularity of life that shapes much of Kitano's work and which, while not represented like in *Boiling Point*, is nonetheless present in *Hana-Bi* in the figure of the girl running around on the beach at the end. Nishi exists outside this circle, using his proximity to death to transcend such repetitions.[13]

It is true that Nishi resists repetition within the story, even warning the punk who reappears by the lake never to show his face again. Nishi does experience recurrent memories of the traumatic shooting (Tanaka's wounding is presented three times in the film), but one could say that Nishi's assumption of responsibility for failing to prevent the incident (and to stop Horibe's shooting), and his decision to act as guardian angel for Tanaka's wife and Horibe, stops these recollections. Nishi, however, is not completely immune from repetition, and thus is never fully transcendent. If his recurrent memories disappear in the film's second half, it is in part because these repetitions have been replaced by another: that of mimesis in the bank robbery. Nishi replicates a police car and then does a performance for the junkman that repeats his own earlier view of a patrol car from the junkyard. The old hand-cranked siren emphasises that this is mimesis and not identity, the irony of course being that since Nishi is no longer on the force, he has to mimic being what he once was. But it still replicates the transcendental viewpoint of the shooting through the similarly detached surveillance camera. What has changed is that Nishi is now within the frame.

This framing of Nishi is crucial to the film. As with previous works, pairs and the number two figure prominently in *Hana-Bi*, whose title itself is split into two. Nishi is paired with Horibe, his wife and even with Tōjō (the yakuza enforcer) through a cut from him gunning down the debtor to Nishi testing his gun. The loan shark Okada's punks come in pairs, as do the carpark attendants. But the number three also reigns over *Hana-Bi*, often working as a framing device. Certain locations appear three times, such as the entrance to Nishi's apartment or Okada's office, and trios are conspicuous throughout, particularly in the form of the family. Through Horibe's family, his paintings, the group seen on the beach, or even the wooden dolls at the inn, all families are composed of two parents and one child. This structure functions in part to underline the missing third term in Nishi's family – the deceased daughter – an absence that is reiterated twice through abandoned child objects at the entrance to the apartment building. One could say that Nishi is caught between the numbers two and three, haunted by a third member when he is in a pair, and opposed by two others when he is in a group of three. When Nishi is in a three shot, he is often framed by the others. Nishi's is frequently a framed existence, and this is evident from the start, when we see a dissolve from the word 'Die!' framed by the parking lot lines, to Nishi's car driving between the lines on the road. His destiny and his framing are tied. When Nishi becomes more and more the subject of Horibe's paintings, even if post facto, his fate is sealed.

Nishi, however, resists or by chance avoids such framing. Although he is captured within the borders of the security camera at the bank, he either has problems with cameras or successfully eludes them after that. He drops his lens cap at the temple and his attempt to do a timed shot with his wife fails. Then he refuses to take a picture at the inn with his wife, who is posed, significantly in front of one of Kitano's large framed paintings. His effort to escape the frame ultimately succeeds through that crane and pan left at the beach at the end that removes Nishi and his wife from the screen, after which they remove themselves from the world of the living.

What Nishi cannot escape, even there, is the frame of the nation. As with *Sonatine*, *Hana-Bi* reiterates Japan as a space one cannot escape from, framed as it is by the sea and the lines of the beach. Unlike *Sonatine*, however, this work more clearly aligns itself with the nation. As Shinozaki Makoto initially pointed out, this is the first of Kitano's films to feature common symbols of Japan such as Mount Fuji, cherry blossoms and old temples.[14] *Hana-Bi* did receive criticism that such symbols served to tailor the film for foreign festivals.[15] Its citation of the nation is more complex, however, since there are moments of national ambivalence in the film. Symbols of tradition like the temple are treated irreverently and the most classical element of the story, Nishi and his wife's journey before death (*michiyuki*), is rendered in a non-classical fashion. The *michiyuki*, which is also used in *Dolls*, is a central narrative device in several famous kabuki and *bunraku* plays, especially *shinjūmono* (double suicide plays) where the couple's journey to commit suicide functions as an opportunity to reiterate the couple's passion, now freed from social ties but inexorably directed towards death. Although Nishi's efforts to escape society resemble the principles of the *michiyuki*, the resulting humour and lack of sexual passion greatly deviates from tradition. In fact, Kitano has offered comments expressing a desire to 'get rid of the typical Asian traits, cultures, and aesthetics in our films'.[16]

Yet his discourse on the film, especially in Japanese, has been more nationalistic, far more than with his previous works. The official pamphlet for the film has him stating, 'I am a Japanese so I'm trying to achieve a Japanese style'. This involved a critique of what the pamphlet called an 'audience indulging in a "peaceful routine"' in postwar Japan. To Kitano,

> In the postwar, Japanese have for a long time only thought of living in ease and pleasure. But if human beings have the right to be happy, they also have the liberty to be unhappy. Given that, I think you can establish a film style based on a way of living directed towards death.[17]

Nishi came to represent an older Japanese 'spirit' that was lost on postwar Japanese, one that he at times likened to 'Bushido, the ancient samurai philosophy'.[18] To Kitano,

> Many present-day Japanese will very possibly see Nishi's behaviour as overly romantic or sentimental, or at least rather out of date. But the way he discharges what he understands to be his responsibilities conforms with an ideal which has existed in Japanese society at least since the Edo period [1600–1867].[19]

That, in his mind, made Nishi 'a man out of synch with the era'[20] like the out-of-season firefly in the snow outside the inn. That the film is sympathetic to Nishi's philosophy is indicated by the pursuing detective's expression of admiration and frustration at the end: 'I could never live like that.' Nishi is a superman in an age become dully average.

This lament for a lost Japaneseness was not solely directed towards a domestic audience. A glance at viewer comments on the Internet Movie Database shows how many foreign viewers interpreted the film though national characteristics, citing 'mono no aware' (a Japanese aesthetic expressing the inherent pathos of life), the 'Oriental mind', or 'Japanese aesthetics' as keys to grasping the film. Again in the pamphlet, Kitano said that 'The issue this time is whether this style, this Japanese sense of feeling, will be acceptable in Europe and America.' He particularly expressed concern over whether the 'spirit' Nishi embodies, especially in his march towards death, would offend foreigners.

> When forced under oppressive conditions, it could be like the spirit of kamikaze pilots. . . . When it is not forced, but is done on an individual basis, I think it's romanticism worth admiration. But romanticism for the nation is bad. That's why I call it poison. If that image overlaps with the image Europeans have of Japanese soldiers during World War II, I fear they could never approve of this film. But if it was a movie where one could feel the romanticism in the problem of that husband and wife on the individual level . . . I felt they could understand it. It's good they didn't make that connection.[21]

This quotation raises two important issues. The first is one of spectatorship. Although Kitano was known for declaring his lack of concern for the audience, his discussions here reveal a greater attention to moulding the film with spectator understanding in mind. He made conscious efforts, both in the film's narrative and in its relation to national themes, not to alienate his viewers. Certainly *Hana-Bi* was Kitano's first film to employ a non-linear narrative structure, one that leaves some scenes, such as Nishi's initial encounter with the carpark attendants, temporally ambiguous. Suzuki Hitoshi may not be out of bounds in saying the film places the past 'adjacent' to the present, but it is excessive to say it then renders time 'null'.[22] *Hana-Bi* is understandable within the structural bounds of art cinema. Its narrative puzzle is not difficult to reassemble, easier perhaps than the brainteaser Nishi and his wife fumble with, because past and present are clearly demarcated. Most of the flashbacks are psychologically motivated and even if Nishi's memories of Tanaka's shooting are initially only brief, they are presented in progressively longer versions that culminate in a full account. Kitano's reiteration of certain shots provides the viewer with landmarks that guide the reconstruction of the narrative path. The non-linear presentation of the story largely ceases by the middle of the film, after which a more conventional parallel editing structure takes precedence.

The other issue is again one of framing. Kitano's statements reveal his awareness that *Hana-Bi* was broaching issues of nationality that were, if not

The framing smile

out of date, possibly offensive to some. His own declarations, as well as structures in the film, describe devices that frame and thus alleviate the problematic nature of these issues. One device is individuation, rendering qualities
which Kitano himself attaches to the nation – at least in the past – now matters
of individual choice and character. Another is death. The director had this to
say about the function of death in this film, if not Japanese society in general.

> There is no doubt that evil is evil in the eyes of the law, but we forgive evil if it is
> accompanied with a resolution to commit suicide (*jiketsu*[23]). However, there was
> a current of such romanticism in the past, when many Japanese soldiers died in
> the name of the emperor. There is something very dangerous about the beautifi-
> cation of such a death. Yet nothing is solved by declaring that the way lots of
> people died is stupid or absurd. Such romanticism flows in the blood of every
> Japanese, and we must face it.[24]

Kitano retains a critical stance against the mass and especially coercive
nature of Japan's construction of suicide, but he nonetheless argues for a
Japanese relation to the practice that serves as a form of moral frame: those
who are willing to die for what they do are excused for their actions. While

there is room for debate on how critical Kitano is towards this racial tradition, it is clear that in *Hana-Bi* Nishi enjoys a moral reprieve for his crimes, the greatest of which are the bank robbery and, we presume, the murder of his wife. It is not only his willingness to die, but also his deep sense of responsibility and care for others that help us excuse him. It is this national romanticism, in effect, that provides the frame that pardons Nishi.

What shapes Nishi's relation to the nation is the additional frame of gender. In one sense, *Hana-Bi* is a film about emasculation. At the start, Nishi has been rendered speechless and largely inactive by the ailing female body (his dead daughter and sick wife). Horibe is also indirectly affected by this body (Nishi's need to care for his wife leads to Horibe's wounding), and he recovers only to then be more blatantly emasculated by his wife, who leaves him. To Abe Kashō, *Hana-Bi* is overlain with cases of paralysis and physical weakness, from Horibe's legs to Nishi's (Takeshi's) face,[25] but the narrative at least offers Nishi moments in which to perform masculinity by taking responsibility for the problems caused by his paralysis, and ultimately directing his own death. The role of his wife in this 're-masculinisation' is complex, however. Some observers did criticise Kitano for offering a female character who is not only weak and silent, but who also says nothing when her unemployed husband suddenly comes into cash, beats up men in front of her and leads her to her death.[26] Kitano, however, spoke of this as a means of adjusting the relationship between Nishi and his wife.

> There is a sense that the wife in *Hana-Bi* knows everything and is letting me do this. It's like I'm playing around in the palm of her hand. Given that, there's a sense of the immensity of women – it's not an equal relationship at all. Cinematically, the man is worried about his wife and takes her on a final trip, trying really hard to do this and that, but the impression is that the wife knows it all and is just letting him do it.[27]

This provides an interpretation of the final scene.

> Perhaps the wife has seen through everything, and there's the sense that she's being kind to him and knowingly following along. In terms of the male–female

relationship, she is maternal, knowing everything and giving him a kind 'Thank you.' A naughty boy has acted recklessly: 'He has done those kind of things while saying it was for me. But I must finally tell him thank you.' It's like they're husband and wife but also something different.[28]

Such statements need not be considered definitive of the film's gender relations. It would be hard to argue, for instance, that the wife has greater power than Nishi. She does not know about all of her husband's financial dealings and is rendered humourously incompetent, if not childish at moments such as when she falls into the snow.[29] Although framing Nishi, rendering his excesses excusable, she herself is framed (as she is by the painting at the inn).

Yet it is precisely because of her cute, somewhat infantile quality that she can function as a frame for Nishi's actions and the film's narrative. Consider, for instance, the scene where Nishi breaks the young girl's kite. Narratively, the girl allows Nishi and his wife to vicariously enjoy a 'daughter' before their deaths.[30] What Nishi does to this 'daughter' is rip her kite. In another context, this would be a callous act. Kitano has spoken about how perspective can make a tragedy seem a comedy, and vice versa,[31] but here he clearly frames spectator interpretation by inserting a shot of the wife smiling at Nishi's hijinks. She is in effect the *tsukkomi* – though a cute and motherly one – that provides a frame dividing this act from real pain. One could argue that she performs a similar function for many of Nishi's actions throughout the film.

For instance, Kitano himself has said that the wife, and the feminine she is made to represent, works to render the romantic nationalism palatable to foreign audiences.[32]

I think there would be nothing more absurd than having two men stand in front of Mount Fuji, but this is a film about a couple. I felt it was all right if it was a woman standing by my side. If it's a man and a woman, it might work even if it's a stereotypical tourist spot. That is, if you give the characters some burden to shoulder, something like having an illness and not knowing how long you have to live, the scene can actually end up seeming kind of sad.[33]

Darrell Davis roundly criticises this move.

> Kitano sells Japanese tradition, the icons of 'Japaneseness', by selling out gender. The 'blatantly stereotypical Asian look' (epitomized by samurai films) that Kitano claims to hate is here domesticated, made palatable to a global market, by feminizing it. This is Orientalism at its most stark: the Orient is always feminized for the West.[34]

To be fair to Kitano, we should underline what he is also reacting against on the domestic front: on the one hand, the hypermasculine aestheticisation of the nation found not only in wartime cinema, but also in sentimental war films produced by Tōhō and Shintōhō after the mid-1950s, where shots of Mount Fuji and cherry blossoms were inserted in stories of young men bravely heading off to die; on the other, the commodification of those same symbols in the postwar era through such domestic tourism campaigns as 'Discover Japan'. Inserting illness and the feminine could work against these stereotypical representations. Yet the feminine frame also projects an image of the nation that is kinder and gentler, one that is aesthetic and can accommodate a little irreverence.

Framing is important to the aesthetic structure of *Hana-Bi* as a whole. Jean-François Buiré confesses a sense that the reality in the film is 'pre-inscribed', already framed before it is filmed.[35] As a somewhat self-reflexive film, *Hana-Bi* presents the boundaries of paintings on screen, even when they are not in the diegetic space. When Horibe envisions a painting, it is shown in a spiralling camera movement backwards that eventually reveals the borders of the work. This camera movement also exemplifies the film's aestheticisation of violence, since it is also used on the white yakuza car after the massacre. Inner frames augment this, not just by demarcating characters in mirrors and windows, but by rendering bloodshed artistic (e.g., the blood on the placemat) and doubling real actions with art (the red paint splashed on the painting). The film itself is book-ended by art, as it both begins and ends with Kitano's paintings.

The degree to which frames are crucial to the film's aesthetics is evident from Kitano's account of his use of colour in the film. *Hana-Bi* was remarkable for its prominent use of a variety of primary colours, moving beyond the generally monochrome colour scheme or the tension between blue and red predominant in his previous films. The bright colours, however, are largely confined to the paintings. Kitano said,

> I hate the colours of buildings and things in Tokyo, so I escape into an image that is sombre and monochromatic. But I do occasionally want to show something with colour. However, colour on the set tends to stick out in terms of the overall pattern of the film. It doesn't fit. If I suddenly include a colour I like in an impressive backdrop, the question arises why it's there, because it doesn't connect with the film as a whole. But with paintings, there's no problem at all in showing colours no matter what they are.[36]

Bright colours on the set threaten not only codes of realism (justification of their use), but also the text's basic structure. Locating them in a frame, rendered distinct from the rest of narrative space, places them in brackets, present but excused for their lack of clear connection. As with the nation and humourous violence, colours become acceptable as an aesthetic element as long as they are bordered.

The focus on aestheticising devices is only to be expected in a film that presents the aesthetic as a central element in its title. The film's American pressbook gave the official interpretation of the title: 'Hana (flower) is the symbol of life while Bi (fire) represents gunfire, and so death.' This opposition, which Tony Rayns called 'a dichotomy which turns out to run through the film',[37] could easily be multiplied into a variety of other, often overlapping divisions, such as beauty versus bloodshed, Horibe versus Nishi, humour versus violence. This dichotomy plays out in the fundamental narrative structure, especially in the emphasis on pairs, and the parallel montage structure shaping the last half. Our question is how the film treats this division. To some the insertion of the hyphen creates divisions that the film never fully resolves, maintaining the play between each pole. Thus to Horike Yoshitsugu,

> It is the intermingling of these oppositional terms – fixed camera and moving camera, explanatory dialogue and utter silence, shots that solely contribute to the

narrative and those that refuse to – that trifles with the lives of the characters
between 'flowers' and 'fire'.[38]

Abe Kazushige similarly argued that the film itself is neither 'hana' nor
'bi' but the hyphen in between.[39] Suzuki sees the movie operating
through combinations of elements separated by gaps, from mismatched
temporalities to the painted juxtapositions of beasts and flowers, that
are still connected by loops and networks of mediation (things relating
through other things).[40] Some saw *Hana-Bi* as ultimately breaking down
these dichotomies, mixing and melding genres (action and melodrama),
moods (violence and sentiment) and personalities.[41] The word 'hanabi'
supported this, offering a concept, fireworks, that harmoniously combines vibrant beauty with sudden violence. One could say the title
paints Kitano as an advocate of montage, combining two terms to create a third unity. *Hana-Bi* does in fact rely on montage to create connections across space and time that do not exist in the individual shots.
The most prominent is the cut from Nishi's lighter to Horibe being
shot, a connection that, while inconceivable in reality, visualises the
responsibility Nishi bears for Horibe's paralysis – as if he himself
pulled the trigger.

The problem with both of these accounts is that they tend to assume that
the terms in these dichotomies are not in a hierarchy. Mixture becomes an
equal concoction, in-betweenness a space of free play. However, as Abe
Kashō argues, 'The paintings as a whole may appear to be "flowers" but they
contain "bi" in their details. Consequently, the title *Hana-Bi* implies not a
relation of opposition, but one of inclusion.'[42] Abe is essentially talking
about framing devices, as many elements, as we have seen, are only established through being framed by other terms. The power relations here are
complex, but the title screen hints at a final force in play. The letters are
presented in blue, but framed at top and bottom by two lines, a motif which
aligns with other frames in the film, from the carpark lines to the tracks of
Horibe's wheelchair in the sand. 'Hana' and 'bi' are thus contained by an
external frame, shaped by the same processes of aestheticisation and
nationalisation we have already seen. The fact that the title is rendered in

roman letters and not Chinese characters (*kanji*) is also significant because it encourages slippage between homophonic terms. Although 'hana' has few homophones (except 'nose', which could refer to Takeshi's paralysed face), 'bi' can designate many other words, the most significant of which is 'beauty' (the title then in effect becoming 'the beauty of flowers'). The framed title is then reduced to two terms aligned with the aesthetic, rendering that the inclusive term in the film's structure.

Hana-Bi does not leave the aesthetic on an abstract level, but locates it in a particular subjectivity. The first image in the film is of a book cover with the English title, 'Kitano Film volume 7'. Bookcovers themselves are framing devices, but this one also emphasises the work as a product of an authorial subject with a continuous oeuvre. The cover then segues into Kitano's paintings, establishing a motif that will dominate the film. If we had sensed that Horibe's paintings are somehow not his own, it is because he is always overwhelmed by Kitano Takeshi. Kitano in *Hana-Bi* is more obviously foregrounding the biographical source of textual enunciation than most art cinema, presenting the artistic subject as someone who can freely enter the work (in the form of Nishi or the paintings), yet remain aloof, in the frame yet somehow outside it. If asked who the transcendental angel is, I would say it is less Nishi than Kitano himself, a suspicion seemingly confirmed by the last image in the film, a painted angel with the Kitano's credit superimposed on top of it.

Hana-Bi thus assumes a more unified subjectivity, both for its auteur and for its characters, than previous Kitano works. This is one of the major differences from *Sonatine*. If that work doubled its empty characters with a theme of authorial self-destruction, *Hana-Bi* offers substantial psychological characters who ultimately function to confirm, not undermine, the authorial status of the director. Although *Kids Return* points to this trend by beginning with the title 'A Takeshi Kitano Film', it is significantly hollowed by the absence of that author in the world of the text. It is this ascension of Kitano to the status of artist that may provide one of the borderlines within his cinematic career.

Perhaps it was this status that was necessary for *Hana-Bi* to cross borders and enter the global market, especially on the tails of the art-cinema genre.

Regardless of how prominent the gangster elements are in *Hana-Bi*, the authority of the art-cinema auteur persists as the overarching term. That is why, for instance, many of the reviews in the United States reiterated the pressbook's emphasis on Kitano's multitalented, practically Renaissance versatility. Yet Kitano's authorial subjectivity was not a natural product of a biological individual, but created through such textual processes as *Hana-Bi*. Crucial among them is the framing of Japanese identity. Just as national symbols like Mount Fuji serve as moments of recuperation and redemption, Kitano's use of such symbols establishes his status as an author. It was as if becoming a film artist, especially in the international sphere, required the assumption of the discourse of Japaneseness, but framing it in the more palatable language of the global art-cinema market, with both the opening book cover and the title appearing in roman letters. This is the look West (Nishi's name actually means 'West') that is necessary for the creation of the East.

Yet Nishi's efforts to escape the frame can still disturb this. On the one hand, they can symbolise the mobility of the authorial subject itself, one that flaunts its transcendental status by craning up and panning left at the end. But note that the final angel has a broken wing, suggesting the author's inability to transcend and contain everything in the textual frame. Nishi's refusal to take a picture with his wife can also be a rejection of the painting behind her, and the oppressively omnipresent authority it represents. Unlike Horibe, who ultimately comes to copy Kitano's work, Nishi completely ignores it, instead painting a work, the car, that is both mobile and less clearly framed. As *Hana-Bi* likens itself to a book, Nishi keeps his distance from words, becoming the mobile signifier that defers its meaning (asking the detective to 'wait just a bit more') and thus attempts to evade the closure of the text. The irony of *Hana-Bi* is that this occurs at the border (the beach and the sea, the limits of the nation), just before the death of such mobility. This may figure as the last outburst of one kind of Kitano Takeshi, before he framed himself as a Japanese auteur.

Kikujiro

With the success of *Hana-Bi*, Kitano Takeshi was now a director firmly on the global stage. A Western audience, however, posed problems for a film-maker who preferred to undermine the expectations of his viewers. He could subvert those spectators as well, but sabotaging expectations could also win, not alienate foreign fans. To Max Tessier, the French Japanese film expert,

> The overwhelming international success of *Hana-Bi* . . . also brought up the question of how Kitano would exploit or not that unexpected success . . . One could fear that he would try to please his western fans by building up his ritual image of the non-speaking violent yakuza to become a kind of icon. However, his newest film, *Kikujiro's Summer* . . . does break this stereotype and proves that Beat Takeshi and Takeshi Kitano are as unpredictable as their own behaviour in this strange world we live in.[1]

Even in Europe, cinematic change was taken as a form of resistance to commercial commodification or the demands of 'Western fans', and thus as a mark of artistic independence.

Subverting foreign definitions of his authorial identity could thus paradoxically serve to reinforce them, but it also created problems in Japan. The plot of *Kikujiro* was surprising to Japanese: a young boy named Masao, living with his grandmother in Tokyo's Asakusa, sets out on the road during summer vacation with a two-bit yakuza called Kikujirō (Beat Takeshi) to see the mother who abandoned him as a baby. They suffer various tribulations along the way, most caused by Kikujirō, until they discover that Masao's mother has remarried and is living a new life. Kikujirō, with the help of some characters picked up along the way, cheers the boy up before taking him back home. This story worried Japanese fans, but not because they expected a gangster movie like their foreign counterparts: it was rather because they did not anticipate a sentimental film. *Kikujiro* faced deep divisions in critical appraisal. While some proclaimed it a masterpiece, others criticised its pacing (finding the film slow) and lack of humour (finding the jokes lukewarm). Even Shibuya Yōichi, the famous music critic who interviewed Kitano on almost every one of his films, clearly disliked *Kikujiro* and constantly pressed the director to discuss its problems.[2] People disagreed about the sentimentalism, in particular about whether the film caved in to conventional forms of emotionality or succeeded in resisting them. Why would a director who constantly changed his cinema to resist categorisation apparently return to conventionality of genre? Was this problem related to the fact that Kitano's pendulum movement now had to deal with multinational expectations? *Kikujiro* is a crucial text for us in considering the practical formulation of Kitano's star and directorial personae in terms of, first, his identity as subversive and, second, how he negotiated his place between the domestic and the foreign. Of particular concern will be how Kitano has recourse to the image of the patriarch – in a film named after Kitano's father – to attempt to manage these new difficulties.

Kitano described *Kikujiro* as taking on conventional stories in order to challenge perceptions of his identity. In the American press notes, he said 'I couldn't help feeling that my films were being stereotyped: "gangster, violence, life and death." It became difficult for me to identify with them. So I decided to try and make a film no one would expect from me.'[3] If Kitano was simply aiming for something different, he could have taken on the very experimental 'Fractal' project he had been speaking about for years. But he thought 'it would be a challenge for me to cope with this ordinary story and try to make it my own through my direction'.[4] He cited classical *rakugo* comic storytelling as a model.[5] Just as *rakugo* artists show their skill and flair less through creating an original story than in adding their own touch to an established narrative, Kitano considered *Kikujiro* to be his opportunity to show his talent through using and twisting conventional stories.

The four main narratives that were discussed in relation to the film were:

1. the novel *Heart: A Schoolboy's Journey* (*Cuore*) originally published in 1886 by the Italian writer Edmondo de Amicis;

2. the *shitamachi* films of Yamada Yōji, particularly the 'It's Tough to Be a Man' series ('Otoko wa tsurai yo') featuring the itinerant peddler Kuruma Torajirō (Tora-san);

3. the road movie; and

4. the long list of films from Chaplin's *The Kid* (1921) to Dennis Dugan's *Big Daddy* (1999), featuring an adult curmudgeon forced to care for a young child, frequently while travelling (the road movie pattern).

Let us consider how *Kikujiro* works with and against these narratives.

In Japanese interviews, Kitano almost invariably cited what was known in Japanese as 'Haha o tazunete sanzenri' (Three Thousand Leagues to Visit a Mother) as the primary narrative structure for *Kikujiro*. 'Haha o tazunete sanzenri' is an episode from Amicis's *Cuore* about an Italian boy who undertakes a long journey to visit his mother working in Buenos Aires. Although Cuore has been popular children's literature since the 1920s in Japan, the 'To Visit a Mother' section was increasingly published separately in the postwar era and become the source of several animated productions, in particular the 1976 television series directed by Takahata Isao (Miyazaki Hayao's longtime collaborator) and the 1999 theatrical feature entitled *Marco* (*Marco: Haha o tazunete sanzenri*, Kusuba Kōzō). *Cuore* became an important representative of Italian national literature through its tales of school children dedicated to parents and country against a background of modern nation-building, an element that may have explained its popularity in prewar Japan. 'Haha o tazunete sanzenri' accorded particularly well with the modern ideological emphasis on the child working hard to live up to the mother's sacrifices within the nuclear family.

Kikujiro obviously borrows this basic story of a boy visiting his mother working far away, even doubling it by having Kikujirō also see his mother. Other similarities include the fact Masao's name resembles that of Amicis's hero (Marco) and that, even though Kitano talked about the picture-diary format as a late addition intended to give structure to a rather loose film,[6] *Cuore* also utilised the journal setup. Yet it seems Kitano used 'Haha o tazunete sanzenri' only to betray its promises. Instead of the emotional reunion with the sacrificing mother, Masao is confronted with a parent who has forsaken him; Kikujirō similarly makes no effort to talk to his own mother. Although the reunion should mark the end of the narrative, *Kikujiro* continues long afterwards, in effect abandoning the *Cuore* story to focus first on the relationship between Masao and Kikujirō, and second, on Kitano's perpetual theme of play. Kitano himself stressed that he attempted to avoid sentimentality by casting Sekiguchi Yūsuke as Masao, a rather nondescript and dumpy boy who lacks the typical cuteness of Japanese child actors.

With regard to the second story pattern, Kitano actually discussed *Kikujiro* in interviews after *Hana-Bi* precisely in terms of Yamada Yōji's work.

> KITANO: The next film is amazing. I'll get rid of the violence . . . and myself do something like Tora-san, something really normal like what Yamada Yōji would shoot.
>
> SHIBUYA: You've gotta be kidding!
>
> KITANO: No, it's true! I want to try making it a bit different depending on how I arrange it. I've got the title *Angel Bell* and the story is just about a boy who lives with his grandmother, discovers his mother is living and goes to visit her.
>
> SHIBUYA: Hey, that's not bad. A road movie!
>
> KITANO: Well there's this yakuza guy who accompanies the boy and they visit the mother together, but the mother has married someone else . . . A lot happens and the boy realises that the most valuable person is his grandmother and the film ends with him running back to her place. It'll have tears and emotion. That's what it'll aim for, but there's something that asks why this is all fake.[7]

Shibuya showed considerable surprise because Kitano had frequently criticised Yamada Yōji's works for their clichéd morality, excess explanation and their depiction of *shitamachi* (see Part I). Kitano's intention to make a 'normal' film like Yamada thus astonished many. A film reinforcing the home community and mixing laughter and tears would certainly fit Yamada's successful formula, but it is significant that *Kikujiro* did not end up as originally planned. Although Masao certainly returns to his grandmother at the end, his desire for home is never strongly shown since the focus has shifted from homesickness towards play on the road. Tora himself can never quite stay at home, but his wanderings always end up commodifying place, as Yamada depicts Tora-san stopping at prominent tourist spots. Kitano, however, avoided showing picture-postcard locations, selecting instead nondescript, aesthetically unremarkable locales.[8] He does offer us a vision of *shitamachi*'s Asakusa, where Kikujirō's wife uses her own money to help a neighbourhood child in need, perhaps proving the strength of communal bonds. But her tiger-print blouse and dyed hair, plus her ease in lying to Masao's grandmother about Kikujirō, is more 'yakuza' than any woman in Tora-san's world. One could argue that *Kikujiro* less utilises the pattern of Yamada's films, than consciously corrects or parodies it.

Kikujirō and Masao are shown travelling more often than Tora, making *Kikujiro* more of a road movie. As such it recalls the travels in *Hana-Bi*, *Boiling Point*, *Sonatine* and *Getting Any?*. Some argued that 'most of Kitano films are road movies',[9] because the director would effectively go on the road with his crew and construct the film according to what he encountered. Others, however, claimed that *Kikujiro* ultimately undermined even this established format. Abe Kashō pointed out that the film lacks the standard image of the road movie: the travelling shots in the vehicle.[10] Apart from a few conversation shots in cars – which fail to reveal much of the passing landscape – *Kikujiro* does not offer us many images of the pair moving in space. The film scholar Umemoto Yōichi argues that the film is actually centred on temporal stagnation, as each attempt at movement is quickly cut off (by, for instance, the many falls in the film), and narrative motion eventually bogs down when the characters begin playing at the water's edge. More precisely, to Umemoto, 'movement and stagnation reveal a cinematic space-time that seemingly renders movement in time and stoppage in time synonymous'.[11] If there is motion in this film, it is either discontinuous and intermittent like in the 'red light, green light' game Kikujirō and the others play, or the circular motion of Masao repeating his run across the bridge (itself a curved structure) at the start and end of the film.

This undermining of the road-movie narrative could signal the difference between *Kikujiro* and the long series of adult-with-children films, some of which are road movies. Kitano rarely if ever associated such works with his film; this was instead an evaluative reference point offered by many foreign observers. To those who praised the film, it was Kitano's ability to take what one critic called 'one of the worst genres',[12] and work with its emotional resonance while avoiding its saccharine schmaltziness, that both proved his versatility and greatness as an artist. The primary way Kitano made this genre 'his own' was by downplaying the 'cute elements'.[13] Where the film differed significantly from the formula was in its refusal to portray the reformation of the loutish Kikujirō. The pattern, from King Vidor's *The Champ* (1931) to Walter Salles's *Central Station* (Central do Brasil, 1998), often centres on character transformation, where the innocent child prompts a down-and-out or uncouth adult to rethink his path, the moment of transformation forming the emotional peak of the film. Kikujirō, however, never exhibits any drastic transformation. Even after showing some kindness to Masao during his encounter with the mother, he reveals the same boorishness subsequently at the festival. The boy has not exactly come of age either, and his fundamental emptiness has not been filled.[14] The film's circular temporality, it could be argued, blocks such transformations in the end.

Not a small number of observers, however, found *Kikujiro* to be as syrupy as the films it was supposedly meant to deviate from. Scenes such as the bus

Looking down

Looking up

stop at night, when Kikujirō notes his similarity to Masao, or at the beach, when the angel descends and Masao holds Kikujirō's hand, bordered on the mawkish or kitschy. If the film was not producing a teary-eyed audience, that was not by design but because, its critics said, it was actually a failure as an effective melodrama, too slow or scattered to build up its emotional resonances.

It is hard to judge claims about the emotionality of a film, complicated as they are by issues of reception. It is sufficient to say that *Kikujiro* was a film that produced quite varied responses, prompting tears in some and the pleasure of unsentimentality in others. One can, however, judge the veracity of claims about the text. For instance, there is reason to doubt arguments denying character transformations in *Kikujiro*. Consider the case of Masao. Some critics complained that he always seems to sulk, but they missed a critical element in the film. Although Kitano primarily pursues a horizontal aesthetics, using flat compositions and lateral motion like in *A Scene at the Sea*, *Hana-Bi* further developed the possibilities of vertical space, especially through crane shots. *Kikujiro* expands on this, using both high-angle and crane shots principally to emphasise character relations. Masao's initial loneliness is underlined, for instance, through the extreme long, high-angle shot of him alone on the football pitch. The impact of such overhead shots is augmented by his tendency to look downward, which communicates his general condition and disappointment. The opposition between up and down, coupled with the fact that Masao is often confined to inner frames (at home, in the sewer pipes), represents a force pressing down on Masao on all sides. What opposes this downward force, and signals a major shift in Masao, is precisely an upward thrust represented primarily by the angel wings on the backpack and the angel bell Kikujirō appropriates from the bikers. One can say that the narrative aim of the film is to get Masao to look up, which he eventually does most significantly by viewing the stars when they camp out and play (this section of the film also features few high-angle shots). He also looks up at Kikujirō, especially on the beach when he first takes his hand after the disappointment with his mother. The shift towards looking up is accompanied by a change in their relationship, as Masao stops calling Kikujirō 'ojisan' (a child's polite appellation for an adult man – also used for the paedophile) and starts saying 'ojichan' (a less polite and more affectionate term). Then, after returning to Tokyo, he finally asks his travelling partner's name. The answer is of course Kikujirō, which is also the name of Kitano's father. On an abstract level, what Masao has found on his trip is not the mother, but the father, which is why Yamane Sadao says the film is not a 'hahamono' ('mother film' – a long-standing Japanese film genre about mothers sacrificing for their children), but a 'chichimono' ('father film').[15]

Masao's change is accompanied by a reciprocal shift in Kikujirō. Abe Kashō argues that, while the film offers Kikujirō as a figure to console Masao, the opposite is more important; citing the ethnographer Origuchi Shinobu's notion of the 'little god' (chiisagami), he likens Masao to child figures from folk mythology who help adults.[16] This is certainly what the boy does at the festival by caring for Kikujirō after he is beaten up. Even the games by the water are not simply for Masao's benefit. The bald biker's suggestion that they begin playing out of pity for the child comes when Kikujirō stands dejectedly after visiting his mother, implying this is as much an attempt to cheer him up as the boy. As Kitano said, in many ways *Kikujiro* is about lonely adults who use a boy to engage in childish play.[17] While it is true that we never see a completely reformed Kikujirō, he is repeatedly shown to be a character who, while often choosing easy money over hard-earned pay, nonetheless diligently learns something if his pride is at stake. Thus he practises his swimming strokes after nearly drowning at the pool, and works hard at juggling until he masters it. Such concrete changes signal that he is capable of transformation, and thus of being caring enough towards Masao to assume the name of the father for a boy who has none.

Kikujiro thus avoids duplicating its primarily generic referent, 'Haha o tazunete sanzenri', by becoming a search for the father. We must ask what results from this shift. It should first be observed that Asakusa is a matriarchal space in the film since the main figures of authority we see are Masao's grandmother and Kikujirō's wife. The lady with the tiger blouse commands influence over not only Kikujirō – who looks down as much as Masao when around her – but also the local teen gang. We are then repeatedly presented with 'the sight of male decline'[18] even after the pair take to the road. The trip to discover the father is an attempt to escape this matriarchal space and free the men from female authority. Concomitant with this narrative is a degradation of the mother. Kikujirō's wife first mentions Masao's mother when she and her husband encounter the boy by the river. Kikujirō blames the mother's absence on 'a man', but the wife retorts, 'She's not like your mother.' But Kikujirō is ultimately proved to be right. This exchange establishes mothers as figures of immorality and betrayal – quite the opposite of what they are in 'Haha o tazunete sanzenri' – an image that is somewhat confirmed in both Masao's and Kikujirō's cases. Kikujirō does not dispute his wife's characterisation of his mother, and her behaviour when we finally see her, shunning others, suggests the poor reputation is deserved, even if her solitude may also earn pity. Masao's mother's marriage is one form of betrayal, but note that Masao already dreamed that she failed to save him from the paedophile. Such poor representations of mothers could serve the film's project of, as one critic stated it, 'weaning the brat Kikujirō, separating him from his mother'.[19]

Escaping from the matriarchal Asakusa can seem to allow for such modes of male behaviour as gambling, violence and all the tricks Kikujirō plays that his wife would stop if she were there (as she does when Kikujirō attempts to pocket Masao's money). However, the road is not necessarily a

Kikujirō's directing look

space of male power: Kikujirō fails at most of his attempts to assert authority and he still encounters women, like the one who gives Masao the winged rucksack, who have some control over their men. It is only after encountering his mother that Kikujirō can finally take command at the camp by the water. Parting from her seemingly allows for an all-male space of play, one that is distinctly homosocial, not homosexual (homosexuality being demonised – some say quite cruelly[20] – in the form of the paedophile), as well as divorced from urban space, if not narrative motion itself.

This space of play resembles earlier such places in *A Scene at the Sea*, *Boiling Point* and *Sonatine*, in its liminality (being at the water's edge) and suspension of narrative progress. However, by eliminating the presence of both death and the feminine, it is a more utopian space, one that is child-like, if not pre-Oedipal, but without descending into death and nothingness like Uehara's male community in *Boiling Point*. *Kikujiro* is a film strongly structured by a child's perspective. The picture-diary structure evinces this the most, not only constructing the events as Masao's recollections, but also effecting the same kind of temporal stagnation we witness in the space of play. Each chapter begins with a title and an image from a narrative event not yet seen. The structure effectively gives the effects of an action before the causes, undermining linear temporality. Masao's visual perspective is offered on several occasions, through regular point-of-view shots or his two dreams, and it provides both motivation for unrealistic aspects of the narrative (such as the angel bell descending to earth) and possibly even the opportunity for Kitano to experiment with film form. The cinematic playfulness is best represented by the 'impossible' point-of-view shots from the bottom of a glass, from a hubcap, or from a dragonfly's multifaceted eye. *Kikujiro* gives the impression of not only depicting a space of play, but also actually embodying that laidback playfulness. Some called it 'an adult movie made by people who never grew up',[21] or sensed in the film's simple and relaxed structure 'the feel of an improvised holiday'.[22] As many noted, including the director himself, most of the characters in this playful world are either childish or at least desire a temporary return to childhood. The most prominent is Kikujirō, an overgrown adolescent bully whose own weaknesses are largely related to his immaturity. There are parallels between Kikujirō and Masao, from their similar upbringing to their tendency to look down.

It would be wrong, however, to say that a more adult authority does not command the film. Masao's perspective structures part of the film, but just as his search for his mother is usurped by Kikujirō's, that man's point of view is often more influential. The best example of this is the encounter with Masao's mother: even though his discovery of her marriage is important narratively, it is Kikujirō's perspective that is pivotal. There is first a medium close-up of the blank face of Masao, then a long, presumably subjective shot of the mother and her new family. But instead of cutting back to Masao, the film shows a long shot of Kikujirō shifting his gaze from the family to Masao. This spatially confirms the object of Masao's gaze, but because the next shot is a close-up of Kikujirō, not Masao, the former's perspective functions as the pivot for the scene. Another single shot of Masao does not appear until after yet another one of the family, and even then it shows a blank face as before. If we see Masao as sad, it is because Kikujirō's gaze writes the narrative on Masao's visage, functioning to direct how we read the scene. Kikujirō then becomes a director in the diegesis. This is a change from him at the beginning, a person who rejects performance (the tap-dancers he berates in the bar), cannot himself perform (his failed attempt to hitchhike by playing a blind man), or remains outside of performance (when the boyfriend imitates the mechanical doll), to him at the end, able to perform (he can now tapdance) and actively staging the scene. He is eventually the authority – the father figure – in the space of play who ensures its security and stability, something that explains why he is less involved in the antics than supervising them from the sidelines.

This figure is familiar to any viewer of Japanese television: this is Beat Takeshi ruling over his 'Army' (which includes Ide Rakkyo and Great Gidayu, who play the bald and the fat bikers respectively). Although *Getting Any?* was a conflicted attempt to deconstruct televisual humour, *Kikujiro* reproduces it rather faithfully, from the sadistic gags to the 'fig leaf' on the naked Ide. So in contradistinction to earlier films like *Violent Cop* or *Sonatine*, which attempted to undermine the persona of Beat Takeshi, this brings it to the fore. In Kitano's words,

> Up until now, I would direct a film while moving Beat Takeshi around. . . .
> I wouldn't let him express his views or have any fun. But this time there's a sense
> that Beat Takeshi has come forward, saying 'May I speak please?''[23]

To one critic, this undermined the emotional force of the film:

> We've seen too many of Takeshi's skits on TV. When there's an emotional scene
> [in *Kikujiro*], the face of Kikujirō disappears and the familiar face of Takeshi
> doing something silly with a straight face appears. Even the Takeshi Army makes
> an appearance then. In this way, we're forced to experience an incomplete pro-
> ject, where we enter the cinematic world of Kikujirō with one foot still in the
> world of Takeshi's comedy variety shows.[24]

Recall that it was spectators imposing the TV image Beat Takeshi on his film
roles that Kitano worked hard to resist in his early films. Why then allow this
practice now? Shibuya Yōichi, complaining that it was hard to identify with
Kikujirō because he was too much like Beat Takeshi, pressed Kitano to admit
the Beat Takeshi tone was introduced for foreign audiences. Kitano
responded:

> There's an image of me on TV in Japan. There are a lot of gestures that people are
> familiar with and ways of talking like you see a lot on TV, right? So the viewers get
> really used to that. Even I get used to it. So I don't know what's new or how to get it.
> I can only depend on the foreign audience. They've never seen anything like this. .
> . . I have read the foreign reviews of my films up until now. They talk about me
> doing a cool man, a tough guy with a restrained performance. They say something
> like this is 'Takeshi's world'. I think I have to pull the rug out from under them, but
> the easiest way to betray their expectations is to do this [TV comedy]. But it does-
> n't pull the rug out from under any Japanese. It's exactly what they expect.[25]

This reveals that *Kikujiro* was in some ways a film intended more for a
foreign than domestic audience.[26] While Kitano attempted to undermine
the expectations of foreign audiences by offering something they had not
seen before, his pendulum swing just provided what Japanese spectators

already knew. Focusing on global viewers, he failed to include domestic audiences in the equation. The authority of the nation was not absent from this space of play.

Although Sera Toshikazu contended that Kitano's choice of nondescript landscapes was an attempt to react against the symbolically Japanese landscapes that populated *Hana-Bi*,[27] Abe Kashō earnestly argued that the "'Japanification" of this film is probably the key to understanding it'. He was referring to the 'distinctly Japanese' angel in the film – the 'little god'[28] – but other signs of 'the folk' populate the work as well, from the *tengu* demons in Masao's dream at the shrine, to some of the mythological figures he views in the stars. But this is a rather sundry collection. The *tengu* dance is performed by a contemporary dance troupe, the Convoy; the figures in the stars range from some of the traditional Seven Gods of Fortune (*shichifukujin*) to Edo-era law officer Tōyama Kinshirō (popular from movies and TV) and a late-nineteenth-century military figure; and the dance staged by Maro Akaji (in Masao's dream) is in the style of Ankoku Butoh, a postwar dance form combining improvisational movement with a strong interest in premodern ritual. *Kikujiro* emits a nostalgic tone, but one that also recalls the entertainment world of 1970s' Asakusa, especially with Beat Kiyoshi appearing for a short repartee with his former partner Beat Takeshi at the bus stop. In this, *Kikujiro* looks forward to *Zatoichi*.

If Kitano had achieved the status of a Japanese artist with *Hana-Bi*, *Kikujiro* reveals the contradictions of that position. The desire to constantly change led to attempts to undermine that identity: the beautiful Japan was opposed by vulgar comedy in a nondescript location, the cool Japanese gangster by the weak and childish miscreant. But Kitano was now a transnational figure, subject to forces extending beyond the borders he was used to. Countering domestic expectations about Beat Takeshi through Kitano Takeshi was difficult as it was, but the split in Takeshi now extended overseas in contradictory ways. Opposing the image of Kitano Takeshi abroad could end up only confirming Beat Takeshi at home. *Kikujiro* revealed that the binary option of either using or opposing conventional narratives, of confirming or undermining expectations, was problematic. That is why

Kikujiro itself ends up being situated, to some so confusedly, on the borders between convention and experiment, commercialism and opposition, television and cinema. Swinging in two dimensions in a now three-dimensional world, Kitano's pendulum left it unclear where Kitano stood or what he really opposed. The role of the trickster became infinitely more difficult and many were left asking what the point was in, as the official pamphlet worded it, 'approving of all the elements he had up until now publicly stated he hated and thus eliminated'. *Kikujiro* appears to both acknowledge and get lost in this both national and personal instability. Its mixtures of traditional and modern, sacred and commercial, underline the inherent hybridity of the nation, but only by also noting its instability and weaknesses. The fatherland here is like Kikujirō himself, obtaining authority only in an unreal, marginal space of play divorced from global realities. *Brother*, we will see, tries to find an answer to this transnational quandary in a Japanised hypermasculinity.

Brother

If *Kikujiro* was a sly attempt to pull the rug out from under foreign spectators, one that ended up revealing the instability of both that strategy and Kitano's trickster identity in a global age, *Brother* was an attempt to deal with the global by force, almost literally invading America to reconstitute the Japanese nation, its cinema and its auteur. This, however, only resulted in exposing more contradictions in Kitano's transnational identity.

Brother was Kitano's first international co-production, and his first work shot outside of Japan. Kitano and his producer, Mori Masayuki, had been in talks as early as 1996 with Jeremy Thomas, the British producer of such movies as *The Last Emperor* and *Merry Christmas, Mr Lawrence* (which featured Beat Takeshi), over the possibility of making a film abroad. These culminated in the creation of a cooperative venture company, Little Brother (with Mori as president and Thomas as vice-president), to produce *Brother*. Especially since few Japanese companies had entered into joint production agreements with foreign companies, the official pamphlet announced the meaning of this arrangement in rather grandiose terms.

> This project takes up the challenge of creating a production method that has never existed before, one melding Kitano Takeshi's auteur-centered filmmaking with the Hollywood production system.
>
> It goes without saying that the realization of this project . . . will greatly influence Kitano Takeshi's film methods, now and in the future, and become a monument opening up new possibilities for Japanese film production in the twenty-first century.

The pamphlet does not specify these influences, but this was unlike any film Kitano had made before. Given the Los Angeles locations and cost involved, Kitano could no longer shift back and forth between film and television work, but had to devote nearly seven weeks to movie production in LA (after filming that many weeks' worth of television programmes beforehand). With a cost of almost ten million dollars, *Brother* was Kitano's most expensive film to date and required budget oversight (including forms of completion insurance foreign to the Japanese industry) and economies of production that the director had not pursued before. In particular, he had to abandon his preference for shooting in order and improvising along the way. This film required a finished script from the start, from which a precise schedule, involving shooting out of order, was constructed and rigidly followed. This was in part necessary in order to accommodate the American cast and crew, which was used to such production methods. Kitano then had to adjust his way of shooting considerably to accommodate the Hollywood environment.

The question is whether this change in the mode of production caused a shift in the structure of Kitano's films. Those who criticised the film often said it did. Some censured it for giving in to Hollywood, becoming 'a highly compromised effort',[1] or, worse yet, 'the thing that [Kitano] had often criticised severely: "an average action flick"'.[2] Others felt that Kitano was trying to meld with Hollywood film-making but failed. *Film Journal International* argued that 'the film's version of America ultimately isn't convincing' and that the 'plot loses steam as Kitano falls prey to the same clichés that mar Hollywood B-movie thrillers'.[3] To others, however, the supposed failures of *Brother* were a sign of resistance to Hollywood methods. As *Libération* described it, 'He did not film in the United States anything other than a yakuza film in perfect conformity with some of his previous examples.'[4] *Brother* was still 'Kitano Takeshi's brand of directing humour and violence', one that undermined the 'pre-established harmony of Hollywood cinema'[5] or functioned as 'a welcome deconstruction of the standard action picture's cathartic celebration of violence'.[6]

The latter position asserted that auteurist spirit overcame the influence of material production conditions. The director claimed the same: 'I shoot films for my own use because I'm my own best audience. That's why it's something completely different from what they make in Hollywood.'[7] Mori also confidently asserted that, 'It's the same way of making a Kitano film as before, only this time there happened to be collaboration.'[8] When asked about the effects of different production conditions, Kitano asserted his ability to appropriate these, using location hunting, for instance, which was done simultaneously with the scriptwriting, as a way to 'mentally shoot in sequence', and eventually 'trying to use editing as a way to resist'.[9] Kitano and Mori stipulated two conditions in negotiations with Thomas: 1) the right of final cut, and 2) the use of Kitano's primary crew members when shooting in the US.[10] Both conditions were met, although Kitano was contractually obliged to deliver a film under two hours in length, which meant scrapping a first cut of 190 minutes, a version he called 'a much more relaxed and laid-back film. The final version became more narratively straightforward and in-your-face.'[11]

In all these discussions, a certain image was created of Kitano Takeshi venturing to Los Angeles and refusing to be affected by it. To some, like Mark Schilling, this was a problem: 'Kitano may have gone to America, but he clearly needed to get out more.'[12] Not a few charged him with a poor understanding of other cultures in the film.[13] But as some commentators noted, one can sense a parallel between the production of *Brother* and the film's own narrative. A gangster named Yamamoto (Beat Takeshi) has to leave Japan for LA when his boss is killed and his gang is forced to merge with the family that killed him. His gangster brother, Harada, actually fakes his death to help him escape. In LA, he finds his half-brother Ken dealing drugs smalltime with some friends, including an African-American named Denny, but when the Mexican mob tries to take control, Yamamoto fights back with yakuza violence. As he becomes buddies with Denny, Yamamoto builds the gang up into one of the major forces in town with the help of Katō, his former lieutenant, and Shirase, a Little Tokyo mobster, only to earn the wrath of the Italian Mafia in the end. The critic Mark Kermode wrote,

Just as Yamamoto understands, but generally declines to speak English, so Kitano's film attempts to inhabit terrain mapped out by the North American film industry (albeit through a British conduit, producer Jeremy Thomas) without engaging in any ongoing dialogue with the compromises for which it has become infamous.[14]

Auteurist continuity was thus similar to the continuity of a yakuza replacing 'Tokyo with L.A., only to recreate his familiar lifestyle in this foreign environment'.[15] Such parallels prompt us to further investigate the issue of continuity in three primary categories: authorship, genre and nation.

When *Brother* was both praised and criticised for returning to familiar Kitano territory, it was most often compared to *Sonatine*, even though, to some, '*Brother* has none of the "philosophical" dimensions of Kitano's *Sonatine* or *Hana-Bi*.'[16] In both *Brother* and *Sonatine*, a mid-level yakuza must leave Tokyo for a different land and in a sense wait for death to arrive. Kitano himself spoke of *Brother* as the 'complete version of *Sonatine*', correcting elements that 'failed' and rendering sections of it more 'popular' (*taishūteki*). Beyond concocting new representations of violence, such as firing a gun through a door peephole, he attempted to improve on scenes such as Murakawa's assault on the hotel. Finding that 'pathetic' (*nasake-nai*),[17] he redid it in *Brother* through the gun battle in the underpass, retaining the strobe effect, but emphasising it through single frames of Yamamoto's men dying off. Yamamoto resembles Murakawa in the way he seems more devoted to play than to protecting his turf. To Umemoto Yōichi, this story 'reproduces the narrative of Kitano's cinema perfectly . . . using playfulness to stagnate the narrative and draw out [Deleuze's] *image temps* from that inertness'.[18]

However, as Abe Kashō argues, Yamamoto exhibits neither the regret of Nishi in *Hana-Bi*, nor the fatigue of Murakawa. He appears to be 'already dead' and lack desire altogether.[19] When he leaves Japan, he is legally dead; his sole pleasure is war unto death, as his smile indicates when he tells Katō there is a battle on in America too. This is not the desire for success or the American dream. Even when the gang defeats the Mexicans and begins to live in luxury, Yamamoto rejects that life by picking a low-class girlfriend and residing in Ken's old ghetto flat. More significantly, Yamamoto essentially ceases to be an active force, doing nothing to expand the business (that is done by Katō and then Shirase) or delay its downfall. Although some reviewers criticised the film's second half for its monotony, it did bleakly convey this desireless doom, becoming 'nothing but an accumulation of scenes of violence that graphically recount only one story and convey only one unique emotion: the slow progression of Death'.[20] Murakawa obtains the catharsis of slaughtering his opponents, but Yamamoto lets his enemy go; *Sonatine* concludes with its hero taking his own life, while *Brother*'s protagonist merely steps outside to die, bereft of even Butch Cassidy's dramatic freeze frame. Although *Brother* presents scenes of play, from basketball in the office to football on the beach, Yamamoto does not participate as much as Murakawa did. At best, he only plays one-on-one games with Denny, a fact that reinforces Yamamoto's solitary disposition.

This does not mean that *Brother* is more unconventional than *Sonatine*. Its temporality is in fact closer to Hollywood's. The shot towards the end, of Yamamoto's car travelling up the desert highway, strongly resembles the image of Murakawa's car on the road, going in and out of sight, but the fact that Kitano cuts to a shot of the boss tied up in the backseat just as the car goes out of view, eliminating dead time on screen – something Kitano refused to do in *Sonatine* – reflects the changes he underwent in coming to America. Becoming more conventional in a Japanese sense was a means of defending himself against Hollywood. While *Brother* was marked as Kitano's return to the gangster genre, it was a yakuza cinema before *Sonatine*. Kitano said,

From smoking as rebellion . . .

... to smoking as authority

> I have been overwhelmed by people's tremendous interest in the behaviour of
> the yakuza. So I wanted to make a film about an authentic, traditional type of
> yakuza. I thought it would be more interesting to set the story in a foreign cultural
> setting rather than to tell the story in Japan, because then the yakuza's behavior
> would appear more striking in the foreign setting.[21]

Two issues are raised here: relating the yakuza to tradition as opposed to the
modern, and framing that through the nation.

Let us consider the first issue. Yamamoto and his lieutenants are much
more invested in yakuza ritual and social structures than earlier figures like
Murakawa or Uehara. Uehara is a loose cannon, embezzling money from the
gang and eventually slaughtering the boss. Even Murakawa, who is more central to the mob hierarchy, appears as an unstable element, signalled through
the trope of the cigarette. When sitting in the club with the gang, Murakawa
is seen smoking well before the boss signals it is okay to light up. This simple
act shows his disrespect for the yakuza hierarchy and his independent streak.
The same trope shows *Brother* to be quite different. Hierarchy is shown when
Katō, for instance, complains early on that an underling has failed to light his
cigarette without prompting. It is this structure that drives Yamamoto to rage

at Shirase at the office when he sees him smoking, presumably without his approval. This is the only time we see Yamamoto vociferously express his authority after their initial success, perhaps precisely to underline that Shirase is not, as he says, a yakuza of the old school.

Yamamoto is defined in the Japan sequences as a mobster who maintains the codes of loyalty. He closely watches over his boss (killing a would-be assassin), protests insults made against his dead leader (pointing out the red tie at the funeral, when black ones are *de rigueur*) and of course refuses to join the family that assassinated his own 'father' (*oyabun*). If *Sonatine* presents a rebellion against a corrupt underworld structure, and thus a critique of the yakuza genre's ascription of chivalric values to the gangster world, *Brother* is more a reaffirmation of the genre's older values. Yamamoto shares qualities with Takakura Ken or Tsuruta Kōji's characters in the Tōei's 1960s' *ninkyō* (chivalric gangster) films, particularly loyalty to the boss and a conflict between duty and friendship (*giri* and *ninjō*). In genre history, he thus precedes the nihilistic Ishikawa Rikio, through whom Fukasaku Kinji announced the 'graveyard of honour'. Perhaps to underline that, Kitano has Watari Tetsuya, the actor who portrayed Ishikawa, appear as a much straighter and more powerful yakuza.

Brother, however, is not a return to the world of *ninkyō* yakuza, and thus retains some of the 'difference' Kitano is noted for. In Tōei yakuza series such as 'Nippon Chivalry' (Nihon kyōkakuden) set in periods before World War II, traditional honour is defined in opposition with modernity. The good yakuza, who maintain communal values of loyalty and wear kimono, are contrasted with those who betray communal trust, wear Western suits and are more capitalist. In *Brother*, however, the traditional/modern structure is less clear. The Jinseikai is no more modern than Yamamoto's Hanaoka gang (its strict, kimono-clad boss in his tatami-matted hall seems, if anything, more traditional than the womanising Hanaoka in a hostess bar). One could argue that it lacks the yakuza ideals of loyalty and fraternity, given that the boss and Hisamatsu, his lieutenant, do nothing to stop Harada from disembowelling himself (Hisamatsu in fact keeps on blithely slurping his noodles, enabling a brutal gag equating noodles and intestines), but initially that is less of a problem than emasculation.

That issue is introduced earlier in the conversation between Yamamoto and Harada after the initial attempt on their boss's life. Harada, insisting times have changed, proposes making a deal with the other side. Yamamoto calls him weak-spirited (*yowaki*). The exchange establishes weakness as an issue not only of declining communal morals, but of the historical loss of masculinity. This is not a problem pressing from outside in the form of another gang (if anything, the Jinseikai are more masculine than Hanaoka), but arising from within. It is partially an issue of identity: Yamamoto in fact berates Harada after he pleads to join the Jinseikai, 'And you pretend to be a yakuza?' Here yakuza are defined as much by masculinity as by their codes of honour. The difficulty arises when brotherhood gets in the way of masculinity. Harada joins the Jinseikai ostensibly for the sake of his men, which angers Yamamoto so much that he almost kills him (significantly, with a sword, not a gun). Yet because of his fraternal affection Yamamoto does not slay Harada. A true yakuza would presumably painfully overlook his mob brother (*ninjō*) and fulfil his duty (*giri*) by killing Hisamatsu alone. That this does not happen indicates a crisis of masculinity that was rarely evident in the Tōei line, and lamenting this loss reveals a desire for the past that *Sonatine* never shows.

One could thus see Yamamoto's trip to America as an attempt to rediscover harmony between yakuza masculinity and brotherhood. Certainly America, with its rooftops, upper-floor offices and open desert, is spatially less restricted than Japan, which may enable the playful fraternity among his crew that is utterly absent in the Jinseikai. As in *Sonatine*, the yakuza can only gain respite from the oppressive Tokyo underworld by fleeing to a foreign coast and playing. Yamamoto, however, remains an ambiguous figure in this space, situated spatially apart from the main group, either at his separate desk, or literally off screen. Failing in his role as paternal boss to the gang, he has in some ways distanced himself from yakuza identity. But he has certainly not given up on such Japanese signs of hierarchy as the term '*aniki*' (brother) or the authority over smoking. One can see in his search for a brother, and finding one in Denny as an alternative to Katō and Shirase, an attempt to reconcile masculinity with fraternity.

Katō may appear to represent ideal loyalty, but he is excessive both in his homosexuality and in his use of violence. While Katō mumbles over Yamamoto's new girlfriend – 'Since when did *aniki* start liking women?' – Yamamoto is more concerned with strictly separating the genders (which is the basis of his counting game with Denny). At the same time, he kills Marina in a scene that mirrors the one where Denny has to shoot him (the latter forces Denny to confront the fraternity/duty conflict, which is largely absent in the former). Denny partially functions to replace all these figures – Marina, Katō and Harada (since he gets Harada's bag) – yet without presenting the threat of homosexuality that Katō does. Katō more consistently maintains yakuza rituals by staying close to the gang and by prompting two generically yakuza rituals: cutting off a finger and sacrificing oneself for one's *aniki*. Kitano ridiculed the former ritual in *Boiling Point*, but treats it more seriously here, especially in the case of Matsumoto, Harada's rival in the Jinseikai. The violence of cutting off a finger is emphasised in *Brother*, to the point that it appears excessive or anachronistic, especially in the American context. Such foregrounding becomes the centring of generic convention itself when Shirase ridicules Katō's threatened act of self-sacrifice as something from a 'yakuza movie'. The comment critiques yakuza film conventions for their unreality while also asserting that Katō's actions are inauthentic (i.e., they must be a bluff). Katō's suicide then is supposed to communicate both his loyalty and the generic formula.

Violence in *Brother* ostensibly operates as a central mode of communication, becoming the means not only for Katō and Harada to relate their inner states to others, but also for Yamamoto to 'talk' to his enemies in a foreign linguistic environment. It is doubtful, however, whether violence can perform these roles. Katō's act is supposed to be the trigger (forgive the pun) for Shirase to align with Yamamoto, but the latter two's lack of true brotherhood is represented by the elision of the proposed handshake between them. The film's exaggerations of violence (Kitano using a loud soundmix for gunfire for the first time) threaten to make it rise above signification and become mere spectacle. That is one reason why we can question whether the Jinseikai have really received Harada's message. Matsumoto, for one, does not show any regret, but rather defers Harada's violent act of signification with just another bloody deed, potentially turn-ing communication into an endless chain of violent free-floating signifiers.

Violence can seemingly enable brotherhood less when it contains specific messages than when it creates relations of exchange and indebted-ness, as it does between Yamamoto and Denny. The nature of this violence, however, renders their brotherhood unequal, contrary to Tsutsumi Ryuichiro's assertion. He is right to analyse *Brother* as ultimately focusing on their pairing, but his structuralist analysis of how the dichotomies of genre versus auteurism and Japan versus America serve only to bring this pairing into relief fails to appreciate how the nation and the auteur shape their relationship.[22] Note that vision is most subject to assault in the film. Denny, of course, is attacked in the eye (after asking Yamamoto, 'Where the fuck are your eyes, motherfucker?') and Jay is shot in the eye while looking through the peephole. Even assaults not necessarily directed at the eyes become attacks on vision through point-of-view structures. In the deaths of both the hitman in the club and the assassin in the sushi bar, Kitano cuts from the victim's perspective just before the bloody deed is done to the physical assault (Yamamoto's bullet, Shirase's hand) directed at the lens (the second even results in a red handprint on screen). This represents a certain power

The unseen enemy

of vision. Yamamoto, for instance, asserts his power through a policy of seeing but not being seen. His authority over Denny is represented by the crooked dice game, where he can peek inside the cup but not Denny. He prefers spaces on the tops of buildings, and uses hidden guns and operates off screen, his location not always known by the spectators. Making the mob boss believe Denny is dead depends on depriving him of his vision. In a film where windows and mirrors proliferate, being able to take away sight is a fount of power. That is in part why Yamamoto and his gang begin to fail at the end: with their big office windows, they not only see, but are also seen by invisible snipers. The Italian Mafia is ultimately victorious because they remain unseen, Kitano not even showing their faces after Ishihara, Shirase's lieutenant, and his men are killed, or when they machine gun Yamamoto.

The cinema spectator can also be defined as seeing without being seen, which means *Brother*'s assaults on the camera are equally directed against the audience, questioning both their power and their frequent detachment from violence. This critique, however, occurs within the context of reaffirming the continuity of two other powers: that of the auteur and of the nation. Kitano's manipulations of what we see through editing – similar to Yamamoto's direction of sight and sound in performing Denny's 'death' – also undermine the viewer's power, but only by transferring it to the force that can control sight: the auteur. Significantly, this force is nationalised in the film. If the story in *Brother* parallels the making of this film, the narrative overarching both is that of World War II. Kitano has delineated some of the links between the film and the war, especially the fact that main characters like Yamamoto, Katō, Shirase and Ishihara were named after prominent wartime military officers. Kitano's or Yamamoto's assault on America is aligned with Japan's assault on Pearl Harbor.[23] Considering this film was directed more at foreign audiences, at least in market terms, the attacks on the viewer become an assault on specifically foreign – possibly American – spectators, while also presenting the fantasy of the American (Denny) forgiving the Japanese for that attack and becoming close friends.

It is true that *Brother* is about brotherhood that can cross national boundaries. This is partially because of gaps and intersections between the various terms used for 'brother' in the film: *'kyōdai'*, *'aniki'*, *'otōto'*, 'brother', etc. 'Kyōdai' is specifically used in the film to signify horizontal relations between yakuza (Harada thus calls Yamamoto that and not 'aniki', which is what Katō uses for Yamamoto). 'Brother' is more expansive, especially when used by African-Americans to designate black or even larger communities. In the film, more restricted relationships like *'kyōdai'* and *'otōto'* (younger brother) ultimately fail. The fact that blood ties are probably the weakest of all fraternal relations is confirmed when Ken flees after learning Denny's mother is dead, abandoning both his blood relative and his street brother. The pleasant irony is that it is Yamamoto and Denny's brotherhood (in the African-American sense) that remains strongest at the end. This aligns with what seems to be the film's anti-racist stance: in what is practically the revenge of the minorities, racist remarks result in quite brutal punishments, as well as such victorious moments as when Yamamoto gloats over his dead enemies, 'I understood "fucking Jap"'.

One should not jump to the conclusion that such a multiracial, transnational brotherhood is antithetical to the World War II narrative. Kitano summarised the film as being about 'minorities like blacks and Mexicans teaming up with the Japanese to beat the shit out of the whites'.[24] On the one hand, this can be the tale of minority empowerment: Kitano said, 'I hope, since it is about people of different ethnic backgrounds getting together and going to war against the big organization or the Establishment, that minorities in America – Asian-American, African-American, whatever – will appreciate and enjoy the film.'[25] It must be noted, on the other hand, that this narrative of non-Caucasians combatting powerful white forces was a staple of wartime Japanese propaganda, used to justify its own domination of Asia. As Oguma Eiji has emphasised, wartime national ideology stressed the international facets of Japanese identity over the exclusivity of blood ties, as such slogans as *'hakkō ichiu'* ('all the world under one roof') preached global brotherhood while accentuating the leadership role for Japan.[26] Denny is then an ideal brother because he calls Yamamoto *'aniki'* and not 'brother', recognising his yakuza superiority while also being his homosocial – not homosexual – buddy. Masculinity and fraternity are united under Japanese dominance.

All this wartime imagery may be Kitano's joke,[27] one similar to his quip after winning at Venice that Japan should align with Italy to fight another war, but that interpretation makes *Brother* a very difficult film to handle. That inscrutability may be the point, however. Umemoto Yōichi wrote in his review of *Brother* about the 'central lack that serves as the motor for Kitano Takeshi's films'.

> *Brother* applies a word to the centre of that lack, a definite word. That word is so resolutely firm that I couldn't believe my ears, but the word is spoken by an old, second-generation Japanese-American bartender at a bar surrounded by the Mafia where the hero played by Kitano Takeshi takes his last stand. 'You Japanese are so inscrutable.' . . . Up until now, Kitano had eluded the threat to his acclaim by opting not to give a word to that lack, thus succeeding in fleeing in the last instant. But this time, the word 'Japanese' has clearly been inserted at the middle of this lack. In his interviews, the word 'Japanese' had especially served to express a difference with foreign spectators, but we interviewers didn't really register that and decided to let it pass. But now the centre, the centre of the lack, that vacant space, was the 'Japanese'. . . .
>
> This is dangerous. That is because when Kitano Takeshi, who was able to become a film auteur precisely by hesitating and daring not to apply the inner reality of a word to that blank, that vacuum, that central lack, inserts the word 'Japanese' into that vacancy, his landscape of nothingness makes us feel the 'beauty' of 'Japan' behind it. I recall Michel Foucault in an interview in *Cahiers du cinéma* in the 1970s, speaking about the nostalgic films flooding France at the time, stressing that excess beauty leads to fascism.[28]

Perhaps we need not go so far as Umemoto and assert a fascist aesthetics in Kitano's recent cinema, but his statement is founded on long-standing critiques of the pernicious relationship between aestheticism and nationalism in Japanese thought and culture. To Umemoto, what made Kitano so politically crucial in 1990s' Japan was not only his thorough refusal to explain his images, thus creating a 'central lack' that always just barely succeeded in escaping the processes of ideologically fixing meaning, but also his radical resistance to calling that emptiness 'Japanese' (or 'Zen', or 'Buddhist', or what have you). This was the difference between emptiness that had been canonised in Japanese art and identity and emptiness radically opposed to ideological signification, between beauty that was placed at the heart of Japanese national feeling and beauty as critique. By calling this emptiness (what is inscrutable) Japanese, Kitano was folding the latter into the former.

It is interesting that it is a Japanese-American who names this inscrutability. One could argue this scene is yet another joke; the man, after all, is framed by the *mise en scène*, distancing Kitano from his statement. But this uncertainty over what the text is saying, one doubled by ambiguities over genre, auteurship and masculinity, eventually ascribes this inscrutability to Kitano Takeshi as well. Through humour or irony, Kitano may mould a frame that helps us cynically refrain from full belief in anything, or equally facilitate the provisional acceptance of everything. But this scene labels that indeterminacy 'Japanese'.

The fact that Yamamoto then ventures outside to die after this statement not only confirms his Japaneseness (his ability to commit suicide), it renders dying itself a national issue. It is true that *Brother* depicts life in Japan quite bleakly in contrast to a more open America, but with the United States never presented as a positive alternative – it is, as Abe Kashō states, merely 'empty'[29] – the choice in the film effectively becomes one between a restricted life and a self-chosen death, both defined as Japanese. This puts a national frame around Kitano's post-accident focus on how to die. It seems as if Yamamoto has come to America to do what Harada has done for him – help a brother (Denny) by hiding his death – but in a more masculine and Japanese way, one that involves a more meaningful death (Yamamoto's demise presumably ensuring the secret of Denny's faked death).

Inscrutability – the inability to be fathomed or found out – is crucial in the film because it aligns with Yamamoto's effort not to be seen, and thus becomes an important part of his authority. Inscrutability, as a national trait, could then justify Japanese dominance. That this national inscrutability is also an aesthetic issue is evident from Kitano's effort to depict cool Japanese. 'Asians in cinema look uncool just by standing next to whites. The pattern is for them to do some kung-fu and get killed easily. I wanted to turn that around and show Japanese who are thoroughly cool (*kakkō ii*).'[30]

Inscrutable

'Cool' in *Brother* is not the same aestheticisation of death that was evident
in postwar kamikaze films, which used conventional national symbols to
melodramatically substitute for deaths never shown, or in Tōei *ninkyō* films,
which ritualised the male protagonist's every movement as he cathartically
confronted the evil yakuza at the end. Some, in fact, accused *Brother* of failing
to achieve this aestheticisation of violence.[31] Kitano, however, believed he
achieved such 'cool'.[32] This aesthetic is partially effected through Yamamoto
Yōji's costumes, which, while not foregrounded enough to become a fashion
show,[33] nonetheless exhibit a uniformity of style (epitomised by the almost
fascistic black suits with white shirts) that exceeds narrative motivation and
becomes aesthetic flourish.

More importantly, the cool is also achieved through a paradoxical combination of inscrutability and stereotype. The statement, 'You Japanese are so
inscrutable', is of course a stereotype if not also an oxymoron. What is
inscrutable cannot by definition be fixed as an object of knowledge, while
stereotype, as its Greek etymology proves, is precisely about fixing. But this
replicates in another form the same issues surrounding Kitano: of discontinuity (the inability to 'catch' Kitano) and continuity (fixing him as an auteur).
The director's image is itself defined as treading the space between

inscrutability and stereotype. Although Kitano said he purposely avoided stereotypes in *Brother* because of Hollywood's history of pigeonholing Japanese,[34] not a few critics found the film rife with ethnic stereotypes, including Japanese ones.[35] While perhaps not intentional, these stereotypes partially result from the same processes of generic foregrounding evident with the yakuza. Just as bringing the yakuza to the United States exaggerated their characteristics, so taking the Japanese abroad prompted the stereotyping of not only Japanese (as Tony Rayns says, 'Kitano goes to LA and becomes more Japanese'[36]), but also the others with whom they are contrasted. To a certain extent, genre and nation operate similarly in *Brother*. Cool, national masculinity is confirmed by transferring it abroad (to where weakness is prevalent, where punks scream over losing a finger, and where a mid-level professional like Yamamoto can easily become a success). While the Italian Mafia ultimately win, theirs is the unfair fight, uncool in part because largely unseen. One has to be seen to be cool, and Yamamoto is paradoxically cool because he is seen as unseen, because he is fixed as someone who cannot be fixed. This overlaps with the definition of Kitano as an auteur, whose variations are increasingly contained because they are defined as uncontainable. When 'aniki' by the end of the film ceases to be a pronoun and becomes a proper name for Yamamoto, Kitano himself becomes the Japanese brother, with Denny's last scene becoming a hagiography to his inscrutable but fraternal coolness.

There remains doubt, however, over whether *Brother* itself is that cool. Although it seems the film's solution to globalism was to invade America with exaggerated Japaneseness, the result was a mishmash of Hollywood, Japan and even European cinema, creating a peculiar beast that the critic Kuroda Kunio, in comparing Yamamoto to Alain Delon's samurai in Jean-Pierre Melville's *Le Samouraï* (1967), terms an 'LA samurai'.[37] Perhaps, instead of being the 'virus' infecting everyone he meets in the USA,[38] Kitano himself was infected, producing what at least in narrative technique is a film closer to the classical style. This may indicate the inherent contradictions in Kitano's global project, but one wonders whether Yamamoto's own lack of energy after his Pearl Harbor indicates the director's own consciousness of this problem. Given the parallels between the film and its making, perhaps this reflects Kitano's lack of interest in producing *Brother* after arriving in Hollywood. Yamamoto's detached stagnation eventually gives way to a Japanese death, but a lingering lethargy still leaves us wondering whether there is not a remaining emptiness that does not earn the name *'aniki'*, 'inscrutable', 'Japanese' or even 'Kitano', a void that still hopes to escape the border.

Dolls

Abe Kazushige intriguingly argues that the theme of 'reuniting with a for-saken past' is not exclusive to the three stories featured in *Dolls*. Just as Matsumoto runs back to Sawako, the fiancée he left to marry the boss's daughter, upon hearing on his wedding day of her suicide attempt and descent into madness; just as Hiro, a yakuza boss who dumped his girlfriend Ryōko decades ago to pursue greater fortunes in the city, discovers her still waiting for him every week in the park; or just as just as Haruna, an idol singer who quit the business after disfiguring her face in a car accident, re-encounters one of her greatest fans in Nukui, so Kitano is reuniting with his own past in the film.[1] The director himself joked that Haruna's accident 'parodies my own experience after the motorcycle accident',[2] and there are many moments in *Dolls* that refer to motifs in previous Kitano works, rang-ing from yakuza assassinations to flower fields, from Japanese festivals to surfboards. Even story actions such as silent couples travelling through Japan or walking right or left across the frame recall *A Scene at the Sea* and *Hana-Bi*, the two works to which *Dolls* is often compared. That is one reason why some critics insisted that 'Kitano Takeshi has only done the same things since debuting [as a director].'[3]

The homology between the narrative and the film's making, however, implies discontinuity in his work. If *Dolls* is 'reuniting with a forsaken past' as much as its characters do, then Kitano must necessarily be confronting a cinema he left behind, but which for some reason has reasserted itself. Abe himself distinguishes between the Kitano of the 1990s and that of the 2000s, arguing that elements of the director's early films, such as the 'utterly minimal form of expression, the insertion of a unique sense of timing, [or] the construction of narrative largely based on the development of repetition', are no longer emphasised. Many noted that the lead actors in each of the three stories are new to Kitano's cinema, although regulars like Ōsugi Ren and Kishimoto Kayoko do appear in small roles. Abe Kashō went so far as to call *Dolls* an 'anti-Kitano' film, one that not only featured the use of zooms and camera movements little seen in his previous work, but that represented a 'letting go of self-restraint'.[4] Many cited the artifice and aestheticism of *Dolls*, especially the striking and to some very Japanese use of seasonal colours, but producer Mori Masayuki claimed this fictionality was the occasion for Kitano to 'free himself' of the reality that he had previously tried to respect.[5]

Not a few critics praised this shift, calling the film's crafting of art and sentiment a 'haunting' example of 'visual poetry',[6] but perhaps an equal number vilified its 'mawkish' and 'caricatured'[7] melodrama, or what was called Kitano's 'continued slipslide down this treacle highway'.[8] Critics who admired the director were at a loss over how to treat a film that appeared to do exactly what Kitano had previously criticised.[9] Several in fact openly wondered whether *Dolls* was not in fact a 'satire' or a 'deadpan black comedy'.[10] Yet seeing that one Japanese review said the film needed Beat Kiyoshi's 'Stop it!',[11] it appeared that *Dolls* lacked such devices as *tsukkomi*, and therefore the frame that could render it parodic or refine its emotionality or aesthetics.

But does *Dolls* really lack such framing devices? Abe Kazushige's observations about the film's self-referentiality imply that Kitano's visual encounter with the past is echoed by the characters' similar act of temporal seeing. In the movie, 'reuniting with a forsaken past' is actually initiated by a glance: the gaze towards the camera of Chūbei and Umekawa, the dolls from the traditional Japanese puppet theatre, *bunraku*, who open the film. The stories that ensue from that act of perception – the tales the two puppets are presumably viewing – also revolve around viewing, as characters mostly recall their neglected pasts through subjective scenes initiated by looks. Given that the entire film is bracketed off by such a process – ultimately concluding with a second shot of the dolls looking – we can say that the dominant structure of *Dolls* is in fact point-of-view editing. With shots of the puppets beginning and ending the film, *Dolls* less abandons framing than makes it central to operations of memory, imagination and viewing. We can argue that, given its self-reflexivity, this is a film about framing. Our questions then must centre on what *Dolls* says about framing, how that framing operates, what is framed and who or what is framing it. This will bring us back to familiar issues such as the nation and aestheticisation, while also raising the question of what Kitano might be seeing as he reunites with the 'forsaken' past of his own cinema.

Abe Kashō uses colour as an example of the freeing of restraint in *Dolls*, and it is true that colour is not framed as it is in *Hana-Bi*, where it is justified by bracketing it off from the rest of the narrative world through picture frames. Here vivid colours are spread throughout the screen, motivated neither by an artist like Horibe nor by the forceful presence of Kitano the auteur (*Dolls* does not begin with Kitano's paintings). Other artists are present instead: first, Chikamatsu Monzaemon (1653–1724), the famed playwright who authored the work *The Courier for Hell* (*Meido no hikyaku*) that is performed at the beginning of the film and that serves as a partial basis for the narrative; second, the *bunraku* artists, the primary of whom (the *omozukai* puppeteer and the *jōruri* musical performers) are customarily in full view of the audience; and third, Yamamoto Yōji, the costume designer. Yamamoto may be the most prominent of these artists because of the central function his costumes play. Although he consciously avoided a 'fashion show' with *Brother*, here he asked Kitano to let him do such a show.[12] Kitano relates that he first planned a much more realistic work until Yamamoto presented the first sample costumes for Matsumoto and Sawako, ones that were not at all true to beggars. Instead of asking Yamamoto to redo them, Kitano decided to go with these costumes by emphasising the framing structure of the *bunraku* puppets.[13] *Dolls* would reverse the usual structure of *bunraku*, in which human beings narrate with dolls, by having the puppets 'imagine' people performing their tale. Chūbei and Umekawa in effect become the puppeteers. This served to motivate many elements in the film. Kitano said, 'during the shoot my sudden openness to a broader colour spectrum panicked some of the veteran members of my crew. I kept telling them these were stories told by dolls, so we could do whatever we liked.'[14] The *bunraku* frame became a very powerful narrative device, justifying not only the use of colour, but also a wide variety of elements in the plot and *mise en scène*, from the costumes to the acting style.[15]

The *bunraku* frame thus operates to naturalise what would otherwise be difficult to accept. That is why it does not function to expose artifice in the

From puppets to viewers

way Abe Kazushige argues it does. Citing *bunraku* as an 'extremely unique
traditional art' in which both the narrative and the artifice of its expression
are in plain view of the audience, Abe considers *Dolls* to be a film that is
similarly 'too honest' (*guchoku*) in laying bare its narrative devices. Far from
joining criticism of the film for its obvious symbolism, its conventional
narrative turns or its orientalist landscape aesthetics – all of which he
recognises – he sees them operating under a form of Brechtian 'estrange-
ment' (*ika* in Japanese), which makes the audience critically aware of these
devices.[16] Abe believes this causes viewers to confront this mawkish honesty
and their desire to look away, a desire expressed in the film through Nukui's
decision to permanently cease looking at Haruna in the present by putting
out his eyes.

The problem with Abe's analysis is not just his failure to develop the
meaning of the dyad to look or not to look, but the fact that *Dolls* is not as
'honest' as he believes it to be. It does not, for instance, maintain the presence of the puppeteers in the diegesis as Shinoda Masahiro's *Double Suicide*
(Shinjū Ten no Amijima, 1969) does, another film that is framed by *bunraku*
theatre, but which pursues the open artifice throughout. *Dolls* drops those
figures even before the narrative properly begins. While the opening

sequence presents *bunraku* on stage in its 'honesty', the crucial shot of Chūbei and Umekawa gazing towards the camera does not. A black screen conceals the puppeteers and silence eliminates the need for the *jōruri*. Here the form of expression is concealed precisely so that the narrative illusion – two inert dolls becoming psychological beings capable of 'imagining' – can succeed. We should imagine what *Dolls* would have been like if the handlers were fully visible in this shot. Perhaps the artifice would have been fore-grounded, but the point-of-view device would have been undermined, breaking up the first construction of subjectivity in a film in which subjec-tive structures dominate. This shot connects with a number of Kitano's efforts to present 'impossible' point-of-view shots like the hubcap in *Kikujiro*. But instead of using this impossibility to undermine subjective structures, Kitano takes advantage of it to expand the realm of the subjective to include even the inanimate. This 'unnatural' structure becomes necessary to frame the film, and to render 'natural' all the artifice that subsequently arises.

If both subjective narration and the artifice that surrounds it are necess-ary in *Dolls*, we must closely investigate their function in the film. *Dolls* exhibits a quite different subjective structure than that of *Hana-Bi*. In the latter, subjective narrative in the form of flashbacks is largely confined to Nishi and to the first half. *Dolls*, however, has flashbacks or subjective visions throughout the film which inhabit different layers. If the dolls occupy the first layer (the objective layer), the second is, for instance, of Matsumoto and Sawako as beggars wandering through Japan after he flees the church and steals her from the hospital (what the dolls first see: the 'present'), the third is of those two in the past (the wedding day), and the fourth is Matsumoto's memory of events before the wedding. The relation-ships between these layers are complex and not all the stories exhibit the same layers. The second through fourth are ostensibly all the subjective vision of the dolls, but it is unclear if the third and fourth, while certainly antecedent in time to the second, are initially the memory of a single char-acter in the second layer. The scene at the church is immediately preceded by a shot of Matsumoto's friends in the present, implying it is their flash-back. However, the long sequence does not end with the friends, confirm-ing their status as narrators, but with a return to Matsumoto and Sawako walking under the blossoming cherry trees. Scenes on the fourth level (or in the case of Hiro, the third level) are more clearly marked as subjective memory: not only do they mostly begin and end with shots of the character reminiscing, they feature devices such as slow motion or disjunctions between sound and image that often, though not always, serve as signs of memory. The relationship between the third and the fourth levels (or the second and third in the latter half of the film) can be complicated, however. An action or word will often spur character memory, but in some cases, such as when the hat blows over the cliff, the memory (of Sawako playing a trick on Matsumoto using a similar hat) precedes what triggers it. In other cases, the memories themselves can be out of chronological order as when we see Hiro's yakuza brother dead before his killing is ordered. Such non-linearity can be explained through character psychology, but some inserts in the film challenge the boundaries of the subjective. For example, there are images of Sawako being found by her parents that Matsumoto could not have experienced, or views of Sawako in the hospital courtyard that Matsumoto could not yet have seen.

Such moments help to create shifts between past and present, memory and imagination, subjective and objective. This is epitomised when, for instance, the subjective structure of Hiro viewing the past of him and Ryōko when they were young suddenly becomes an objective present when he spots Ryōko in the park. Just as with the beggars' final trip to the ski lodge where they had once announced their engagement, a subjective journey in time overlaps with an objective spatial relation in the present. The boundaries between these levels are not lost completely, however; as with *Hana-Bi*, we can ascribe a time or status to most of the scenes by the end of the film. What gives the strong impression that all these levels flow into one another is the fact that structures of looking tend to invade many of the film's forms of narrative. The multiple stories and levels are linked in a variety of ways. The parallel between Chūbei/Umekawa and Matsumoto/Sawako is rendered obvious (to some, too obvious) when the latter couple sees the former in the snow country wearing their *dotera* coats. Matsumoto and Sawako appear briefly in the other two stories and the disabled son of Hiro's yakuza brother appears in two scenes with the bound beggars. Nukui

Unmatched gazes again

lives next to Ryōko and we even hear Haruna's song playing on Matsumoto's cell phone. These spatial connections are augmented on the level of film form by linked gazes that are spatially less clear. Many of the transitions between the stories are marked by unresolved or impossible acts of looking. The first episode with Hiro ends with him in a close-up looking off screen (presumably at Ryōko). What is seen in the next shot, however, is the shanty Matsumoto has built under a bridge. That episode then ends with the couple gazing off screen at the cliff, a shot that is followed by the first appearance of Nukui being led to the beach by Haruna's aunt. That part of the third story then ends with a close up of Haruna gazing (presumably at Nukui), followed by a cut to Matsumoto and Sawako. This chain of unanswered gazes mostly ends at this point (though it continues within episodes), probably because the looks have finally been answered by others as the couples reunite.

   Dolls is a film of gazes because each of the characters is seeking the other who can look back. The return gaze is crucial in the case of Matsumoto and Sawako because her inability to return his glances is a sign of her insanity; it is only her look back at the camera after the nightmare under the bridge that signals a possible change. There are still problems with her vision, however, because the next scene features her sharing glances with the man from her dream with the *hyottoko* comic mask. The couple only really look at each other when they are outside the ski lodge. The tragedy of all three stories is that this exchange of glances will be severed by death and Ryōko and Haruna will begin looking off into space again. Even Matsumoto and Sawako, while together at the end, are suspended from a branch looking in the same direction, not at one another. Perhaps ironically, it is only Chūbei and Umekawa, the dolls who in reality cannot see, that are still able to exchange looks in the final shot.

In this drama of looks, the story of Nukui and Haruna stands out for a number of reasons, the primary being that it is a narrative that rejects the gaze. The two never exchange glances because they only truly meet after Nukui has put out his eyes and Haruna has refused to let any fans see her disfigured face. Before then, their gazes are mostly mediated. The only possible occasion for Haruna to look at Nukui before the accident is when her manager points him out from the car and a shot of him is inserted between ones of Haruna. That image is probably not her subjective shot because it actually repeats portions of a previous shot that was probably her manager's vision (his voice is actually narrating the scene). Nukui is also not shown clearly looking at Haruna. He arrives late at the television studio and focuses mostly on her book at her autograph session. Nukui's subjective shots do not even feature the flesh-and-blood Haruna. His only flashbacks are of the autograph session or of failing to catch Haruna at the studio. Even the repeated shots of Haruna singing her song are not clearly marked as Nukui's. Images of her on television are placed between shots of him dancing, but even if we accept them as mental images, they are from television, not direct reality. The final images of her he imprints on his retina are some of the strongest subjective shots in the film, but they are similarly mediated, coming from her photo book, not herself. Perhaps it is inevitable that a fan's relationship to a star is mediated, but Kitano emphasises this mediation. Haruna's interactions with others are mediated by her manager or her relatives, while Nukui also often relates to Haruna through his rivalry with Aoki, so much so that one wonders whether he is more in love with outdoing Aoki than with Haruna herself.

The story of Nukui and Haruna is fundamentally different both in content and form. If the film's narratives are supposedly unified by the theme of 'reuniting with a forsaken past', this one has little past to speak of since the two were never together to begin with. If one of these two has a forsaken past, it is Haruna, reversing the gender roles of the other two stories. Her memories, however, are not privileged with subjective shots like Matsumoto and Hiro. At best, we could say that most of the first section of their story is her flashback since it begins with a look off screen at the beach and, after Nukui blinds himself, features a similar shot later on. It is a peculiar flashback, however, since it centres not on Haruna but Nukui, and seems to end before the subsequent bracketing shot. They appear to be individuals who are divided not only from each other but also from their past. This is underlined by one of the primary formal dissimilarities between this story and the others. In a film featuring camera movements and couples, one of the privileged moments is a semi-circular camera dolly around the couple. It is first seen in the second image of the film with Chūbei and Umekawa, and is repeated with both Matsumoto and Sawako (at the hospital) and Hiro and Ryōko (on the bench in the past), but not with Nukui and Haruna. Such a camera movement appears only when Haruna is alone on television. Perhaps Nukui shares in this moment, since it is one of the two shots inserted between images of him dancing, but again, this only emphasises how much this couple's past and present, objective and subjective, are fundamentally divided and mediated.

In a film featuring repetition – of similar stories, of similar camera movements, etc. – what is narratively and structurally different necessarily stands out as significant. The pivotal nature of Nukui and Haruna's story is further emphasised by how it is placed in the centre: it is the last of the stories to be introduced and the first to end through the death of one of the lovers. Chūbei and Umekawa may be focusing on that story as revolving around the problem of looking and the mediation of sight. It may also be Kitano's most self-reflexive tale, since it features not only the accident and television, but also Kitano's driver in real life (who plays Nukui). What then is seen in this episode?

Clearly it shares much with the other stories. With no images of them as a happy couple, love is not presented as sweetly romantic (even the cloyingly cute scenes of Matsumoto and Sawako's past do not speak strongly for romance). Sawako's love literally drives her insane, and that of Nukui and Ryōko borders on the abnormal, repulsing not a few viewers.[17] *Dolls* may critique the selfishness of Matsumoto and Hiro, but Nukui's actions are also presumptuous, if not self-indulgent. Reviewers could write that the film confirmed 'love's strange power to survive change and even death',[18] but these love relationships are largely one-sided, considering, for instance, that there is no evidence that Haruna loves Nukui in return. The analogy with the dolls also complicates the depiction of love. Although only Matsumoto and Sawako are directly related to Chūbei and Umekawa, their similarities with the other couples make the latter dolls as well. To many, that was a metaphor for the fatefulness of love, as even Matsumoto and Sawako, after recognising their mutual affection, are chased away and literally hung up like two marionettes after a performance. Most critics read Kitano as the puppeteer here, and a rather cruel one, as he called *Dolls* one of his most violent films to date because death acts capriciously and without reason.[19] One wonders how romantic sentiment can emerge from this. Yamane Sadao argued that *bunraku* was a perfect fit for Kitano because 'all the actors on screen in any Kitano film have been moved around like dolls'.[20] Perhaps Kitano's challenge was similar to that of *bunraku*: how to create emotional characters out of stone-faced performers. Saruwatari Manabu argues that emotion arises from the characters' decisions, as the sacrificial option to become a doll becomes a sign of love.[21] The film's final irony, however, is that only Chūbei and Umekawa, the dolls who commit suicide in the Chikamatsu story, remain alive and together at the end.

Taking a hint from that, perhaps the romantic revolves not around whether characters are dolls, but what kind of dolls they are. This is where the difference of the Nukui/Haruna story proves crucial. Of all the characters in the film, it is Haruna who is the most doll-like. Her main competitor for that honour, Sawako, is only attached to a string because she does not follow her handler; Haruna, however, shows no sign of resisting her managers, at least up until the accident. Her existence is mediated by television and the idol industry, and her body defined by repetition (her musical performance is a repertory of machine-like gestures). Nukui is similarly marked by repetition, not only through his traffic guard job (where all he does is swing a flashing light), but also by his commitment to reproducing an image in his own mind that itself was the product of reproductive technology (the photo book). Nukui himself is just another duplication machine.

Cyclical repetition constitutes a theme throughout the entire film, one introduced at the beginning through the circular camera movements, the revolving *jōruri* stage, and even the editing that repeats portions of the same action (this happens at least twice: with the *jōruri* performers and with Nukui on the beach). Cyclicality is a hallmark of Kitano's work, but here it is grounded in both the temporality of the four seasons and the narratives of reliving the past. Repetition in the Nukui/Haruna story, however, is different because, without a clear past, the two never re-enact a significant action or revisit an important place from a previous time. Theirs is repetition trapped in the present. In a film where time and looking are closely interconnected, Nukui is effectively freezing an eternal now in his mind by opting not to view a changed Haruna. Haruna, who herself has one eye covered, effectively encourages this in all her fans by hiding her transformation, leaving them to only repeatedly look at photographic duplications of an unchanging, mass-produced idol face.

Theirs is love in the age of mechanical reproduction, but that modernity, or even postmodernity, stands in contrast with the two other stories, which are both deeply imbricated with the past. As Abe Kashō notes, none of the three stories is very original, based in one way or another on well-known if not outdated tales. Matsumoto and Sawako's narrative resembles less Chikamatsu's double suicide tale than *shinpa* melodrama;[22] Hiro's story combines *shinpa* with yakuza film narratives; and that of Nukui and Haruna resembles Tanizaki Jun'ichirō's *Shunkinshō*, a short novel about a man who puts out his eyes when the blind *koto* (Japanese zither) player he loves is disfigured. While Kitano keeps the first two narratives largely unchanged, creating noticeable disjunctions between the contemporary setting and the old-fashioned stories, the third has been significantly transformed from being an aestheticist tale of devotion to artistic aura to a disturbing narrative of repetition breeding repetition in an age without an aura.

The televisual dolls of Nukui and Haruna are thus also distinct from the traditional world of *bunraku* where it takes a decade just to learn how to operate a puppet's feet. That world, however, is the one looking at Nukui and Haruna. In a film composed of flashbacks, we should remember that the standard for looking in the film – the gaze of the two puppets – creates another significant reversal: just as it renders the dolls the puppeteers, it has the past 'recalling' the present, the traditional contemplating the modern. Such a reversal strongly resembles that of the nation, that creation of modernity that is rendered a transcendent continuity with the past by inventing the perspective of tradition moulding the present.[23] *Dolls* was another of Kitano's later films that was often discussed in relation to Japaneseness. From its first showing at the Venice Film Festival, it was criticised as aestheticised orientialism pandering to foreign tastes.[24] The film's producers were very conscious of this criticism, even arguing against it in the pressbook: 'If there is a tendency to understand [this film] as 'catering to European "Japonisme"', it is considerably mistaken. One can rather say that *Dolls* is the answer Kitano Takeshi produced in opposition to European 'Japonisme'. The press material does not make clear the content of this 'answer', but the producer Mori Masayuki claimed it was a message directed at Japanese not foreign viewers:

From the moment that he said he would film the four seasons of Japan, the issue of Japanese mentality came up. This was made with Japanese, not overseas, audiences in mind. With things Japanese disappearing from Japan, the film placed the mentality of the Japanese in the foreground.[25]

Mori is speaking as if the film itself is 'reuniting with a forsaken past' and asking Japanese to recall the Japaneseness they once had but had forgotten. Kitano said that,

What this story tries to get at is not just 'love' but any kind of intense relationship: between a nation and a citizen, say, or between a yakuza godfather and one of his loyal soldiers. That strong kind of bond. It's not fashionable to speak of it nowadays and it's not as visible as it once was, but I suspect it still exists, just out of sight.[26]

Dolls attempts to put such bonds in sight, to recall relationships like that with the nation that postwar Japan has been blind to. Nukui's story is then problematic to the degree that it has lost sight of that past, replacing it with the endless consumption of mass-produced images.

If it is anything like the relationships in the film, however, the bond with the nation is not always romantic and may in fact border on insanity. Yet remember that *Dolls* is a film structured through framing. Just as the romanticism of these relationships can, in spite of their cruelty and insanity, arise through their differences (from each other, from their surroundings, from contemporary Japan), so their beauty stems from how they are framed. As Kitano said, 'Ultimate love, if you think about it, is just a cruel and selfish infatuation. But just as falling blossoms or fall foliage can be beautiful, love can shine to the degree it is headed towards destruction.'[27] Violence and death thus function as the aestheticising frame, but that is certainly not uncommon in Japanese aesthetics and became nationalised during World War II. The danger of *Dolls* is that it beautifies the insanity of nationalism through aestheticism, reproducing the way the national body (*kokutai*) in Japan has long been defined through and justified by the aesthetic.

Perhaps Kitano too is reuniting with his forsaken Japaneseness after becoming too globalised with *Brother*, but as we speculated at the beginning, the past he encounters is as much cinematic as it is national. We have noted the structural similarities between *Dolls* and earlier films, but it is important to underline how those constitute Kitano's past. *Dolls* revives the issue of looking that was central to *A Scene at the Sea* and *Sonatine*, but it structures it in fundamentally different ways. The fact that *Dolls* looks at the beach from the sea, as well as at the sea and the characters from the beach, is enough to signal how it reverses *A Scene at the Sea*. If that film fundamentally divided looking from the performance seen, finding a precarious abyss in the interstices of montage that questioned the unity of looking, *Dolls* has the performance (the dolls) look back, creating a model of subjectivity where not only can dolls have an internalised vision, but where the entire world seen by the puppets can be rendered subjective. The look at the camera, which in *Sonatine* was the ultimate sign of emptiness or even of death, becomes a sign of internal plenty (aesthetic fullness) to the degree that must frame these stories. The framing device of the puppets looking founds, rather than undermines the stories, unlike Masaki's toilet reverie in *Boiling Point*. By the time of *Dolls*, the look that frames the film becomes more and more that of Kitano Takeshi the auteur, the ultimate puppeteer, who himself requires subjectivity to found his artistic cinema. In *Dolls* he reunites with a past he had forsaken, but just as the dolls encounter a modernity that is their opposite, but still envelop it in their aesthetic world, so Kitano absorbs the difference of the past in his auteur personality: the director who is free to reinvent himself with each film.

The beginning of *Dolls*, however, with the puppeteers hidden from view, makes it clear, perhaps even intentionally, that to create this internalised nation, this traditional perspective, or even this auteurist subjectivity, the surrounding artifice must be hidden from view; a certain blindness (of history, of modernity, of the constructed nature of subjectivity) is necessary in order for vision to occur. For the dolls to look (at beauty, at Japan), they must be placed in front of a black background, as if they are out of space and time – as if tradition and the nation can be envisioned only when estranged from history. *Dolls* is neither Brechtian nor non-Brechtian because it straddles the abyss between the two: for it to reflect upon itself, it must first be partially blind; yet for it to be blind, it must be crucially conscious of the problem of looking and what is visible or not. It would be wrong to suppose that the audience of *Dolls* misses the fact that the puppeteers have disappeared from view. Kitano may have needed to hide them in order to construct his beautiful subjective narrative of love and nation, but they remain in memory, as that forsaken past that threatens to return some day – although not at the end of *Dolls* – to remind us of the artificiality, the kitschiness, even the insanity of present-day narratives of devotion and Japan.

Zatoichi

When asked in an interview after *Dolls* whether he was interested in being named a 'living national treasure' (*ningen kokuhō*), Kitano Takeshi quipped, 'I'd love the idea of receiving such honourary titles while I'm alive. My dream is to accept them all and then hoodwink them, pull a trick so scandalous that they'd strip me of all the titles at once.'[1] Such a joke spoke of both Takeshi's mischievousness and his aversion to official culture. Although he had won international film awards and produced films like *Hana-Bi* and *Dolls* with serious artistic intentions, there remained the urge to pull the rug out from under his high-class admirers. *Zatoichi* was perhaps one such effort, a film consciously directed both cinematically and thematically at popular culture, one that represents a swing in the Kitano pendulum away from fine art and towards mass entertainment. It in fact became Kitano's most successful movie at the box office, reaping in ¥2.85 billion in domestic receipts, a sum significantly higher than his previous films.[2] The irony was that the film also earned a Silver Lion for directing at the Venice Film Festival. A film concerned with social class and popular culture, it was also his most polished work, combining genre conventions with auteurist flourishes in a manner amenable to a broad audience. As a result, more people saw *Zatoichi* than any of his other movies. The question remains, especially in a movie where blindness takes centre stage, what spectators actually saw. In a different fashion to *Dolls*, *Zatoichi* takes up the issue of looking and problematically links it to class, cinema and nation.

Zatoichi resembles *Violent Cop* in a number of ways: both begin with a side shot of a man facing screen left that is interrupted by unexpected violence, and both were works Kitano did not plan himself. Saitō Chieko, the president of Saitō Entertainment, a company based in Asakusa that managed a number of strip and theatre halls, had asked Kitano to both direct and star in the film. Saitō was a financial backer of Katsu Shintarō, the actor who became synonymous with the Zatōichi character in twenty-six films between

1962 and 1989 and nearly one hundred episodes of the TV programme. The series began at Daiei, but later moved to Katsu Productions, the independent company the actor started in 1967. Saitō helped fund Katsu Productions in the 1970s, and thus incurred considerable debt when it went bankrupt in 1981. Saitō Entertainment now owned the rights to the Zatōichi line and had been seeking to make a new version to recoup its losses, even proposing a film that would star Takeshi (Saitō had known him since the late 1990s), but be directed by Miike Takashi. Eventually Saitō's request that Kitano both direct and star made the film a reality. Saitō not only invested in the project, but pressed Kitano to use two of her star performers, Tachibana Daigorō (as Osei) and Saotome Taichi (Osei as a child), who both appear in *taishū engeki*, a less refined and more popular version of *kabuki* and classical dance.

Kitano's condition for accepting the project was that, while he would keep the basic outline of the character (a blind masseur who is also a master swordsman), he wanted the freedom to do what he wanted beyond that. Just as Kitano had agreed to helm *Violent Cop* and proceeded to undo the basic premises of the script, so it is said he took on the Zatōichi institution, if not the genre of the *jidaigeki* itself,[3] and manipulated it with such 'sheer barefaced cheek' and 'cinematic chutzpah' he put 'Tarantino's *Kill Bill . . .* in the shade'.[4] By outdoing even that most contemporary of directors by flamboyantly crossing genres, Kitano was making someone else's project 'vintage Kitano'.[5] He wanted to 'go in a completely different direction with an alternative, anti-Katsu Shintarō version'.[6] Starting from his long-held wish to avoid being seen as imitating others, he added the blond hair and the red cane as elements that would disassociate his Zatōichi with Katsu's, and pursued narrative and aesthetic strategies that would 'radically change the style of historical film'.[7]

Most observers, however, held the position, one not refuted by Kitano, that *Zatoichi* was actually not much of a departure either from the original franchise or the *jidaigeki* genre. The general plot outline largely conformed to the formula of the series. Zatōichi (Beat Takeshi) wanders into a post town where an evil gang, led by a mysterious leader but managed publicly by Ginzō and the merchant Ōgiya, is abusing the populace. The blind masseur teams up with an old woman named Oume, her nephew Shinkichi, and two wandering geisha, Okinu and Osei (the latter is actually a man), out to revenge their parents, to defeat the villains and expose the boss. As with many Zatōichi films, the masseur has a main rival, this time the samurai Hattori Gennosuke, who hires out his sword to Ginzō as he cares for his sick wife Oshino.

Yamane Sadao carefully lists all the elements in *Zatoichi* that would be familiar to *jidaigeki* fans:

1. Introducing the major characters and their situations in the first scene.
2. The masterless samurai with a sick wife (the first Zatōichi film, *The Tale of Zatoichi* [*Zatōichi monogatari*, 1962], featured a rival samurai who was sick himself).
3. The fencing match in front of the lord becoming a source of humiliation.
4. Siblings whose family was killed by an evil gang and are out for revenge.
5. A man assuming female disguise to enact revenge (a centrepiece of the *Actor's Revenge* [*Yukinojō henge*] films, such as Ichikawa Kon's version in 1963).
6. The children hiding under the floorboards and escaping danger.
7. The *shamisen* concealing a hidden sword.
8. Orphaned children doing performances to stave off starvation.
9. Villains in league with merchants who use any means to suppress their rivals.
10. Gangs beating up peasants for protection money.
11. Escaping the bad guys by donning a straw cloak and pushing a cart.
12. A celebration in song and dance after the villains have been routed (evident in Kurosawa Akira's *Seven Samurai* [*Shichinin no samurai*, 1954], but common in B-movies like those starring Takada Kōkichi at Shōchiku or Tōei).[8]

The last point is the most contentious given that even Yamane stresses that he has never seen *jidaigeki* with tapdancing before. Yet when confronted with an interviewer who insisted on the modernity of *Zatoichi*'s contents, Kitano stressed that that 'transvestites, or the lunatic running around, or even tap-dancing are not new in Japanese history' and that even kabuki uses stomping feet to emphasise certain moments.[9] We can add that rhythm features prominently in many *jidaigeki*, particularly Makino Masahiro's films. The final battle in *Takadanobaba Duel* (*Chikemuri Takadanobaba*, 1937), directed by Makino and Inagaki Hiroshi, is practically staged like a dance number.

If Kitano perhaps inherited the spirit of one of Japan's great popular film-makers, he also confessed to a number of homages to Kurosawa Akira in the film, particularly Zatōichi's swordfight in the rain (referencing the end of *Seven Samurai*), the spouts of blood (recalling the conclusion of *Sanjuro* [*Tsubaki Sanjūrō*, 1962]) and a crazed character in his own dream world (referencing *Dodesukaden* [1970]).[10] The connection with Kurosawa was reinforced by the fact that his daughter, Kurosawa Kazuko, served as costume designer on the film, as well as by the coincidence, often reported in the Japanese papers, that the Venice award was received on the anniversary of Kurosawa's death. In commenting on that to the press, Mori Masayuki reported that Kurosawa had sent a letter to Kitano just after *Hana-Bi* writing, 'I entrust you with the future of Japanese cinema.'[11] The implication was that *Zatoichi* had carried on Kurosawa's torch.

Kitano considered *Zatoichi* to be proof that he had acquired the film-making skill to now make a relatively normal film. 'This time', he said, 'it was like I was being told, "You're a craftsman, so make a craftsman's film (*shokunin eiga*)." So figured I'd show off my skills, like I could bend bamboo or something.'[12] Working now as a director for hire, he compared the situation to his rebellious *manzai* days, when he would do a normal show only when someone paid them to come to their town to perform. This time it was to be a normal entertainment film. 'I must have shot about twice as much as I usually do. I edited it as you're supposed to, moved the camera and had them memorise lines. This was the most serious I've been. You have to do a job for hire properly.'[13] The production of *Zatoichi* was thus closer to contemporary Hollywood practice than previous works like *A Scene at the Sea*: there was a script, with fewer changes on the set, shots planned out beforehand to accommodate the complicated fight scenes, multiple cameras for some scenes, a shorter average shot length[14] and the use of computer graphics. As evidence of his efforts to 'stick to it' (*nebaru*), he closely directed the actors and shot multiple takes, something he rarely did before. On the one hand, *Zatoichi* was the entertainment film of a craftsman (not an auteur) faithful to the practices of the *jidaigeki*; on the other, it was a work brazen in its cheek, a mark of the individuality of the artist Kitano Takeshi. This duality led to some rather peculiar statements, such as one declaring that the finale 'both mocks and celebrates traditional Japanese period dramas'.[15] What that means is unclear, but it underlines how it was not always clear what spectators were looking at in *Zatoichi*. Perhaps one of the sources of *Zatoichi*'s popularity is its ability to appear in such contradictory roles. That, I would contend, lays at the root of the film's thematics, particularly its stances towards class, nation and the problem of looking itself.

The issue of class was central to how Kitano's *Zatoichi* differed from Katsu Shintarō's. Katsu and Kitano had much in common and knew each other personally before Katsu died of cancer in 1997. Both were born in Tokyo's *shitamachi* and trained in popular performing arts (Katsu was a *nagauta*[16] singer), both were actors who started their own companies and took charge of their own work, and both had maverick personalities that sometimes conflicted with social norms (Katsu was arrested several times for drug possession). Katsu's style, however, was wet, earthy and emotional compared to Kitano's dry humour. His masseur sometimes descended into humour and self-parody, but within a humanistic emotional framework absent from Kitano's film. Katsu's Zatōichi made friends in the towns he visited and even had women fall in love with him; parting with such a community – or even the baby he cares for in *Fight, Zatoichi, Fight* (Zatōichi kesshōtabi, 1964) – founded the melodrama and underlined the tragedy of his social position (being a yakuza and sometimes an outlaw). Kitano's Zatōichi does find companions in town, but he is more distant than Katsu's, a fact emphasised by his absence from the communal tapdancing at the end. Katsu's Zatōichi may have missed that too, but only to force the woman who loves him to forget about such a disreputable character; Kitano's masseur is absent because he does not fit naturally into society.

The contrast is centred in the fact that Katsu's narratives, like those of many postwar *jidaigeki*, revolve around the conflict between *giri* and *ninjō*,

Katsu's *Zatōichi* (*Zatoichi and the One-Armed Swordsman*)

Kitano's Zatōichi – The Strongest

between duty and human feeling.[17] This is often the conflict between society (one's social obligations) and the individual (one's personal feelings) and so Katsu's masseur is ultimately tragic because social mores exile him even though his moral code is ultimately social. Such conflicts are utterly absent from Kitano's Zatōichi because he is less in society than above it. He does kill the villains and sides with the little people, but these codes are never in conflict with other obligations because Zatōichi has no social duties. As Yamane notes, Zatōichi does not bear the burdens of the past that create emotional conflicts for the other characters; his sole extended flashback is of the swordfight in the rain, which does little to elucidate his past. In the critic Shinada Yūkichi's words, Kitano's Zatōichi is a 'protecting angel',[18] hovering above the characters and only occasionally descending to help. In the ads, he is 'The Strongest'.[19] While the premise of a blind masseur as master swordsman is patently unrealistic, Katsu's Zatōichi was still an imperfect human being who physically bore the trauma of his blindness. While a rainstorm could pose problems for him because of the sound, it does nothing of the sort for Kitano's Zatōichi, who is so powerful he has the luxury, the ending implies, to choose to be blind. Kitano declared, 'I really hate [Katsu's] kind of earthy human dramas',[20] so the Zatōichi he

created was, in his own words, 'the biggest evil appearing in the film',[21] a
'sort of killing machine'.[22] Trying to cheat the blind masseur in gambling
was one of the staples of Katsu's series, but he never methodically slaugh-
tered everyone in the room like Kitano's masseur does. He in fact tried to
put down his sword several times for the benefit of others, attempts that
eventually failed because of the contradictions he bore. Kitano's Zatōichi
confronts no contradictions, but just kills and kills. Some viewers found
him 'scary' or 'monstrous',[23] but the fact that his victims are one-dimen-
sional villains (except for Hattori) probably explains why many spectators
still thought this 'killing machine' to be 'good humored'[24] or a heroic
defender of justice.[25]

Noting the difference between the two versions, Ahn Min Hwa has
offered a pointed political critique of Kitano's Zatōichi. Although the older
Zatōichi to her embodies the tensions of postwar Japanese conservatism by
both criticizing and waxing nostalgic for a Japanese past, she praises its util-
isation of a marginal hero to focus attention on the class conflicts of the
1960s and 1970s. Citing contemporary critics, she notes how Zatōichi's
blindness is the mark both of his oppression (and the reason for discrimination) and of a logic in which the very objects of denigration become the
source of resistance. This is one reason, she argues, that Katsu's Zatōichi
achieved popularity among lower-class Asian spectators, thus becoming a
kind of transnational 'third cinema' that transcended the film's national
elements. Kitano's Zatōichi, she argues, may seem to introduce critical
forms of cultural hybridity like tapdancing in a Shintō shrine, but the critique fails because Zatōichi is constructed as an all-powerful figure who may
solve social problems, but never experiences them. The cultural hybridity
does not appeal to a transnational underclass, but rather works to rewrite
Japanese tradition for Western consumption, reinforcing the structure of
Japanese modern self-formation, in which Japan is constructed by absorbing the gaze of the West, in effect becoming Japan by performing for
Western consumption.[26]

This is a very intriguing analysis of Katsu's Zatōichi, and echoes some
critiques of the construction of national identity in Kitano's work. As a textual analysis of Kitano's *Zatoichi*, however, it is rather sparse. For instance,

it does not fully consider the issue of class in the film. Social divisions appear initially in the form of hierarchies of power and oppression: Ginzō's men abuse and exploit the farmers, the proprietor of the Matoya commands the old man who works for him, and so on. Some of these structures are discriminatory, as Zatōichi is subject to abuse purely because of his blindness. It becomes clear that the Kuchinawa gang is quite conscious of hierarchy, with Ōgiya doing anything to curry favour with the magistrate, even if it means killing a blind man. Most telling is the one clue that Matoya is not the head of the Kuchinawa gang. Although he gives the broken flask to the old man inside the tavern to throw away, Matoya later finds it on the windowsill outside; clearly the old man – the real leader of the Kuchinawa – refuses to do menial labour, passing it on to his underling.

Against those who assert dominance in economy, labour and possibly culture, *Zatoichi* proffers blindness and the folk. When asked by Matoya why he is feigning blindness, Zatōichi claims the blind can better understand people's feelings. This raises issues of perception I will return to later. Here it is a populist statement: Zatōichi is asserting that real self-denigration – truly living on the bottom unlike the Kuchinawa leader – is the best way to

The fecund folk

understand the people. Given Zatōichi's transcendent status, these are almost the words of a bodhisattva, an enlightened one who foregoes buddha-hood to help the suffering. But this masseur is no pacifist. He is aware of class conflict and serves as the people's avenging angel.

The people is loosely defined here as the folk. It is in effect everyone except the villains, but the focus is especially on those marginal to Japanese political and economic power such as transvestites, prostitutes, masseurs, entertainers and farmers, ones excluded either for their outmodedness or for their social difference. *Zatoichi* resembles *Getting Any?* in its respect for old-time *geinin* (entertainers). Performances are scattered throughout the film from Osei's dancing (which cites Asakusa popular theatre) to the room entertainers (*ozashikigei* like the comedian performing in the inn), from spinning top artists (*komamawashi*) to *shamisen* music. Even the seemingly Western tapdancing fits in this marginal world given how Kitano praised the Stripes, the artists who led and choreographed the last scene, for inheriting the tap style not of whites like Fred Astaire and Gene Kelly, but of African-Americans.[27] Yet the marginal class is largely aligned with the folk broadly defined. Given Takeshi's biographical background and Saitō's connections, the folk as entertainment is clearly rooted in Asakusa. Shinkichi's bungled swordsmanship and much of the swordfight choreography (done mostly by Kitano) were based on the tricks the director learned as an Asakusa comedian.

Zatoichi is easy to read as a valorisation of Asakusa culture, but other aspects spread the definition of the folk beyond that. The most significant is the straw votive figure, which first appears at the beginning when Zatōichi is walking by the fields. At that point it serves as background for the rural set-ting but, in a curious scene, Zatōichi is later shown restoring the figure after some children had played with it. Having no narrative purpose except per-haps to divert Zatōichi from the road Ginzō's men will take to burn Oume's house, the scene is largely superfluous, but as such it begs for interpret-ation. First seen alongside a female figure, the straw man is a fertility sym-bol, bearing an erect penis and placed in a newly tilled field. In a broader sense, it can be tied to vitality,[28] lending that liveliness both to the tapdanc-ing rhythms heard when the figures are first introduced, and to Zatōichi, when there is a dissolve from the figure to the masseur carrying Oume's basket. The association may be curious, given how much death Zatōichi brings to the town, but presumably this is death in the name of life. It is significant that the film focuses on the male figure, putting importance not only on erection (forgive the pun) in the life of the village (re-erecting the figure, rebuilding Oume's house), but also on patriarchy, as the female votive is shunted to the side. Zatōichi aligns himself with the figure and its culture by saving it from the children. On the one hand, this may be Kitano's critique of the childish play that inhabits most of his films, one reflecting the more 'serious' stance he assumed with this entertainment film; on the other, it links Zatōichi's defence of the marginal with a defence of traditional folk beliefs. In this, *Zatoichi* is an extension of the ethnographic world that began with *Kikujiro*.

Such a concern for the folk potentially undermines the depiction of class by essentially reducing complicated social divisions to a unified folk. Difference is then shifted from synchronic conflict towards diachronic narratives of loss and restoration. The issue ceases to be one of the powerful against the marginalised, and becomes one of returning the community, divided by the violent usurpation of power, to a past classless society. Kitano called *Zatoichi* a 'dry' (*kawaita*) work that 'reeks of the modern',[29] and many observers saw it 'embedding the dynamic heartbeat of the modern inside the body of the traditional',[30] but the framing structure is still the traditional, the folk to which the film seeks to return. Kitano also spoke of the film in nostalgic terms as a work recalling his days in Asakusa. Everything in the film, including the character of Zatōichi and the tapdancing (which Kitano first learned in Asakusa), is 'the past. I just filmed it in today's world. There's not much new there.'[31]

In auteurist terms, the film was 'reviving "Beat Takeshi, the Entertainer (*geinin*)" ',[32] but some also hoped it would restore Japanese cinema itself. *Zatoichi* was discussed in the Japanese press as offering a new form of swordplay (*tate*) that emphasised the impact of blade cutting flesh over the spectacle of clanging swords. The director considered this as one way to produce 'a feeling of fast action' matching 'the contemporary speed of the modern film',[33] but he also portrayed this as a return to Japanese authenticity. He complained,

What's more sad is the fact that even the Japanese period films are copying the
Hong Kong style movements which makes it more confusing and more messed
up. . . . What I did with *Zatoichi* was to restore and then to reinterpret the authentic mannerism and movement of swordfighting that they used, not in movies but
in the real art of combat.[34]

His *tate* was supposedly new not because it emulated Hong Kong action, but
because it brought the already fast motions of real Japanese swordplay to the
screen. At least one critic hoped this would help Japanese cinema worldwide:

One can sense in Kitano's version of *Zatoichi* a clear strategic consciousness of
chanbara as a form of action that can combat Hollywood. What is important is
modern *tate* that is based in tradition, and only Japanese cinema can do that.[35]

Zatoichi again seemed posed on the border between performing nationality for foreign spectators, finding authentic Japaneseness in what will cap-
ture overseas markets; and seeking to restore for Japanese 'the heart of
Japanese in an older, better age, one that modern Japanese are forgetting'.[36]

The unseeing seer – Zatōichi/the camera–attacks

Kitano said his decision to not explain Zatōichi, instead relying on Japanese audiences' common knowledge of him, was proof that he was not catering to foreign audiences.[37] This complicates Ahn's thesis, but we should consider it alongside one of the dominant themes of the film: the invisible. Foreign spectators may not be shown Zatōichi's background, but there is a lot the film does not show. Although *Zatoichi* is conscious of class, it complicates that with a hierarchy that is itself hard to see: the Kuchinawa's power structure is actually the reverse of what it seems to be. This may be a lesson in the hidden dimensions of class domination, but problems of perception extend beyond the Kuchinawa to Osei and Zatōichi. Many items hide things in the film, ranging from Zatōichi's cane sword to Okinu's *shamisen*.

These could be examples of the unreliability of sight in a film where the lead character appears to be blind. Vision is not only doubled through mirrors and reflections, it can be oppressive, especially through the male sexual gaze (the magistrate's look at Osei) or instances of surveillance. When a chain of gazes forms at Ginzō's dice parlour, it seems looks really could kill, and Zatōichi's counterattack, shot mostly through a point-of-view structure, makes it seem as if the camera eye is literally cutting up the characters. In a world where vision equals power, authority tries to conceal itself (as it does in *Brother*), either through disguising its hierarchical structures or, as with the shop owner molesting Osei as a boy, simply doing evil out of sight. Most frightening is when those in power, like Matoya and his ninja, take advantage of what is invisible, especially off-screen space. Within this realm of violent vision, it makes sense that Zatōichi deprives the man responsible for this bloody world, the real boss, of sight. The powerless can best fight back by complicating sight and, like Zatōichi, taking advantage of blindness.

Zatōichi replaces sight with sound and smell, but these are less of an option for the film *Zatoichi*. It instead pursues the possibilities of not seeing. Consider the scene where the comedian gives a performance for Zatōichi, Shinkichi and the two geisha at the inn. It is one of several jokes revolving around the masseur's blindness, but the performance itself significantly centres on the inability to see. The comedian, alone, takes advantage of the *fusuma* screen to conceal part of his body and pretend, using his own hands, that someone is pulling him. This is an example of the positive creation of off-screen space, where the interaction of the visible and the invisible produces an extra phenomenon that is pleasurable only to the degree that it is not seen.

This positive use of the unseen is mostly associated with examples of performance inside the diegesis. Many of the characters are performers whose artistry partially depends on the practical ability to conceal. Shinkichi can never be Osei, even though he tries at one point, because hiding his face in make-up is not enough: he needs the talent of showing and not showing. Such a lesson applies to Hattori as well. It seems he loses the match in front of his lord because he fights out in the open, following the rules. The ronin, however, while not necessarily hiding his tactics, bends the rules and fights dirtily. Hattori learns from this and assumes a sword style that is rougher and more pragmatic; he even tries his own performance trick by using Zatōichi's backhand grip against him. He fails because the masseur is an even better performer and parries his trick with another, using a normal sword grip against the unsuspecting Hattori. This is a world where the better performer – the one better at concealing – wins.

Zatoichi, like *Dolls* before it, is a strongly self-referential film as the performers on screen utilise some of the same tricks as the film.[38] Kitano has

Productive invisibilty

stressed the importance of this self-reflexive spectacle. To him, Zatōichi is a killing machine in part

> because I wanted this film to be a frame for all sorts of entertainments: comedy, action, dance, music. The characters and the actors are there to show their talents, their art – what they are best at. For me, the spectacle in *Zatoichi* was as important as the central narrative problem was for the protagonist. If I had put more of an accent on the human aspect of Zatōichi, I would have had to develop the other characters more.[39]

It was partially because he wanted to emphasise the other characters as performers, thus putting the spotlight more on their talents than on their emotional make-up, that he refrained from developing the web of human interactions around Zatōichi.

In the words of one reviewer, *Zatoichi* 'showcases its own artifice and theatricality',[40] and thus places performances at every corner of the film. With Kitano using traditional Japanese architecture to create inner frames, many events occur within a proscenium, and even the final dancers all perform on stage facing some unseen spectator. In an interview, Kitano said his desire to show artifice was so strong he filmed a shot where the camera tracks back from the dancers to reveal the film crew. This certainly would have been a Brechtian moment, one that 'would allow the audience to feel it's only a movie', but he chose to cut it because it would have been 'too rude to the audience'.[41] This revives one of the central issues of *Dolls*, but his decision not to use that shot in *Zatoichi* may provide a different take on the issue, one revolving around the question of performance and invisibility.

Showing the artifice satisfies the desire to see everything. That desire is accommodated in the film mostly through computer graphics. Kitano was reluctant to use them, but they nevertheless appear prominently in *Zatoichi*, especially in the fight scenes. They tread the borderline between realism and artifice, on the one hand, giving 'the film an almost cartoon-like tone', emphasising the contemporaneity of its artifice;[42] on the other, extending the realism by having blades 'really' slice bodies in line with what today's spectators expect. This was a different aesthetics from the one that prized not showing over showing. The former was evident in how Kitano presented bloodshed in earlier films like *Boiling Point*, where the aftermath of violence is sometimes depicted more fully than the violence itself. The swordfights, however, show us all or more than we would want to see, including what a pre-digital cinema could not show. Here *Zatoichi* seems a concession to a different kind of film-making that Kitano had not yet pursued, one that had become synonymous with Hollywood cinema.

In this *Zatoichi* comes closest to accommodating a Hollywoodised spectator seeking to command everything through vision, but it is never self-reflexive enough to expose this viewer. What it does instead is offer an alternative aesthetics that resists or plays with the desire to see, that valorises Zatōichi's decision to be blind. This is another philosophy of entertainment, in which not seeing is pleasurable precisely because it enables an imaginative game of hide-and-seek involving both performer and spectator, allowing creation out of nothing in a way that acknowledges the fact of performance, but not so much that it undermines the creativity of performance (and spectatorship). Here talent (*gei*) is spread between performer and audience, forming a community where everyone, in a sense, gets on stage and dances at the end.

The association of this community with older Japanese entertainments, if not the folk, indicates it could serve as a kind of Japanese national resistance to Western forms of spectatorship. Modern Japanese history has been a story of performing for the Western other, or of internalising that foreign gaze when performing for oneself; *Zatoichi* repeats that to the extent it expresses the desire both to see and to present the Japanese folk for unseen spectators. But as a film fundamentally divided between genre and auteur, traditional and modern, Japan and the West, *Zatoichi* simultaneously presents an alternative strategy of performance where concealment and masquerade are part and parcel of the show for the West. Ideally, all spectators, Japanese and Western, should get in on the global act, where the world is in fact a stage. But in the film's popular nationalism, that must involve restoring a Japanese past against a digital present, albeit a past that may not be that old, that may be centred in Asakusa, and that may, like Asakusa itself, involve hybrid mixtures of traditional and modern, Japanese and Western.

Zatoichi thus presents two quite contradictory visions of performance and spectatorship. If there is one figure who may transcend and resolve these it is Zatōichi, or the man who plays him, Kitano Takeshi. The masseur alone is able to rise above class and even the folk, being the only one off stage during the dancing because he alone can take up the position of the absent viewer. He could make Kitano 'The Strongest' as well, privileging him in a global age as an artist who can freely move between Japanese traditional entertainments and Hollywood digital cinema, becoming the model for a Japan that does not just display itself, but can cunningly say no and hide its wares. Such a figure is certainly attractive in an age of disorder, a 'protecting angel' who can descend and solve Japan's problems. But he is also someone hard to identify with,[43] who does not fit in the entertainment community he himself has helped create. That is perhaps why Kitano, after demoting himself from the artist of *Dolls* to the craftsman of *Zatoichi*, cannot resist but trip up his 'strongest' figure at the end. Zatōichi stumbles precisely on what is not seen, and this is Kitano's warning to a world bent on mastering the environment through vision: 'No matter how much you open your eyes, what can't be seen can't be seen.'[44]

Takeshis' Conclusion

This book has presented two Kitano Takeshis: one the auteur in the traditional sense who produces one recognisable, possibly evolving text over his career; the other a trickster who repeatedly undermines expectations and defines himself by changing style and thematics from film to film. It has not been my aim to adjudicate these two images because clearly they are yet another of the dualities in Kitano's films, including life and death, seeing and being seen, self and other, and conventional and alternative. One could resurrect auteurism by arguing that the consistencies outweigh the alterations; or see the variations as evidence of the true *différance* of signification, constantly deferring the ascription of identity to either the authorial subject or the text. But it seems Kitano's films, if not also the discourses around them, both official and unofficial, have increasingly accommodated these two positions, accepting them even in their contradiction. Kitano's works may indeed constitute a single text, not one modelled on the bourgeois novel, as in auteur theory, but on the *manzai* act with its dialogic conflicts.

With many of the dualities in Kitano's cinema, especially in his later work, framing structures have operated to unite opposing terms through creating hierarchies or subsuming the terms in a transcendental third term. This is the case with the two Kitano Takeshis: in concert they have elevated Takeshi's status to someone who is both an auteur and someone who self-consciously critiques auteurism, who pursues his unique worldview and yet escapes any who would define it, who is both a master director and can play with that very concept. One of the results of these two Kitano Takeshis is to further concentrate attention on Takeshi. If a normal auteur can be reduced to that single text or thematics, Kitano rises above even that, his themes becoming simply another tool he masterfully plays with. Kitano then becomes the ultimate focal point of all his work – not his themes or cinematic style – the transcendental frame that, perhaps like the angels in Kitano's films, accommodates all differences.

It then comes as no surprise that his twelfth film makes him and his multiple images its subject. *Takeshis'* can serve to both represent a growing focus on Takeshi as well as a self-reflexive commentary on these multiple Takeshis and how they have been framed. That is one reason I did not give *Takeshis'* its own chapter but have used it as a frame enclosing the two versions of Kitano Takeshi I have described. As a means of concluding, I would like to briefly consider how *Takeshis'* frames the two Takeshis if not Kitano's career up until this point. Its own contradictions, I hope, can illuminate both the problems Kitano has come to represent, as well as the challenges they pose for us.

Takeshis' was not the first Kitano film to be called a summary of his work, but this time even the director claimed he was finished with his style, junking previous periodisations of his career to claim this was the definite end of his first period of film-making.[1] He called it a 'mixture of *Getting Any?* and *Boiling Point* filmed more seriously',[2] and the official pamphlet narrated *Takeshis'* as a walk through Kitano's past work.[3] The film was replete with the iconography of his previous films, from the Okinawan beach to the taxi driver. The beginning of his directorial career was even cited through a film called *White Heat* (Shakunetsu), in which the Beat Takeshi character stars, which was actually the original title for *Violent Cop* before it was changed to lure Beat Takeshi into the project.

Takeshis' could be Takeshi's effort to narrate his own history, if not his own self, but as usual, this involves rupture and self-critique. *Takeshis'* was originally conceived after *Sonatine* under the title 'Fractal', but Mori Masayuki had long refused to give it the green light. By his own account, Mori said the concept didn't make sense until after *Zatoichi*, as the experimental piece that 'destroyed' that popular work.[4] The original 'Fractal' had the structure of a dream within a dream, but not the two Takeshis. The former engineering student explained his conception of the fractal as 'the part and the whole all possessing the same form', and his example was the dialogue at the *rāmen* noodle restaurant, which was to invade the entire film, spoken word for word by different characters in different situations.[5] Introducing the multiple Takeshis was probably another form of the fractal: they are parts that share the same form as the whole, like the *Takeshis'* poster with small images composing a bigger Takeshi, or like Kitano's oeuvre in an alternative conception of the auteurist corpus, with each of his films, while different, sharing the same form as the larger entity, Kitano Takeshi.

This may not hold water as an analytic methodology, but it does press us to investigate how the film describes this entity. From the two posters to the opening title, a motif of mirrored duality shapes the narrative structure. At the centre of this is the pair of Beat Takeshi and Kitano Takeshi, but many other pairs, from the fat comedians to the colours blue and red, populate the film. The primary story involves one side of the pair imagining the other. Initially, we think it is the unsuccessful actor Kitano imagining becoming the famous TV personality Beat Takeshi, or more precisely, the character he has played. That supposition, however, is undermined when, after the actor Kitano wakes up from his reverie and tries to kill Beat Takeshi, it is the TV star who then wakes up, revealing that Kitano's dream was actually Beat Takeshi's.

This structure, in which an existing frame of reference (Kitano's dream) is undermined by another (Beat Takeshi's dream), is likened by the director to the cylindrical *Baumkuchen* cake, where one layer is repeatedly enveloped by another. It is also conceivably like Kitano's career, as each new film superimposes one definition of his film-making on another. The structure also resembles a common Kitano editing trope, where he cuts between two characters looking at the camera. Just as each of these shots is both a subjective shot (what one character sees) and an objective shot (the image of the person looking), here each character is both the dreamer and the dream of the other dreamer. That more complicated structure, however, is not sustained for, as again with many of Kitano's dualities, if not his career, these doubled imaginings are framed, this time by Beat Takeshi's dream. Although that may undermine some of what we might know (rendering much of what we know about Kitano just Beat Takeshi's imagination), this frame makes this supposedly 'incomprehensible' film much easier to understand.

We then might ask ourselves the motivation for Beat Takeshi imagining Kitano Takeshi, both in terms of character psychology and artistic intent. The Kitano character's fantasy is simple to comprehend, involving an emasculated loner dreaming of manliness achieved through guns, women and money. The star's motivations are less clear since he, presumably, already has these. Perhaps this is a manifestation of narcissism or, as some charged, of a 'masturbatory private film'.[6]

Beat Takeshi's mastery of his own desire is undermined on several fronts, however. First, the fantasy is repeatedly frustrated by both women (particularly Kishimoto Kayoko's characters), who betray and emasculate the men, and by death. This may revive the death wish of Kitano's early work, but in a film where violence is often without consequence, death is never final (since the dead come back to life). Second, there are moments before Beat Takeshi's fantasy begins that already question this fantasy, such as the brief image of Kyōno Kotomi having sex in Kitano's apartment (how could Beat Takeshi imagine this if he had not met Kitano yet?). Beat Takeshi's command over his own vision is thus questioned. In fact much of what Beat Takeshi dreams is 'suggested'. The fantasy of Kitano the convenience-store clerk actually begins right after the manager speculates that the meek actor must be working at such a store. It is as if the fantasy is not Beat Takeshi's own, but prompted by others, emasculating the dreamer when he's dreaming of masculinity. In a film in which viewers get shot at by performers, viewing a dream is far from being a safe fulfilment of desire.

Yet although *Takeshis'* offers many moments that are bizarre and absurd, the film is not surrealist in Breton's sense. While scenes like the taxi ride through the bodies border on the disturbing, *Takeshis'* is mostly contained within a comedic frame that renders threats funny and violence harmless. Despite Mori's claims of its destructive nature, a number of critics pointed to the film as evidence that Kitano, in this work if not also in his cinema as a whole, was actually not that subversive.[7] *Takeshis'* is a far smoother film than *Boiling Point* or *Getting Any?*, in part because, despite the narrative of loneliness and frustration, it is imbued with a rather pleasingly consistent rhythm, which Kitano apparently dictated on the set as 140 beats per minute. This was a film to be enjoyed for that continuous flow: both Kitano and Mori urged spectators not to think about the movie, but to experience it with their body.[8] *Takeshis'* thus resurrected the concept of the primitive that some used to describe Kitano in his early films; here, however, that attribute is shifted from the director to the audience, from being an original state to becoming something assumed partly through forgetting previous modes of cinematic reading.

With the last scene returning us to Beat Takeshi's fictional movie, *Takeshis'* self-consciously signals the victory of the fictional over the real, the conventional over the experimental, circularity over rupture. This set of frames keeps the conflict between Beat Takeshi and Kitano Takeshi in check. Circularity in Kitano has always smelled of fate, of characters weakened and trapped by a spinning world larger than them, and in *Takeshis'* Kitano appears to be lamenting the eternal return of Beat Takeshi. Not only has he not succeeded in killing him, as he might have tried with his early films, but the film presents an ironic reversal: it is now Beat Takeshi inventing Kitano Takeshi, not vice versa. With the Beat Takeshi character active in both film and television, the problem depicted in *Takeshis'* seems to be less the victory of television over cinema, than the oppressiveness of media celebrity, in which doubles proliferate, others 'misrecognise' you, and performances are already read (and, in the case of the acting audition, rejected) before you even start. The title is in the possessive form, but what seemingly owns this film is less Beat Takeshi and Kitano Takeshi than the multitude of

Takeshi as the defeated Japanese soldier

The powerful Americans

Takeshis circulating in the media, perpetually returning even if one escapes as far away as Okinawa.

Takeshis' could then be Kitano's justification for constantly fleeing the media expectations created of him. This tale of fate, however, offers little hope for a successful escape. Although Kitano looms over this film with his face and name, he is like the angel with the broken wing in *Hana-Bi*, a transcendental figure who cannot fly. One could argue that this was inevitable given how Kitano enacted his politics of fluid identity. Kitano could have pursued a politics of positionality as described by Stuart Hall, one where identity is not grasped as a given essence, but accepts difference through strategic shifts in position. Hall, however, contrasts this with a vulgar Derridean pursuit of constant flow and deconstruction. To speak and to mean, he argues, we must occasionally assume a stance, all the while maintaining a tension between movement and position.[9] Kitano exemplifies the failure that results from choosing flow over the occasional stance. His desire to subvert established categories was commendable, but his moves were so frequent that, instead of undermining media expectations, he proliferated the number of media Takeshis until they engulfed him, augmenting the circulation of *tarento* currency not subverting it. Especially when his later films ended up subverting a defined politics of subversion by adopting elements of dominant cinema, he threatened to denigrate the positions he previously took. Takeshi's case shows there are limits to being a trickster, especially when its tendency to escape a position can be appropriated by a dominant cynicism that in contemporary Japan serves to legitimise inertia.

In Takeshi's case, the result of a politics of fluid identity is less the critique of identity than the elevation of Takeshi himself. As if to verify that, *Takeshis'* was advertised as a '500% Takeshi experience with zero impurities'.[10] The fate of being trapped in multiple Takeshi media was ultimately sold as a pleasurable experience for the audience, as if an amorphous but manifold Takeshi, and not his worldview or cinematic style, was all that was left to market. This could be another form of hegemony, one similar to the form Hall attributes to Thatcherism and its ability to accommodate difference, not through an open and strategic positionality, but through a closed system that essentially speaks different words to difference audiences. If Thatcher proffered a vision of unified Britain in this fashion, Takeshi sells Takeshi by offering different Takeshis to various audiences, keeping it 500 per cent pure precisely by emptying them of substantial meaning.

Takeshis' reveals that Kitano is not pleased with this situation, but the film places blame in disturbing areas. The movie is actually framed by two scenes: the 'Beat Takeshi' movie that ends *Takeshis'* and the scene from World War II that begins it. The latter also greets the Beat Takeshi character after he wakes from his Kitano Takeshi dream and effectively introduces the final frame. The World War II scenes can function as the frame of a subjective sequence, rendering everything from after the title until Beat Takeshi wakes up the dream of the prostrate Japanese soldier confronted by an American, just before he is presumably killed. The Beat Takeshi film returns after that. This is again a narrative of emasculation, but one that clearly marks the violence as national, with Japan suffering at the hands of America. With the Beat Takeshi film emerging from that, it is as if *Takeshis'* is connecting the all-enveloping system of media personality, if not the world of images that swallow up any reality, to America's postwar emasculation of Japan. *Takeshis'* supposedly works to expose this situation as well as to resist it. One author in the official pamphlet celebrated the film as the triumph of Beat Takeshi in 'returning to his original subjectivity', thumbing his nose at foreigners by making a movie they could not understand but that 'we Japanese', familiar with the real Beat Takeshi, can easily comprehend.[11]

If this interpretation of the framing devices is correct, they offer a simplistic analysis of postwar media culture and echo rightwing attempts to blame Japan's contemporary weaknesses on products of American dominance such as the 1947 Constitution. This poverty of analysis may symbolise not just the rise of nationalism from the mid-1990s on, but also the inadequate theorising that has surrounded Kitano's films in Japan, if not Japanese cinema as a whole, one that has reduced the complexities of image production in an increasingly globalising yet also nationalistic postwar world, for instance, to crude oppositions between television and cinema.

What proves fascinating about watching Kitano's films, however, is the realisation that they are too complex and sophisticated – and often contradictory – to be contained by any frame the theoretician or even Kitano can impose. I have hoped that the structure of this book, while framing discussion, has also allowed some of these complexities and contradictions to escape. *Takeshis'* is, as its title shows, a film about possession, but one that questions possession as the ownership of dreams repeatedly shifts. The ownership/framing of *Takeshis'*, if not Kitano's career, is also problematised by a director who has experienced the contradictions of postmodern media culture more than any theorist or film-maker, knowing both its oppressive dominance and its pleasures, both the means of commercial success and possible avenues of subversion. Kitano may again be thinking with his body, but his cinema of doubles and diversions, emptiness and escape, and nothingness and nationalism has itself figured as a sometimes blind and sometimes brilliant practical exploration of the multiple and contradictory valences of the image, the author, the star, the nation and identity in a postmodern, globalising world. Kitano remains fascinating not because he offers us a single vision of our complex world but because he, like the poster for *Takeshis'*, encompasses the many images of that, allowing us multiple perspectives. In this, he both proclaims his transcendence with bravado and recognises his own handicaps. If Kitano has achieved anything, it is the consciousness of difference among his audiences: that 'Beat

Takeshi' is not all there is to his image, and that 'Kitano Takeshi' is not one author.

This is ultimately a challenge for us, the audience. *Takeshis'* foregrounds the humiliation of the clown, making it one of the reasons for the Kitano character to kill Beat Takeshi. When the clown outside the store angrily asks Kitano – and us, the audience – what we are looking at, *Takeshis'* connects with many of Kitano's attacks on the viewer, linking them with both a portrait of the violence of comedy, performance and spectatorship, and a project to trip up if not also cripple the audience. At times he may do that to lord over his stunned viewers, but also acknowledging his own handicaps and humiliation, Kitano is not capable of leading us to answers and overarching visions. His cinema challenges us to crawl on our own, confronting both the differences and the contradictions of his own films and those of a world that his work both represents and resents.

NOTES

Introducing Two Takeshis

1. Abe Kashō, *Kitano Takeshi vs Beat Takeshi* (Tokyo: Chikuma Shobō, 1994). This has been translated into English, with additional articles, as *Beat Takeshi vs. Takeshi Kitano*, eds William O. Gardner and Daisuke Miyao (New York: Kaya Press, 2005). There Abe's name is rendered Casio Abe, but since I refer to the Japanese originals, I follow the name used in American libraries when cataloguing his work.

2. Daisuke Miyao, 'Telephilia vs. Cinephilia = Beat Takeshi vs. Takeshi Kitano', *Framework* vol. 45 no. 2 (Autumn 2004), pp. 56–61.

3. See his interview with Tsukushi Tetsuya, 'Wakamonotachi no kamigami: Bīto Takeshi', *Asahi jānaru* vol. 26 no. 25 (15 June 1984), pp. 43–7. For his use of the same concept with regard to film, see Kitano Takeshi, 'Mizuumi mitaina umi ga ii', *Cahiers du cinema Japon* no. 23 (March 1998), p. 83.

4. 'Fukkatsu Takeshi "Motto nebaru"', *Asahi shinbun*, evening edition, 2 February 1995. In other interviews, he has spoken of working with three characters: the 'comedian Beat Takeshi', the 'serious actor Beat Takeshi' and Kitano Takeshi 'the director': see Matthew Turner, 'Kitano in London', <www.kitanotakeshi.com/index.php?content=resources&id=56>.

5. Quoted in Maruyama Kazuaki, *Sekai ga chūmoku suru Nihon eiga no hen'yō* (Tokyo: Sōshisha, 1998), pp. 220–1.

6. The title of the first English-language book on Kitano published by Tadao Press in 1999.

7. Quoted in Katsuta Tomomi, 'Chōfu yūkan: Dokuritsukei eiga', *Asahi shinbun*, evening edition, 14 June 2005.

8. To use Chris Rojek's terms: *Celebrity* (London: Reaktion Books, 2001), pp. 17–18.

9. Richard Dyer, *Stars*, new edition (London: BFI, 1998), p. 99.

10. For an account of postmodernity and flexible accumulation, see David Harvey, *The Condition of Postmodernity* (Oxford: Blackwell, 1989); for a theorisation of the schizophrenic nature of postmodernity, see Fredric Jameson, *Postmodernism, or the Cultural Logic of Late Capitalism* (Durham, NC: Duke University Press, 1991). For a review of debates of the problem of the individual in stardom, see Su Holmes, '"Starring . . . Dyer?": Revisiting Star Studies and Contemporary Celebrity Culture', *Westminster Papers in Communication and Culture* vol. 2 no. 2 (2005), pp. 6–21.

11. Joshua Gamson, *Claims to Fame: Celebrity in Contemporary America* (Berkeley: University of California Press, 1994).

12. Mitsuhiro Yoshimoto, 'Image, Information, Commodity', in Xiaobing Tang and Stephen Snyder (eds), *In Pursuit of Contemporary East Asian*, (Boulder, CO: Westview Press, 1996), pp. 123–38.

13. Office Kitano manages such *tarento* as Zomahoun, who appears in *Takeshis'* as the mysterious African with a headlight.

14. See Mark Schilling's interview with Kitano in *Contemporary Japanese Film* (New York: Weatherhill, 1999), p. 96.

15. Tony Rayns, 'Puppet Love', *Sight and Sound* vol. 13 no. 6 (June 2003), p. 18.

16. Tom Mes and Jasper Sharp, *The Midnight Eye Guide to New Japanese Film* (Berkeley, CA: Stone Bridge Press, 2005), p. 160.

17. His name has been rendered both Yanagijima and Yanagishima, but the former is what he uses on his business card.

18. See, for instance, Higuchi Naofumi's response to the questionnaire, '*Dolls* kōkai chokuzen kinkyū ankēto', *Kinema junpō*, no. 1366 (15 October 2002), p. 43.

19. Horike Yoshitsugu, 'Jitensha no kioku', *Yuriika* vol. 28 no. 12 (October 1996), p. 233.

20. Jean-François Buiré, 'Hana-Bi', *Lycéens au cinéma* (2000–1), p. 10.

21. Nakano Midori, 'Yappari nan da ka, henna hito', in Kitano Takeshi (ed.), *Komanechi! Bīto Takeshi zenkiroku* (Tokyo: Shinchōsha, 1998), p. 227.

22. For such confessions, see Turner, 'Kitano in London', or 'Dai 1-kai Kyoto Eigasai "Kitano Takeshi, gakusei to kataru"', *Kinema junpō* no. 1293 (1 October 1999), p. 75.

Part One
Kitano Takeshi: The Auteur

1. See Shinozaki Makoto's comments in his interview with Kitano: 'Hana-bi, Kitano Takeshi', *Studio Voice* no. 263 (November 1997), p. 42.

2. A view forwarded by Henrik Sylow, who manages the Kitanotakeshi.com website: 'SV: Kitano/Kijujiro/ Buffoon—Addition re Furansu-za', KineJapan mailing list, 12 August 2006.

3. See Niizawa Hiroko, *Bīto Takeshi ron* (Tokyo: Gakuyō Shobō, 1995).

4. For a well-balanced account of Takeshi's life, see Okazaki Takeshi, 'Takeshi to Takeshi no iru hodō', *Yuriika* (rinji zōkan) vol. 30 no. 3 (February 1998), pp. 87–95, 143–51, 194–203. This is my main source in relating Takeshi's biography.

5. 'Kitano Takeshi intabyū', *Dolls*, official theatre pamphlet, pp. 18–21.

6. Kitano Masaru, 'Kitano-ke no hitobito', in Kitano Takeshi, *Kikujirō to Saki* (Tokyo: Shinchōsha, 2001), p. 124.

7. For instance, Kitano calls *Kikujiro* a 'shy film' (*tere no eiga*) because he was always too embarrassed to take the extra step and go for the tears. See Kitano Takeshi, *Takeshi ga Takeshi o korosu riyū* (Tokyo: Rokkingu On, 2003), p. 211.

8. Actress Kanno Miho, who starred in *Dolls*, said, 'I think he's such a shy person that he cannot depict love without depicting violence': 'Kanno Miho', *Kinema junpō* 1366 (15 October 2002), p. 36.

9. Bīto Takeshi, *Watashi wa sekai de kirawareru* (Tokyo: Shinchōsha, 1999), pp. 82–99.

10. 'Dai 1-kai Kyoto Eigasai "Kitano Takeshi, gakusei to kataru"', *Kinema junpō* 1293 (1 October 1999), p. 88.

11. Kitano has been ambiguous on this topic. He once told Tony Rayns, A journalist asked if it was true my grandfather was Korean. I answered honestly that I could well be one-quarter Korean. I got this idea because when my mother scolded me she used to say, 'What can we expect? You are the grandson of a Korean!' . . . I concealed this belief . . . until I reached some level of maturity and began earning my own living. Then I asked my mother once again if it was true . . . She answered, 'Worse than that! He was an abandoned child, a foundling!' . . . It seems to be true that my father didn't know his own parents, which means he had a very low social standing in Japan. Tony Rayns, 'Papa Yakuza', *Sight and Sound* vol. 9 no. 6 (June 1999), p. 17.

12. See Niizawa, *Bīto Takeshi ron.*

13. Tomohiro Machiyama, 'A Comedian Star Is Born', in Brian Jacobs (ed.), *'Beat' Takeshi Kitano* (London: Tadao Press, 1999), p. 107.

14. Tsukushi Tetsuya, 'Wakamonotachi no kamigami: Bīto Takeshi', *Asahi jānaru* vol. 26 no. 25 (15 June 1984), p. 46.

15. Kitano Takeshi and Tony Rayns, 'The Kitano Talkshow (IFFR 04)', <www.kitanotakeshi.com/index.php?content=resources&id=54>.

16. Matsukura Hisayuki, *Utatta, odotta, shabetta, naita, warawareta* (Tokyo: Gomu Bukkusu, 2002), p. 180.

17. Okazaki, 'Takeshi to Takeshi no iru hodō', p. 146.

18. Nibuya Takashi, '"Warai" to "bōryoku"', *Yuriika* (rinji zōkan) vol. 30 no. 3 (February 1998), p. 164.

19. Bīto Takeshi, *Gozen 3-ji 25-fun* (Tokyo: Ōta Shuppan, 1986), quoted in Okazaki, 'Takeshi to Takeshi no iru hodō, p. 144.

20. Ōta Shōichi, *Shakai wa warau* (Tokyo: Seikyūsha, 2002), p. 71.

21. Andrew Horton, 'Introduction', *Comedy/Cinema/Theory* (Berkeley: University of California Press, 1991).

22. Steve Neale and Frank Krutnik, *Popular Film and Television Comedy* (London; Routledge, 1990), pp. 79–80.

23. Bīto Takeshi, *Manzai byōtō* (Tokyo: Bungei Shunjū, 1993), quoted in Okazaki, 'Takeshi to Takeshi no iru hodō', pp. 148–9.

24. As described by Yoshikawa Ushio, 'Shōgeki no Tsū Bīto', in Kitano Takeshi (ed.), *Komanechi! Bīto Takeshi zenkiroku* (Tokyo: Shinchōsha, 1998), p. 217.

25. Quoted in 'Akashingō, minna de watareba kowaku nai', *Asahi shinbun*, 'be shūmatsu' section, 30 August 2003.

26. See, for instance, Kamata Satoshi's comments in a roundtable discussion with Tsurumi Shunsuke and Satō Tadao, 'Tsū Bīto wa kikenna chōkō ka', *Asahi jānaru* vol. 23 no. 28 (1 May 1981), pp. 24–31.

27. Kobayashi Nobuhiko, *Nihon no kigekijin* (Tokyo: Shinchōsha, 1982), pp. 315–16.

28. See Tsurumi's comments in 'Tsū Bīto wa kikenna chōkō ka'.

29. Takayama Hiroshi, 'Shimainya warau zo', *Yuriika* (rinji zōkan) vol. 30 no. 3 (February 1998), p. 159.

30. Kitano has stressed this. See, for example, the interview 'Kodomo o dashi ni kodokuna renchū ga ōsawagi', *Kinema junpō* no. 1285 (1 June 1999), pp. 36–8.

31. Horike Yoshitsugu, 'Bīto Takeshi to wa dare ka', *Yuriika* (rinji zōkan) vol. 30 no. 3 (February 1998), pp. 108–19.

32. Takada Fumio, '"Tokyo bunka" toshite no katarigei', *Yuriika* vol 30 no. 3 (rinji zōkan) (February 1998), p. 140.

33. Yoshimoto Takaaki, 'Taishū bunka '83', in *Sōtai genron*, by Yoshimoto and Kurimoto Shin'ichirō (Tokyo: Tōjusha, 1983), pp. 216–17.

34. Asada Akira, 'Infantile Capitalism and Japan's Postmodernism', in Masao Miyoshi and H. D. Harootunian (eds), *Postmodernism and Japan* (Durham, NC: Duke University Press, 1989).

35. Ōta, *Shakai wa warau*, p. 181.

36. For more on the phenomenon of the *shōjo*, see Ōtsuka Eiji, *Shōjo minzoku-gaku* (Tokyo: Kōbunsha, 1989); or Sharon Kinsella's 'Cuties in Japan' and John Whittier Treat's 'Yoshimoto Banana Writes Home', in Lise Skove and Brian Moeran (eds), *Women, Media and Consumption in Japan* (Honolulu: University of Hawaii Press, 1995), pp. 220–54, 275–308.

37. Jacques Rancière, 'Le mouvement suspendu', *Cahiers du cinéma* no. 523 (April 1998), pp. 34–6.

38. Saruwatari Manabu, 'Kitano Takeshi/Bīto Takeshi no sekai', *Tōhoku kōgyō daigaku kiyō II Jinbun shakai kagaku hen* no. 22 (2002), pp. 1–16; Bob Davis, 'Takeshi Kitano', *Senses of Cinema*, <www.sensesofcinema.com/contents/directors/03/kitano.html>.

39. Ōta, *Shakai wa warau*, p. 182.

40. Chuck Stephens, 'Comedy plus Massacre', *Film Comment* vol. 31 no. 1 (January–February 1995), pp. 31–4.

41. Yomota Inuhiko, *Nihon eiga no radikaruna ishi* (Tokyo: Iwanami Shoten, 1999), p.61.

42. Machiyama Tomohiro, 'A Comedian Star Is Born'. p. 106.

43. Yoshimoto, 'Taishū bunka '83', p. 217.

44. Ōsawa Masachi, *Kyokō no jidai no hate* (Tokyo: Chikuma Shobō, 1996), pp. 38–72.

45. Fredric Jameson, *Postmodernism, or the Cultural Logic of Late Capitalism* (Durham, NC: Duke University Press, 1991).

46. Yumiko Iida, 'Between the Technique of Living an Endless Routine and the Madness of Absolute Degree Zero', *positions* vol. 8 no. 2 (2000), pp. 423–64.

47. Niizawa, *Bīto Takeshi ron*, pp. 23–44.

48. For a history of this, see Victor Koschmann, 'Intellectuals and Politics', in Andrew Gordon (ed.), *Postwar Japan as History* (Berkeley: University of California Press, 1993), pp. 395–423.

49. See Bīto Takeshi, *Takeshi no 20-seiki Nihonshi* (Tokyo: Shinchōsha, 1999).

50. See, for instance, Takeshi's *Watashi wa sekai de kirawareru*, pp. 193–209.

51. Bīto Takeshi, *Hadaka no ōsama* (Tokyo: Shinchōsha, 2003), p. 110.

52. Bīto Takeshi, 'Bīto Takeshi "aikokushin" o kataru', *Sapio* vol. 10 no. 2 (4 February 1998), p. 17.

53. Kitano called for rethinking prewar Japan in 'Nihon eiga wa ore ga sasaeru', *Chūō kōron* vol. 112 no. 14 (1997), p. 262.

54. For examples of this, see 'Dai 1-kai Kyoto Eigasai' or Mark Schilling's interview with Kitano in *Contemporary Japanese Film* (New York: Weatherhill, 1999), pp. 99–100.

55. Darrell Davis, 'Reigniting Japanese Tradition with *Hana-Bi*', *Cinema Journal* vol. 40 no. 4 (Summer 2001), p. 59.

56. For this and other critiques of Beat Takeshi, see Media Clip (ed.), *Dakara Takeshi wa kirawareru* (Tokyo: Ningen no Kagakusha, 1992), especially the essays by Nisho Kan and Zenjī Nankin.

57. Machiyama, 'A Comedian Star is Born', p. 105.

58. Quoted in Suga Hidemi, 'Shōsetsu o kakanai shōsetsuka', *Yuriika* (rinji zōkan) vol. 30 no. 3 (February 1998), p. 168.

59. Fukuda Kazuya, 'Deguchi no nai zetsubōkan', in Takeshi Kitano, (ed.), *Komanechi! Bīto Takeshi zenkiroku*, pp. 289–97.

60. Davis, 'Reigniting Japanese Tradition', p. 58.

61. Mitsuhiro Yoshimoto, 'Image, Information, Commodity', in Xiaobing Tang and Stephen Snyder (eds), *In Pursuit of Contemporary East Asian Culture* (Boulder, CO: Westview Press, 1996), pp. 123–38.

62. Abe Kashō, *Kitano Takeshi vs Beat Takeshi* (Tokyo: Chikuma Shobō, 1994), p. 41.

63. Mori Masayuki, 'Mori Masayuki', in Kakeo Yoshio (ed.), *Eiga purōdūsā ga omoshiroi* (Tokyo: Kinema Junpōsha, 1998), p. 65.

64. Kitano's statement at the Kitano Takeshi International Symposium: see my 'And the Beat Goes On', *Daily Yomiuri*, 3 October 1996.

65. 'Kodomo o dashi ni', p. 39.

66. See Kitano's interview with Hasumi Shigehiko: 'Kitano Takeshi intabyū', *Bungakukai* vol. 59 no. 6 (June 2005), pp. 244–5.

67. This is how Kitano teaches narrative to students, now that he has become a professor of film at the Tokyo National University of Fine Arts and Music.

68. See Mori Masayuki's comments in 'Kitano-gumi no genba de nani ga okotte iru no ka', *Yuriika* vol. 30 no. 3 (rinji zōkan) (February 1998), pp. 72–86.

69. Mark Schilling, 'Kitano Takeshi, asobu', *Premiere* vol. 2 no. 5 (May 1999), p. 57.

70. Kitano Takeshi, 'Mizuumi mitaina umi ga ii', *Cahiers du cinema Japon* no. 23 (March 1998), p. 72.

71. For details on the cinematography of Kitano's films, see John Pavlus's article on Yanagijima Katsumi: 'Global Village', *American Cinematographer*, vol. 85 no. 6 (June 2004), pp. 14, 16–17.

72. With *Takeshis'*, Yanagijiima Katsumi, Isoda Norihiro and Takaya Hiroshi reported few changes in Kitano's style. But Yanagijiima, when pressed, noted that Kitano is definitely shooting more

takes and a greater variety of shots:
'E de "taikansuru" Kitano eiga', in
Sōryoku tokushū Kitano Takeshi (Tokyo:
Kadokawa Shoten, 2005), pp. 108–15.

73. Few talk of Kitano's influences and he
himself said he saw few movies in his
youth. Abe Kashō (*Kitano Takeshi vs Beat
Takeshi*) and Yomota Inuhiko (*Nihon
eiga no radikaruna ishi*) stress the
importance of Ōshima Nagisa, who
directed Takeshi in *Merry Christmas, Mr
Lawrence*, in shaping Kitano's treatment
of actors (especially 'Beat Takeshi'), the
use of at least one fresh actor per film,
and possibly his interest in Okinawa
and other minority cultures. Some have
taken the original title for *Sonatine*,
'Okinawa Pierrot', as indication of his
interest in Jean-Luc Godard (e.g.,
Pierrot le fou, 1965) (Machiyama, 'A
Comedian Star Is Born', p. 113),
although Kitano confessed he could not
understand him. In the end, his
inconsistent statements about his film
experience have enabled commentators
to construct him as a true original.

74. '*Dolls* kōkai chokuzen kinkyū ankēto',
Kinema junpō no. 1366 (15 October
2002), pp. 40–4.

75. Bīto Takeshi, *Watashi wa sekai de
kirawareru*, p. 10.

76. Kitano Takeshi, 'Kondo wa igai ni
shinken ni yaru ka mo wakannee na',
Représentation no. 3 (1992), p. 172.

77. Abe, *Kitano Takeshi vs Beat Takeshi*,
pp. 3–49.

78. 'Dai 1-kai Kyoto Eigasai', p. 78.

79. Kitano Takeshi, 'Kitano Takeshi
eigajutsu', *Switch* vol. 9 no. 4
(September 1991), p. 41.

80. Mutō Kiichi, *Shinema de hīrō: Kantoku
hen* (Tokyo: Chikuma Shobō, 1995),
p. 22.

81. Hasumi Shigehiko, *Kantoku Ozu Yasujirō*
(Tokyo: Chikuma Shobō, 1983).

82. Shinozaki Makoto, 'Fukigen ni
tatakaitsuzukeru monotachi', *Cahiers du
cinema Japon* no. 0 (Summer 1991),
pp. 86–97.

83. Hasumi Shigehiko, 'Kitano Takeshi,
mata wa "shinshutsu kibotsu" no koji',
Mube, <www.mube.jp/pages/critique_1.
html>.

84. Kitano's painting style, which is
childish but resembles Henri Rousseau,
also manifests this primitiveness.
Kitano consciously cites Rousseau in the
beach scene in *Takeshis'*.

85. As with Ozu, Hasumi rejected the
notion Kitano was a minimalist:
'"Sunahama no sakka" Kitano Takeshi',
Sonatine, official pamphlet.

86. Following Kitano's statement that blue
is a base colour used to punctuate other
colours, Daisuke Miyao has investi-
gated the symbolic conflicts between
blue and red (and sometimes yellow) in
the films up to *Hana-Bi*. He shows how
the 'poetically functional' use of colour
shifts from film to film, although red
appears most consistently associated
with violence. See his 'Blue vs. Red:
Takeshi Kitano's Color Scheme', *Post
Script* vol. 18 no. 1 (Autumn 1998),
pp. 112–27.

87. Yamane Sadao, *Eiga wa doko e iku ka*
(Tokyo: Chikuma Shobō, 1993),
pp. 159–60.

88. Yamane Sadao, *Eiga no bō* (Tokyo:
Misuzu Shobō, 1996), p. 598.

89. Kitano, 'Kitano Takeshi eigajutsu',
     p. 38.
90. Ibid., p. 41.
91. See Yamane's comments in *Dare ga eiga
     o osorete iru ka* (Tokyo: Kōdansha,
     1994), pp. 138, 148 – a collection of
     correspondences between Yamane and
     Hasumi. Hasumi's response was to
     iterate that 'Only the taciturn nature of
     "zero point films" can, in a way more
     eloquent than all forms of verbosity,
     expose the naked form of cinema itself'
     (p. 160).
92. Kitano, 'Kitano Takeshi eigajutsu',
     pp. 41, 43.
93. Suzuki Hitoshi's *Gamen no tanjō*
     (Tokyo: Misuzu Shobō, 2002) contains
     a fifty-two-page essay on *Hana-Bi*.
94. Shinozaki, 'Fukigen ni tatakaitsuzukeru
     monotachi', p. 89. In later years,
     Shinozaki withdrew this claim.
95. Kasahara Kazuo, 'Kore wa ehagaki no
     renzoku suraido de aru', *Eiga geijutsu*
     no. 363 (Winter 1991), pp. 60–3.
96. The 'script' a month before filming
     started – only seventy-nine lines long –
     is printed in *Eiga geijutsu* 363 (Winter
     1991), pp. 56–8.
97. Kasahara, 'Kore wa ehagaki', pp. 62–3.
98. Shinozaki, 'Fukigen ni tatakaitsuzukeru
     monotachi,' p. 90.
99. Kitano said that the lack of dramatic
     change between Shigeru and Takako in
     A Scene at the Sea, or the lack of a
     conclusive home run, either in the
     game or in the battle with the yakuza in
     Boiling Point, is more realistic. See
     Shinozaki's 'Fukigen ni tatakaitsuzukeru
     monotachi' or 'Kitano Takeshi
     eigajutsu'.

100. 'Kitano Takashi kantoku intabyū',
     Kinema junpō no. 1068 (15 October
     1991), p. 40.
101. Suwa Nobuhiro and Aoyama Shinji,
     'Cinema as a Natural Phenomenon', in
     Viennale '00 (Vienna: Vienna
     International Film Festival, 2000),
     pp. 246–54.
102. Umemoto Yōichi, 'Umerareyō tosuru
     kūhaku no fūkei', *Cahiers du cinema
     Japon* no. 31 (2001), pp. 276–7.
103. Miyahara Kōjirō, 'Tasha no shōgeki,
     shōgeki no tasha', in Uchida Ryōzō,
     Imēji no naka no shakai (Tokyo: Tokyo
     Daigaku Shuppankai, 1998), pp. 49–78.
     Miyahara did an experiment with 200
     of his students, showing *Sonatine*'s
     Russian roulette scene twice and asking
     them to describe Murakawa. The
     responses said he was 'like a thing',
     who has 'forgotten this thing called his
     self', whose 'mind has flown off
     somewhere', and who 'has no will and
     is just some thing laying there
     exposed'.
104. Aoyama Shinji, 'Yo wa ika ni shite
     Gareru shito ni nari shika', *Cahiers du
     cinema Japon* no. 21 (1997), p. 175.
105. Ibid., p. 168.
106. For an analysis of Japanese images of
     blackness, see some of the articles by
     John G. Russell, starting with 'Race
     and Reflexivity: The Black Other in
     Contemporary Japanese Mass Culture',
     Cultural Anthropology vol 6. no. 1 (1991).
107. Ishihara Ikuko, 'Kiyoku, subayai,
     kagekina shi', *Kinema junpō* no. 245
     (15 January 1998), p. 57.
108. Davis, 'Reigniting Japanese Tradition',
     p. 72.

109. The Okinawan film-maker Takamine Gō has told me of his praise for *Sonatine*'s radical depiction of Takamine's home island compared to that of conventional mainland directors.

110. Isolde Standish, *Myth and Masculinity in the Japanese Cinema* (Richmond: Curzon, 2000), p. 190.

111. Mark Schilling, 'Hits and Memories: Reinventing the Yakuza Film', *Japan: People, Power & Opinion* no. 1 (October–November 2001), pp. 87, 95.

112. Nakamura Hideyuki, 'Gaishō no e/Zōyo no monogatari', *Yuriika* (rinji zōkan) vol. 30 no. 3 (February 1998), pp. 61–71. He defines this wound as an excessive and disturbing physicality that prevents the spectator from identifying or entering the space of these films.

113. Yvonne Tasker, *Spectacular Bodies* (London: Routledge, 1993).

114. Kitano Takeshi 'Ore wa Nihon eiga no gan,' *Yuriika* (rinji zōkan) vol. 30 no. 3 (February 1998), pp. 10–38.

115. 'Even if the guy watching says, "Takeshi, I don't get it at all—this film's terrible", I'll just nod my head and say, "OK". I have absolutely no inclination to change it.' From 'Owarai no ma', *Eiga geijutsu* no. 368 (Summer 1993), p. 13.

116. Sono Shion, 'Kitano Takeshi wa gyangu eiga sakka de aru', *Gendaishi techō* vol. 37 no. 7 (1994), pp. 84–7.

117. All of Kitano's films up to *Kikujiro*, with the exception of *Getting Any?*, made the top ten in the respected *Kinema junpō* poll of critics (*Violent Cop* 8th, *Boiling*

Point 7th, *A Scene at the Sea* 6th, *Sonatine* 4th, *Kids Return* 2nd, *Hana-Bi* 1st, *Kikujiro* 7th). *Brother*, however, finished at number 23, *Dolls* at 12 and *Takeshis'* at 14. (*Zatoichi* was 7th.)

118. See many of the comments in the '*Dolls* kōkai chokuzen kinkyū ankēto'.

119. Kimura Tatsuya, 'Kitano Takeshi', in Mutō Kiichi *et al.* (eds), *Nihon-sei eiga no yomikata 1980–1999* (Tokyo: Firumu Ātosha, 1999), pp. 78–9.

120. See Frodon's comments in 'Kaigai no eigajin ga kataru "Nihon eiga no kanōsei"', *Invitation* no. 0 (December 2002), p. 52.

121. David Bordwell, *Narration in the Fiction Film* (Madison: University of Wisconsin Press, 1985). I want to thank Ian Conrich for suggesting this, although I believe further analysis is needed. While a film like *Boiling Point* does exhibit the constraint typical of parametric films, there are questions about how 'ordered' it is, particularly whether it exhibits the strict 'theme and variation' structure of other parametric directors like Ozu and Bresson.

122. 'Dolls,' *TheGline.com*, <www.thegline.com/dvd-of-the-week/2003/07-28-2003.htm>.

123. From Hasumi Shigehiko's comments in the pamphlet for the Takeshi Kitano International Symposium and Retrospective held at the 1996 Tokyo International Film Festival.

124. Horike Yoshitsugu attempts an uneven and in the end a-political theorisation of Kitano through Deleuze's notion of a body without organs: 'Jitensha no

kioku', *Yuriika* vol. 28 no. 12 (October 1996), pp. 233–42.

125. Abé Mark Nornes, 'The Postwar Documentary Trace', *positions* vol. 10 no. 1 (2002), pp. 39–78.

126. Tony Rayns, 'Puppet Love', *Sight and Sound* vol. 13 no. 6 (June 2003), p. 18.

127. Davis, 'Takeshi Kitano'.

128. See the interview 'Kitano Takeshi kantoku', *Kinema junpō* 1245 (15 January 1998), p. 44. Kitano speaks about his own film history – albeit in a revisionist way – at the end of *Takeshi ga Takeshi o korosu riyū.*

129. Yamane Sadao, 'Kitano Takeshi, eiga to no akusen kutō', *Kinema junpō* no. 1153 (1 February 1995), p. 107.

130. 'Kitano Takeshi-san, tsugi wa motto janpu', *Yomiuri shinbun*, 26 September 2002.

131. Tsutsumi Ryuichiro, 'Finding an Alter Ego: The Triple-Double Structure of *Brother*', *Iconics* no. 8 (2006), pp. 135–57.

132. Higuchi Naofumi, 'Sturēto nō cheisā', *Kinema junpō* no. 1443 (15 November 2005), p. 157.

133. For a more extensive account of these issues, see my 'The Industrial Ichikawa', in James Quandt (ed.), *Kon Ichikawa* (Ontario: Cinematheque Ontario, 2001), pp. 385–97.

134. Mori, 'Mori Masayuki', p. 70.

135. Mori Masayuki quoted in Maruyama Kazuaki, *Sekai ga chūmokusuru Nihon eiga no hen'yō* (Tokyo: Sōshisha, 1998), p. 223.

136. See Katsuta Tomomi, 'Chōfu yūkan: Dokuritsukei eiga', *Asahi shinbun*, evening edition, 14 June 2005. Kitano's

success has returned him to major distribution.

137. A term used by Davis, 'Reigniting Japanese Tradition', p. 70.

138. As argued by Umemoto Yōichi, 'Kitano Takeshi Kokusai Shinpojiumu', *Cahiers du cinema Japon* no. 20 (April 1997), pp. 10–11.

139. Davis, 'Reigniting Japanese Tradition', p. 75.

140. That manga-like world was emphasised by the comic-book-like design of the *Takeshis'* pressbook at Venice.

Part Two
Another Kitano Takeshi: The Films

Violent Cop

1. The Army/*Gundan* members arrested with Takeshi included Yanagi Yūrei, Guadalcanal Taka and Dankan. While they were never prosecuted, Takeshi was convicted and sentenced to six months in prison, suspended for two years.

2. The public reason for Fukasaku's withdrawal was scheduling problems, particularly Takeshi's desire to film every other week, but Okuyama says it was Takeshi's insistence on filming without rehearsals and doing only one take per shot: Okuyama Kazuyoshi, 'Bīto Takeshi e no ketsubetsu', *Bungei shunjū* vol. 71 no. 9 (1993), p. 285.

3. From the preface of an interview with Beat Takeshi by Akimoto Tetsuji: 'Bīto Takeshi intabyū', *Kinema junpō* 1016 (15 August 1989), p. 86.

4. Okuyama, 'Bīto Takeshi e no ketsubetsu', p. 286.

5. Ibid.

6. For the former, see Yamaguchi Takeshi,
    'Inshitsuna gendai o tsuku!!', *Kinema
    junpō* no. 1016 (15 August 1989),
    pp. 88–9; for the latter, see Osugi's
    comments in 'Gei no aru eiga, nai eiga',
    Image Forum no. 114 (October 1989),
    p. 124.

7. Tommy Udo, 'Violent Cop', in Brian
    Jacobs (ed.), *'Beat' Takeshi Kitano*
    (London: Tadao Press, 1999), p. 19.

8. Yamane Sadao, 'Katsugeki no saranaru
    yukue', *Kinema junpō* no. 1018 (15
    September 1989), p. 205.

9. Nozawa Hisashi, 'Fukasaku-gumi
    toshite no *Sono otoko, kyōbō ni tsuki*',
    Shinario vol. 45 no. 9 (1989), pp. 8–9.

10. Since Kitano never specifically rewrote
    Nozawa's script, the *Kinema junpō* script
    is just a transcription of the completed
    film made by Tanaka Hideko.

11. Shinozaki Makoto, 'Fukigen ni
    tatakaitsuzukeru monotachi', *Cahiers du
    cinema Japon* no. 0 (Summer 1991),
    pp. 86–97.

12. Four pages' worth of scenes were cut
    from the twenty-nine-page script
    published in *Shinario*, although some
    were shifted to before or after this
    scene.

13. Abe Kashō, *Bīto Takeshi vs. Kitano
    Takeshi* (Tokyo: Chikuma Shobō, 1994),
    pp. 58–63.

14. Shinozaki, 'Fukigen ni tatakaitsuzukeru
    monotachi', pp. 93–4.

15. See, for instance, Jasper Sharp, 'Sono
    otoko, kyobo ni tsuki Violent Cop', in
    Justin Bowyer (ed.), *The Cinema of
    Japan and Korea* (London: Wallflower,
    2004), p. 135.

Boiling Point

1. Morita Ryūji, '"Bōryoku" "shitsugo"
    "shi" "warai"', in Yodogawa Nagaharu
    (ed.), *Kitano Takeshi* (Tokyo: Kinema
    Junpōsha, 1998), p. 60.

2. A word used by Asakura Kyōji,
    'Oshimareru buntai no "yurusa"', *Eiga
    geijutsu* no. 361 (Spring 1991), p. 86.

3. Mike Bracken, 'The Birth of an Auteur:
    Takeshi Kitano's Boiling Point',
    CultureDose.net, <www.culturedose.net/
    review.php?rid=10004713>.

4. Words culled from user reviews at the
    Internet Movie Database,
    <www.imdb.com> and Minna no
    shinema rebyū <www.jtnews.jp>.

5. Iguchi Noboru uses this logic to counter
    those who consider the film a 'failure':
    'Taberu yō ni miyo!', in Yonezawa
    Kazuyuki (ed.), *Masters of Takeshi*
    (Tokyo: Shūeisha, 1999), pp. 158–61.

6. Sera Toshikazu, *Sono eiga ni haka wa
    nai* (Okayama: Kibito Shuppan, 2000),
    p. 204.

7. Yomota Inuhiko, *Nihon eiga no
    radikaruna ishi* (Tokyo: Iwanami
    Shoten, 1999), p. 68.

8. Abe Kashō, *Bīto Takeshi vs. Kitano
    Takeshi* (Tokyo: Chikuma Shobō, 1994),
    pp. 83–110.

9. To help viewers, the voiceover in the
    trailer repeatedly pronounces the title:
    San tai yon ekkusu jūgatsu.

10. Shinozaki Makoto, 'Fukigen ni
    tatakaitsuzukeru monotachi', *Cahiers du
    cinema Japon* no. 0 (Summer 1991),
    pp. 86–97.

11. Yamane Sadao, 'Zero-chiten no
    katsugeki', *Kinema junpō* 1044 (15
    October 1990), p. 159.

12. Jerry Palmer, *The Logic of the Absurd* (London: BFI, 1987).

13. Tony Rayns, '3–4 x Jugatsu', *Sight and Sound* vol. 4. no. 8 (August 1994), p. 52.

14. Some read the opposite 'message' in the film: the danger of a loner trying to prove something. See Peter Stack, 'Cold Blooded Killer in "Boiling Point"', *San Francisco Chronicle*, 30 July 1999.

15. Iguchi, 'Taberu yō ni miyo!', p. 161.

16. See especially Shinozaki, 'Fukigen ni tatakaitsuzukeru monotachi' and Abe, *Bito Takeshi vs. Kitano Takeshi*.

17. See, for instance, Rayns, '3–4 x Jūgatsu' and Bracken, 'The Birth of an Auteur'.

18. See, for example, Nomura Masaaki's review in *Kinema junpō* no. 1046 (15 November 1990), p. 163; or fan reviews like 'Boiling Point': <www.thegline.com/dvd-of-the-week/2001/03-10-2001.html>.

A Scene at the Sea

1. Sera Toshikazu, *Sono eiga ni haka wa nai* (Okayama: Kibito Shuppan, 2000), p. 210.

2. Tommy Udo, 'A Scene at the Sea', in Brian Jacobs (ed.), *'Beat' Takeshi Kitano* (London: Tadao Press, 1999), p. 28.

3. For instance, Sera, *Sono eiga ni haka wa nai*, pp. 210–18.

4. For example, Sano Kazuhiro, 'Zeiniku o sogiotoshi, "ningen" ni semaru', *Eiga geijutsu* no. 363 (Winter 1991), pp. 32–3.

5. Sasaki Atsushi, 'Nani mo utsutte nai, nani mo katatte nai', in Yodogawa Nagaharu (ed.), *Kitano Takeshi* (Tokyo: Kinema Junpōsha, 1998), p. 68.

6. Jasper Sharp, 'A Scene at the Sea', *Midnight Eye*, <www.midnighteye.com/reviews/scenesea.shtml>.

7. 'Kitano Takashi kantoku intabyū', *Kinema junpō* no. 1068 (15 October 1991), p. 40.

8. 'Koi monogatari eiga ni chōsen', *Asahi shinbun*, 23 May 1991.

9. 'Kitano Takashi kantoku intabyū', pp. 40–1.

10. 'Koi monogatari eiga ni chōsen'.

11. 'Kitano Takashi kantoku intabyū', p. 40.

12. Yamane Sadao, *Eiga no bō* (Tokyo: Misuzu Shobō, 1996), p. 598.

13. See the roundtable discussion with Kitano: 'Kitano Takeshi kantoku to katarō', *Eiga geijutsu* no. 363 (Winter 1991), pp. 8–23.

14. See viewer review sites like Minna no shinema rebyū, <www.jtnews.jp/>.

15. Noboru, 'Nihon eiga Ano natsu, ichiban shizukana umi', *Asahi shinbun*, 5 October 1991.

16. Sera, *Sono eiga ni haka wa nai*, p. 211.

17. Ibid., p. 213.

18. Kitano called it his 'coldest film'. See Shibuya Yōichi's interview in *Kurosawa Akira, Miyazaki Hayao, Kitano Takeshi* (Tokyo: Rokkingu On, 1993), p. 253.

19. As the director Negishi Kichitarō argues in 'Kitano Takeshi kantoku to katarō', p. 13.

20. See, for instance, Yamane Sadao's comparison between *A Scene at the Sea* and *My Son: Eiga wa doko e iku ka* (Tokyo: Chikuma Shobō, 1993).

21. 'Ano natsu, ichiban shiawase datta bokutachi', *Eiga geijutsu* no. 363 (Winter 1991), p. 53.

22. He spoke of this as creating a 'third-person narration', compared to the 'first-person' perspective of the first films. Shibuya, pp. 253–4.

23. 'Kitano Takeshi kantoku to katarō', p. 11.

24. See Shibuya, *Kurosawa Akira*, p. 253, and 'Kitano Takeshi kantoku to katarō', p. 11.

25. Abe Kashō, *Bīto Takeshi vs. Kitano Takeshi* (Tokyo: Chikuma Shobō, 1994), pp. 114–19.

26. See for instance, Sera, *Sono eiga ni haka wa nai*, p. 217, or Sasaki, 'Nani mo utsutte nai'.

27. 'Kitano Takeshi kantoku to katarō', p. 12.

28. 'Ano natsu, ichiban shiawase datta bokutachi', p. 52.

29. Horike Yoshitsugu, 'Ano natsu, ichiban shizukana umi', *Yuriika* (rinji zōkan) vol. 30 no. 3 (February 1998), p. 308.

30. See Sera, *Sono eiga ni haka wa nai*, pp. 248–9.

31. See the director interview in the official pamphlet.

32. Aoyama Shinji, '"Mohō" to "kinsen, mata wa zōyo", "hōkō tenkan", "kinen satsuei", soshite "owari" ', in Yonezawa Kazuyuki (ed.), *Masters of Takeshi* (Tokyo: Shūeisha, 1999), pp. 162–5.

33. Hasumi Shigehiko, *Kantoku Ozu Yasujirō* (Tokyo: Chikuma Shobō, 1983).

34. 'Kitano Takeshi kantoku to katarō', p. 14.

35. See for instance, Yoshida Tsukasa, 'Zurui eiga *Ano natsu, ichiban shizuka na umi*', *Aera* (12 November 1991), p. 74.

36. Niizawa Hiroko, 'Warugaki jun'ai eiga, daiseikō', *Eiga geijutsu* no. 363 (Winter 1991), pp. 30–1.

37. To accept silence as a sign of subjectivity would problematise Shigeru and Takako's subsequent point-of-view shots, since all are accompanied by sound.

38. While the film occasionally cuts to a narrative effect before showing its cause, it offers these causes eventually, unlike *Boiling Point*.

39. Yoshimi Takashi, '"Mubōna tsunagi" ni makikomarete iku', *Eiga geijutsu* no. 363 (Winter 1991), pp. 38–9.

40. The only possible exception is a shot during the first tournament that shows the lovers in the foreground and the sea in the back. The announcer implies a heat is underway, but the surfers are not visible.

41. One exception is when Shigeru sees the four surfers set for their heat in the first tournament. This is narratively significant because the missing surfer is Shigeru, but the fact that the spectator is as ignorant as Shigeru renders this subjective shot peculiarly empty.

42. See 'Ano natsu, ichiban shiawase datta bokutachi', pp. 45, 53.

43. Aoyama, '"Mohō" to "kinsen, mata wa zōyo"'. Perhaps out of deference to Kitano, Aoyama delicately avoids terms such as 'national ideology'. The implication is clear, however.

Sonatine

1. Tamura Tsutomu was the central participant in the roundtable talk 'Gakusei eiga ka, "sakka no eiga" ka', *Eiga geijutsu* no. 368 (Summer 1993), pp. 19–33.

2. Ibid., p. 21.

3. Ibid., p. 32.

4. Ibid., p. 26.

5. Ibid., p. 31.

6. See the comments by Tamura and the director Matsuoka Jōji in 'Gakusei eiga ka, "sakka no eiga" ka', p. 24.

7. Mark Schilling, *Contemporary Japanese Film* (New York: Weatherhill, 1999), p. 341.

8. Miyazawa Akio, 'Sonachine', in Yodogawa Nagaharu (ed.), *Kitano Takeshi* (Tokyo: Kinema Junpōsha, 1998), p. 81.

9. For an overview of these debates, see J. Victor Koschmann, *Revolution and Subjectivity in Postwar Japan* (Chicago, IL: University of Chicago Press, 1996).

10. Abe Kashō, *Bīto Takeshi vs. Kitano Takeshi* (Tokyo: Chikuma Shobō, 1994), pp. 139, 187.

11. Yamane Sadao, *Eiga no bō* (Tokyo: Misuzu Shobō, 1996), p. 623.

12. Abe, *Kitano Takeshi vs Bīto Takeshi*, p. 181.

13. Ueno Kōshi, *Eiga zenbun* (Tokyo: Ritoru Moa, 1998), p. 115.

14. Ueno Kōshi, 'Eiga kantoku Kitano Takeshi no hokō', *Shinario* vol. 49 no. 7 (1993), pp. 26–7.

15. See Abe, *Kitano Takeshi vs Bīto Takeshi*, and Koreeda Hirokazu, 'Aozora no shita de tamureru Tanatosu shōdō', in Yonezawa Kazuyuki (ed.), *Masters of Takeshi* (Tokyo: Shūeisha, 1999), pp. 166–9.

16. See Hasumi Shigehiko's essay, '"Sunahama no sakka" Kitano Takeshi', in the official pamphlet.

17. Abe, *Kitano Takeshi vs Bīto Takeshi*, p. 188.

18. See, for instance, Yokoo Tadanori, 'Sonachine ni wa yosoku fukanōna rizumu ga aru', in the official pamphlet.

19. See Arai's comments in 'Gakusei eiga ka, "sakka no eiga" ka' and 'Kitano Takeshi vs Emoto Akira', *Eiga geijutsu* no. 368 (Summer 1993), pp. 6–18.

20. Koreeda, 'Aozora no shita de tamureru Tanatosu shōdō', pp. 166–9.

21. Ibid., p. 169.

22. 'Kitano Takeshi intabyū', *Kinema junpō* 1108 (15 June 1993), pp. 63–7.

23. See David Bordwell, *Narration in the Fiction Film* (Madison: University of Wisconsin Press, 1985).

24. One can only suppose this relation from Miyuki's later remark about the blue car being her husband's.

25. Yomota Inuhiko, *Nihon eiga no radikaruna ishi* (Tokyo: Iwanami Shoten, 1999), p. 76.

26. David Bordwell, *Ozu and the Poetics of Cinema* (Princeton, NJ: Princeton University Press, 1988).

27. Hase Masato, *Eizō to iu shinpi to kairaku* (Tokyo: Ibunsha, 2000), pp. 181–7.

28. Yomota, *Nihon eiga no radikaruna ishi*, p. 77.

29. Hasumi, '"Sunahama no sakka" Kitano Takeshi'.

30. For more on representations of Okinawa in recent Japanese film, see my 'From the National Gaze to Multiple Gazes', in Laura Hein and Mark Selden (eds), *Islands of Discontent* (Lanham, MD: Rowman and Littlefield, 2003), pp. 273–307.

31. For example Miike Takashi's *Ley Lines* (1999) and Kurosawa Kiyoshi's *Barren Illusion* (Ōinaru gen'ei, 1999).

Getting Any?

1. Yamane Sadao, *Eiga no bō* (Tokyo: Misuzu Shobō, 1996), p. 659.
2. From the introduction to the special section on *Getting Any?* in *Kinema junpō* no. 1153 (1 February 1995), p. 106.
3. 'Minikui tsura motsu nengen ni aijō', *Asahi shinbun*, 23 February 1995, p. 10.
4. Sera Toshikazu, *Kono eiga ni haka wa nai* (Okayama: Kibito Shuppan, 2000), p. 224.
5. Kitano Takeshi, *Minnā yatteru ka!* (Tokyo: Fusōsha, 1995), p. 8.
6. Many of these can be found in the roundtable talk 'Eiga e no shāpuna hihyō o gyagu ni mo mukete hoshikatta', *Eiga geijutsu* no. 375 (Spring 1995), pp. 43–56.
7. The film director Ishii Katsuhito expresses his confusion over the film and criticises the editing.
8. See Shinohara Tetsuo's comments in 'Eiga e no shāpuna hihyō'.
9. Yamane, *Eiga no bō*, p. 660.
10. Kitano, *Minnā yatteru ka!*, p. 8.
11. Inagawa Hōjin, 'Kūkyona zōshoku ni yotte "zetsubō" o seisansuru', *Cahiers du cinema Japon* no. 15 (Spring 1995), p. 7.
12. Sera, *Sono eiga ni haka wa nai*, pp. 228–9.
13. For instance, Morita Ryūji, 'Miru mono no kitai o koppamijin ni uchikudaku kyūkyoku no kuso eiga', *Eiga geijutsu* no. 375 (Spring 1995), pp. 60–2.

14. Sera, *Sono eiga ni haka wa nai*, pp. 224–5.
15. Yomota Inuhiko, *Nihon eiga no radikaruna ishi* (Tokyo: Iwanami Shoten, 1999), p. 85.
16. See, for instance, Ian Whitney, 'Getting Any?', *Dual Lens*, <www.duallens.com>, or Tommy Udo, 'Getting Any?', in Brian Jacobs (ed.), *'Beat' Takeshi Kitano* (London: Tadao Press, 1999), p. 29.
17. Mutō Kiichi, *Shinema de hīrō: Kantoku hen* (Tokyo: Chikuma Shobō, 1995), p. 54.
18. Daisuke Nishimura, 'Takeshi Kitano', *Tokion* no. 46 (March/April 2005), pp. 66–9.
19. Ōta Shōichi, *Shakai wa warau* (Tokyo: Seikyūsha, 2002).
20. Henry Jenkins, *What Made Pistachio Nuts?* (New York: Columbia University Press, 1992).
21. Yamaguchi Takayoshi, 'Warawasetai no ka, warawasetaku nai no ka, dō de mo ii no ka?', in Yonezawa Kazuyuki (ed.), *Masters of Takeshi* (Tokyo: Shūeisha, 1999), pp. 170–3.
22. Steve Neale and Frank Krutnik, *Popular Film and Television Comedy* (London: Routledge, 1990).
23. Yamaguchi, 'Warawasetai no ka', p. 173.
24. 'Eiga e no shāpuna hihyō', p. 45.
25. The Trio's Minakata Eiji is cast to type, unlike in *Sonatine*, where he played the hitman.
26. 'Eiga e no shāpuna hihyō', p. 51.
27. A point made by Tanaka Yōzō and Watanabe Takayoshi in 'Eiga e no shāpuna hihyō'.
28. Abe Kashō, *Nihon eiga ga sonzaisuru* (Tokyo: Seidōsha, 2000), p. 261.

29. Some viewers claimed the film is funnier when viewed on TV.

30. Nibuya Takashi, '"Warai" to "Bōryoku"', *Yuriika* vol. 30 no. 3 (rinji zūkan) (February 1998), pp. 166–7.

31. Bob Davis, 'Takeshi Kitano', *Senses of Cinema*, <www.sensesofcinema.com/ contents/directors/03/kitano.html>.

Kids Return

1. For such parallels, see 'Oira no jibunshi', in Kitano Takeshi (ed.), *Komanechi! Bīto Takeshi zenkiroku* (Tokyo: Shinchōsha, 1998), pp. 298–308. The same dialogue appears in *Takeshis'*.

2. Beat Takeshi, *Kid Return* (Tokyo: Ōta Shuppan, 1986). 'Kid' is in the singular, so much of the content relates to Takeshi himself. The poems have little relation to the film.

3. Kitano Takeshi, *Takeshi ga Takeshi o korosu riyū* (Tokyo: Rokkingu On, 2003), p. 158.

4. Kitano quipped that such a response in the face of failure showed how stupid he and the kids were. See Mutō Kiichi, 'Kitano Takeshi', in *Shinema de hīrō: Kantoku hen* (Tokyo: Chikuma Shobō, 1995), p. 60.

5. Hoshina Tatsuaki, 'Eiga kantoku Kitano Takeshi no jikogo no henshin', *Aera* (24 June 1996), p. 62.

6. Kitano, *Takeshi ga Takeshi o korosu riyū*, p. 114.

7. See, for instance, Ueno Kōshi, *Eiga zenbun* (Tokyo: Ritoru Moa, 1998), pp. 330–4; or Abe Kashō, 'Zankokusa no kyōi ni shutsugenshita "kyakuhonka no eiga"', *Eiga geijutsu* no. 379 (Summer 1996), pp. 19–21.

8. Tsukamoto Shin'ya cites the music as one reason for seeing the ending as positive: ' "Dōbutsu" moshiku wa "mushi" toshite no Kitano Takeshi', in Yonezawa Kazuyuki (ed.), *Masters of Takeshi* (Tokyo: Shūeisha, 1999), pp. 174–7.

9. See Yamane Sadao's essay in the film's official pamphlet.

10. Abe Kazushige, 'Kitano Takeshi Sonachine to Kizzu ritān', *Kokubungaku* vol. 42 no. 4 (March 1997), pp. 11–16.

11. Horike Yoshitsugu, 'Jitensha no kioku', *Yuriika* vol. 28 no. 12 (October 1996), pp. 233–42.

12. Abe Kashō, 'Zankokusa no kyōi', p. 21.

13. His example is of Sachiko taking up smoking, which communicates a larger shift in time: Hiroshi's demise. Ueno, *Eiga zenbun*, pp. 334–7.

14. Yomota Inuhiko, *Nihon eiga no radikaruna ishi* (Tokyo: Iwanami Shoten, 1999), p. 88.

15. See, for instance, Boris Trbic, 'Kids Return', *Senses of Cinema*, <www.senses ofcinema.com/contents/cteq/01/15/kid s_return.html>; or Mike Bracken, 'Beat Takeshi Kitano's Kids Return', *Culture Dose.net*, <www.culturedose.net/ review.php?rid=10002334>.

16. This is one reason offered by Kitano in an interview with Tony Rayns, 'The Harder Way', *Sight and Sound* vol. 6 no. 6 (1996), p. 24.

17. For instance Kawamoto Saburō, 'Nigeba no nai wakamonotachi no 'haiiro' no seishun', *Kinema junpō* no. 1198 (1 August 1996), pp. 47–9.

18. Tony Rayns, 'Kids Return', *Sight and Sound* vol. 7 no. 5 (1997), p. 46.

19. Takahashi Yōji argues as much in 'Kizzu Ritān', in Yodogawa Nagaharu (ed.), *Kitano Takeshi* (Tokyo: Kinema Junpōsha, 1998), pp. 90–6.

20. Kawamoto, 'Nigeba no nai wakamano-tachi', p. 49. Emphasis in the original.

21. Sera Toshikazu, *Sono eiga ni haka wa nai* (Okayama: Kibito Shuppan, 2000), p. 234.

22. Kitakōji Takashi, 'Okinawa de no natsuyasumi', *Kinema junpō* no. 1198 (1 August 1996), pp. 55–7.

23. See the 'Production Notes' in the official pamphlet.

24. Mutō, 'Kitano Takeshi', p. 62.

25. Sera, *Sono eiga ni haka wa nai*, p. 233.

26. Kitano, *Takeshi ga Takeshi o korosu riyō*, pp. 104–5.

27. Bīto Takeshi, 'Kids Return 2', in Kitano Takeshi (ed.), *Komanechi! Bīto Takeshi zenkiroku*, pp. 257–95.

Hana-Bi

1. Kitano Takeshi , 'Venechia o seisu', *Brutus* no. 396 (15 October 1997), p. 73.

2. Kitano Takeshi , 'Hana-bi, Kitano Takeshi', *Studio Voice* no. 263 (November 1997), p. 42.

3. Ibid., p. 42.

4. Abe Kashō, *Nihon eiga ga sonzaisuru* (Tokyo: Seidosha, 2000), p. 274.

5. Jacqui Sadashige, 'Fireworks: Hana-Bi', *Magill's Cinema Annual* vol. 18 (1999), p. 160.

6. See Shinozaki Makoto's comments in his interview with Kitano: 'Hana-bi, Kitano Takeshi', p. 38. See also Darrell Davis, 'Reigniting Japanese Tradition

with *Hana-Bi*', *Cinema Journal* vol. 40 no. 4 (Summer 2001), pp. 55–80; and Aaron Gerow, '"Nihonjin" Kitano Takeshi', *Yuriika* (rinji zōkan) vol. 30 no. 3 (February 1998), pp. 42–51.

7. Anthony Leong, 'Fireworks (Hana-Bi)', *The Eyepiece Network*, <www.eyepiece. com/ent/9804/980410al.asp>.

8. Roger Ebert, 'Fireworks', *Chicago Sun-Times*, <www.suntimes.com/ebert/ ebert_reviews/1998/03/032002.html>.

9. Yomota Inuhiko argues that by the end, the narrative is 'swallowed up' in the logic of the paintings: *Nihon eiga no radikaruna ishi* (Tokyo: Iwanami Shoten, 1999), p. 93.

10. Kitano, 'Hana-bi, Kitano Takeshi', p. 43.

11. Gavin Smith, 'Takeshi Talks', *Film Comment* vol. 34 no. 2 (March/April 1998), p. 32.

12. Kitano, 'Venechia o seisu', p. 73.

13. Abe Kazushige, '"Hana" to "bi" no aida ni nani ga aru no ka', *Ronza* no. 32 (December 1997), p. 169.

14. Kitano, 'Hana-bi, Kitano Takeshi', p. 39.

15. See, for instance, Akiyama Noboru, 'Otoko no anākīna shinjō ni shōten', *Asahi shinbun*, 29 January 1998, p. 17.

16. Milestone press kit for *Hana-Bi*, quoted in Davis, 'Reigniting Japanese Tradition', p. 55.

17. Kitano, 'Venechia o seisu', p. 73.

18. Smith, 'Takeshi Talks', p. 32.

19. Kitano Takeshi, 'Silent Running', *Sight and Sound* vol. 7 no. 12 (December 1992), p. 29.

20. Kitano Takeshi, 'Hana-Bi no naka no "Benjo no rakugaki"', *Geijutsu shinchō* vol. 48 no. 12 (December 1997), p. 87.

21. Kitano Takeshi, 'Mizuumi mitaina umi ga ii', *Cahiers du cinema Japon* no. 23 (March 1998), p. 70.

22. Suzuki Hitoshi, *Gamen no tanjō* (Tokyo: Misuzu Shobō, 2002), pp. 236, 234.

23. Kitano uses *jiketsu* (literally, 'self-decision') here and in Horibe's painting, not the more common term, *jisatsu* (literally, 'self-killing'). The former was the euphemism for suicide during World War II.

24. Kitano, 'Venechia o seisu', p. 74.

25. Abe, *Nihon eiga ga sonzaisuru*, pp. 274–7, 295–303.

26. Takano Fumie, 'Nattokudekinai joseizō', *Mainichi shinbun*, Aichi edition, 26 December 1997.

27. Kitano Takeshi, *Takeshi ga Takeshi o korosu riyū* (Tokyo: Rokkingu On, 2003), pp. 165–6

28. Kitano, 'Mizuumi mitaina umi ga ii', p. 74.

29. Kitano said he chose Kishimoto because she was 'cute and gave the impression of being a child'. Kitano, 'Venechia o seisu', p. 78.

30. Her role as the daughter is evident from the fact she is played by Kitano Shōko, Kitano's real-life daughter. She appears under the name Matsuda Shōko, borrowing her mother's maiden name.

31. Smith, 'Takeshi Talks', p. 32.

32. See the interview with Kitano in Hasumi Shigehiko's *Eiga kyōjin, kataru* (Tokyo: Kawade Shobō Shinsha, 2001), p. 314.

33. Kitano, 'Hana-bi, Kitano Takeshi', p. 39.

34. Davis, 'Reigniting Japanese Tradition', p. 72.

35. Jean-François Buiré, 'Hana-Bi', *Lycéens au cinéma* (2000–1), p. 10.

36. Kitano Takeshi, 'Ore wa Nihon eiga no gan', *Yuriika* (rinji zōkan) vol. 30 no. 3 (February 1998), p. 16.

37. Tony Rayns, 'Flowers and Fire', *Sight and Sound* vol. 7 no. 12 (December 1997), p. 28.

38. Horike Yoshitsugu, 'Hana-Bi', *Yuriika* (rinji zōkan) vol. 30 no. 3 (February 1998), p. 317.

39. Abe, '"Hana" to "bi" no aida', p. 168.

40. Suzuki, *Gamen no tanjō*.

41. See, for instance, Sadashige, 'Fireworks: Hana-Bi'; or Kenneth Turan, 'Fireworks', *Los Angeles Times*, 20 March 1998.

42. Abe, *Nihon eiga ga sonzaisuru*, p. 276.

Kikujiro

1. Max Tessier, 'Kikujiro's Summer', *Cinemaya* no. 44 (1999), p. 29.

2. See Kitano Takeshi, *Takeshi ga Takeshi o korosu riyū* (Tokyo: Rokkingu On, 2003).

3. Quoted in Andrew Sarris, 'All about My Mother in Japan', *New York Observer*, 12 June 2000, p. 19.

4. Quoted in Sarris, 'All about My Mother'.

5. See Kitano's interview in the official pamphlet for the film.

6. Kitano, *Takeshi ga Takeshi o korosu riyū*, p. 201.

7. Ibid., pp. 179–80.

8. A point made by Abe Kashō: Casio Abe, 'Kikujiro', in Brian Jacobs (ed.), *'Beat' Takeshi Kitano* (London: Tadao Press, 1999), p. 38.

9.   Nishiwaki Hideo, '"Tabi" ni "asobu"
     Kitano eiga', *Kinema junpō* no. 1285
     (1 June 1999), p. 42.
10. Abe, 'Kikujiro', p. 38.
11. Umemoto Yōichi, 'Teitaisuru idō',
     Cahiers du cinema Japon no. 28
     (Summer 1999), p. 163.
12. David Perry, 'Kikujiro', *Cinema-Scene.
     com* 2.35 (2000), <www.cinema-scene.
     com/archive/02/35.html#Kikujiro>.
13. Andrew Saunders, '*Kikujiro*:
     Tapestries', *Senses of Cinema* (2000),
     <www.sensesofcinema.com/contents/
     00/10/kikujirotap.html>.
14. As argued by Umemoto, 'Teitaisuru idō'.
15. Yamane Sadao, 'Takakura Ken to Kitano
     Takeshi', *Kinema junpō* no. 1292
     (1 September 1999), p. 155.
16. Abe Kashō, *Nihon eiga ga sonzaisuru*
     (Tokyo: Seidosha, 2000), p. 309.
17. Kitano Takeshi, 'Kodomo o dashi ni
     kodokuna renchū ga ōsawagi', *Kinema
     junpō* no. 1285 (1 June 1999), p. 33.
18. Geoff Gardner, 'Kikujiro', *Senses of
     Cinema* (2000), <www.sensesofcinema.
     com/contents/00/10/kikujiro.html>.
19. See Konno Yūji's 'Tenshi – gaki x
     natsuyasumi' in the official pamphlet .
20. Kuroda Kunio, 'Kikujirō no natsu',
     Kinema junpō no. 1288 (15 July 1999).
21. Ibid.
22. G. Allen Johnson, '"Kikujiro" Touching,
     but Lacks the Master's Touch', *San
     Francisco Examiner*, 9 June 2000.
23. Kitano, 'Kodomo o dashi ni', p. 39.
24. Ishitobi Noriki, 'Kikujirō no natsu',
     Asahi shinbun, Nagoya edition, 16 June
     1999.
25. Kitano, *Takeshi ga Takeshi o korosu riyū*,
     pp. 207–8.

26. This may explain why *Kikujiro* was not a
     great commercial success at home.
27. Sera Toshikazu, *Sono eiga ni haka wa
     nai* (Okayama: Kibito Shuppan, 2000),
     p. 242. The official pamphlet, however,
     states the journey is coloured by the
     'warm, original landscape of Japan'.
28. Abe, 'Kikujiro', p. 38.

Brother

1.   David Wood, 'Career Profile: Takeshi
     "Beat" Kitano', *BBCi*, <www.bbc.co.uk/
     films/2001/03/20/career_profile_takes
     hi_kitano_article.shtml>.
2.   Miyamura Naoyoshi, 'Bōryoku byōsha
     no yasuuri', *Kinema junpō* no. 1330 (15
     April 2001), p. 161.
3.   Daniel Eagan, 'Brother', *Film Journal
     International* (1 May 2001),
     <www.filmjournal.com>.
4.   Olivier Séguret, 'Étanche Kitano',
     Libération (5 September 2000).
5.   Fukunaga Seiji, 'Kitano Takeshi,
     Nichieibei gassaku eiga *Brother* o totta',
     Yomiuri shinbun, evening edition (23
     January 2001).
6.   Cynthia Fuchs, 'Identity Politics', *Pop
     Matters*, <www.popmatters.com/film/
     reviews/b/brother.shtml>.
7.   Quoted in Katsuta Tomomi, 'Shinsaku
     Brother o kanseisaseta Kitano Takeshi-
     san', *Mainichi shinbun*, Osaka evening
     edition, 9 December 2000.
8.   Mori Masayuki, 'Hariuddo de
     gassakusuru', *Kinema junpō* no. 1324
     (15 January 2001), p. 58.
9.   Kitano Takeshi, *Takeshi ga Takeshi o
     korosu riyū* (Tokyo: Rokkingu On,
     2003), pp. 242–3.
10. Since *Brother* was classified as a low-

budget production, rules about the use of non-union labour were less strict.

11. Quoted in Daniel Steinhart, 'Return of the Yakuza', *Film Journal International* (1 June 2001), <www.filmjournal.com>.

12. Mark Schilling, *The Yakuza Movie Book* (Berkeley, CA: Stone Bridge Press, 2003), p. 172.

13. See, for instance, Serdar Yegulalp, 'Brother', *TheGline.com*, <www. thegline.com/disc-of-the-week/ 2002/11-16-2002.htm>.

14. Mark Kermode, 'Brother', *Sight and Sound* vol. 11 no. 4 (April 2001), pp. 40–1. Robert Whiting makes a similar point in the official pamphlet for the film: 'Underworld Honor Provides the Film's Unifying Force'.

15. Peter Wilshire, 'When Worlds Collide: Takeshi Kitano's Brother', *Metro Magazine* nos. 131/132 (2001), p. 149.

16. Tony Rayns, 'To Die in America', *Sight and Sound* vol. 11 no. 4 (April 2001), pp. 26–7.

17. Kitano, *Takeshi ga Takeshi o korosu riyū*, pp. 238–9.

18. Umemoto Yōichi, 'Umerareyō tosuru kūhaku no fūkei', *Cahiers du cinema Japon* no. 31 (2001), pp. 276–7.

19. Abe Kashō, *Nihon eiga no 21-seiki ga hajimaru* (Tokyo: Kinema Junpōsha, 2005), pp. 32–6.

20. Nachiketas Wignesan, 'Déjà mort', *L'Avant-scène du cinema* no. 496 (November 2000).

21. Quoted in Steinhart, 'Return of the Yakuza'.

22. Tsutsumi Ryuichiro, 'Finding an Alter Ego: The Triple-Double Structure of Brother', *Iconics* 8 (2006), pp. 135–57.

23. See Rayns, 'To Die in America'.

24. Fukunaga, 'Kitano Takeshi'.

25. Kitano Takeshi, '"Beat" Comes to America', *Cinéaste* vol. 26 no. 3 (Summer 2001), pp. 32–3.

26. Eiji Oguma, *A Genealogy of 'Japanese' Self-Images*, trans. David Askew (Melbourne: Trans Pacific Press, 2002).

27. Kuroda Kunio wondered whether Harada's hara-kiri was not a joke that threatened to undermine the entire film: 'Brother', *Kinema junpō* no. 1329 (1 April 2001), pp. 152–3.

28. Umemoto, 'Umerareyō tosuru kūhaku', pp. 274–5.

29. Abe, *Nihon eiga no 21-seiki*, p. 35.

30. Fukunaga, 'Kitano Takeshi'.

31. See, for instance, Osugi, 'Kitano eiga', *Asahi shinbun*, 14 April 2001.

32. Kitano Takeshi, 'Kitano Takeshi kantoku intabyū', *Kinema junpō* no. 1324 (15 January 2001), p. 58.

33. In pursuing a degree of realism, Yamamoto said he wanted to avoid costumes that stood out like in a fashion show. See Yamamoto Yōji, 'Futari no "Yamamoto"', in Bītō Takeshi (ed.), *Komanechi! 2: Brother daitokushū*, (Tokyo: Shinchōsha, 2000) pp. 84–5.

34. Satō Yūki, 'Brother Kitano Takeshi', *Kinema junpō* no. 1323 (1 January 2001), p. 29.

35. See, for instance, Tom Mes, 'Brother', *Midnight Eye*, <www.midnighteye.com/ reviews/brother.shtml>. A number of commentators on the Internet Movie Database had similar complaints.

36. Rayns, 'To Die in America'.

37. Kuroda, 'Brother', p. 153.

38. Rayns, 'To Die in America'.

Dolls

1. Abe Kazushige, 'Kako no sairai to baka shōjiki', *Bungakkai* vol. 56 no. 12 (December 2002), pp. 309–11.

2. Tony Rayns, 'Puppet Love', *Sight and Sound* vol. 13 no. 6 (June 2003), p. 19.

3. See Higuchi Naofumi's response to the questionnaire, '*Dolls* kōkai chokuzen kinkyū ankēto', *Kinema junpō* no. 1366 (15 October 2002), p. 43.

4. Abe Kashō, *Nihon eiga no 21-seiki ga hajimaru* (Tokyo: Kinema Junpōsha, 2005), pp. 154–6.

5. Quoted in Tozawa Misa, 'Kitano Takeshi kantoku no *Dolls* kōkai', *Mainichi shinbun*, Osaka evening edition, 12 October 2002, p. 2.

6. David Rooney, 'Dolls', *Variety*, 23 September 2002.

7. Michael Atkinson, 'Life on a String in Takeshi Kitano's Sentimental Triptych', *The Village Voice*, 5 December 2004.

8. Chuck Stephens, 'Dolls', *Film Comment* vol. 40 no. 6 (November–December 2004), p. 72.

9. For instance, Yamaguchi Takeshi noted that Kitano had earlier criticised Leos Carax's depiction of love between homeless people in *Les Amants du Pont-Neuf* (1991), as '*kusai*' (mawkish): '*Dolls* kōkai chokuzen kinkyū ankēto', p. 44.

10. See 'Dolls', *TheGline.com*, <www.theg line.com/dvd-of-the-week/2003/07-28-2003.htm>, or Andrew Cunningham, 'Dolls', *Midnight Eye*, <www.midnight-eye.com/reviews/dolls.shtml>.

11. Todoroki Yukio, 'Dolls', *Kinema junpō* no. 1367 (1 November 2002), p. 112.

12. See the interview with Yamamoto in the official pamphlet.

13. Kitano Takeshi, *Takeshi ga Takeshi o korosu riyū* (Tokyo: Rokkingu On, 2003), pp. 274–303.

14. Rayns, 'Puppet-Love', p. 20.

15. Kitano thought that the bound beggars would only work if they were a story viewed by dolls. See 'Eiga kantoku Kitano Takeshi, shinkyōchi idomu', *Asahi shinbun*, evening edition, 9 October 2002.

16. Abe, 'Kako no sairai', pp. 310–11. Jonathan Romney also calls the use of *bunraku* 'a Brechtian gesture': 'Dolls', *Sight and Sound* vol. 13 no. 6 (June 2003), p. 42.

17. A number of fan reviews emphasised their revulsion for these characters: for instance, Taku and Tomo at J-Fan Cinema, <www.j-fan.com/cinema/cinema.cgi?action=viewrev&selected=10>.

18. Anton Bitel, 'Dolls', *Movie Gazette*, <www.movie-gazette.com/cinereviews/283>.

19. Kitano Takeshi, 'Venechia Eigasai Kitano Takeshi kantoku kyōdō kisha kaiken', *Kinema junpō* no. 1366 (15 October 2002), pp. 34–5.

20. Yamane Sadao, 'Gamen to "e"', *Kinema junpō* no. 1370 (15 December 2002), p. 102.

21. Saruwatari Manabu argues that Haruna and Ryōko are dolls who chose to become human: 'Kitano Takeshi *Dolls* shiron', *Tōhoku kōgyō daigaku kiyō II: Jinbun shakai kagaku hen* 25 (March 2005), pp. 1–11.

22. *Shinpa* theatre developed in the late nineteenth century as a more modern alternative to *kabuki*, focusing on

contemporary stories of women
suffering from the class or patriarchal
family system.

23. For more on the invention of tradition,
see Eric Hobsbawm and Terrence
Ranger (eds), *The Invention of Tradition*
(Cambridge: Cambridge University
Press, 1992); and Stephen Vlastos
(ed.), *Mirror of Modernity* (Berkeley:
University of California Press, 1998).

24. The critics Terawaki Ken, Yamaguchi
Takeshi and Watanabe Takenobu all
blamed Kitano for becoming too eager
to please foreign critics: 'Dolls kōkai
chokuzen kinkyūankēto', pp. 42–4.

25. Quoted in Tozawa, 'Kitano Takeshi
kantoku no *Dolls* kōkai'.

26. Quoted in Rayns, 'Puppet Love'.
pp. 19–20.

27. 'Eiga kantoku Kitano Takeshi'.

Zatoichi

1. Caroline Vié, 'Takeshi, la rencontre',
Brazil 6 (April 2003).

2. *Brother*'s ¥888 million was his previous
record for domestic box-office
revenue. However, the Motion Picture
Producers Association of Japan only
announced distribution earnings (the
distributor's take of the total box
office) until 2000. *Violent Cop*'s ¥780
million was only Shōchiku's share;
given that distributors take between
40–60 per cent of the box-office take,
it probably made about ¥1.3 billion at
the theatre. Statements that *Zatoichi*
was Kitano's first hit film at home were
thus incorrect.

3. The *jidaigeki*, or period film, refers to
films set before the opening-up of

Japan to the West, the most popular of
which are *chanbara*, or swordfight
films.

4. Mark Kermode, 'Zatoichi', *Sight and
Sound* vol. 14 no. 4 (April 2004),
p. 72.

5. Sharon Mizuta, 'The Blind Swordsman:
Zatoichi', *Pop Matters* (3 June 2004),
<www.popmatters.com/film/reviews/b/
blind-swordsman-zatoichi.shtml>.

6. Kitano Takeshi, 'Kitano Takeshi intabyū',
Bungakkai vol. 59 no. 6 (June 2005),
p. 235.

7. Quoted in Michel Ciment, 'Créer un
tempo', *Positif* 513 (November 2003).
Set designer Isoda Norihiro also said
the director told him to avoid the
jidaigeki's usual colour scheme: see his
interview in the official pamphlet for
the film.

8. See Yamane Sadao's essay, 'Kitano
Takeshi to goraku jidaigeki no kankei',
in the official pamphlet.

9. See Matthew Turner, 'Kitano in
London', <www.kitanotakeshi. com/
index.php?content=resources&id=56>.

10. Kitano Takeshi, 'Intabyū Kitano
Takeshi', *Kinema junpō* no. 1389 (15
September 2003), pp. 34–7; or 'Sekai
no Kitano, arata na sainō', *Yomiuri
shinbun*, evening edition, 8 September
2003.

11. '"Eiga wa seikō, shō wa omake" Kitano
Takeshi, sutaffu ni 'arigatō', *Yomiuri
shinbun*, 7 August 2003.

12. Kitano Takeshi, *Takeshi ga Takeshi o
korosu riyū* (Tokyo: Rokkingu On,
2003), p. 330.

13. 'Eiga kantoku Kitano Takeshi', *Yomiuri
shinbun*, 2 September 2003.

14. The average shot-length (ASL) for *Zatoichi* is about 8.1 seconds, nearly 40 per cent shorter than that for *Dolls* (13.2 seconds).

15. Kermode, 'Zatoichi', p. 72.

16. A form of narrative singing that was most popular around the turn of the nineteenth century.

17. For more on *giri* and *ninjō* in postwar *jidaigeki*, see David Desser, 'Toward a Structural Analysis of the Postwar Samurai Film', in Arthur Nolletti, Jr and David Desser (eds), *Reframing Japanese Cinema* (Bloomington: Indiana University Press, 1994), pp. 145–64.

18. Shinada Yūkichi, 'Takeshi wa "shugo tenshi" de aru', *Asahi shinbun*, evening edition, 4 September 2003.

19. The tag line for the film emphasised his superhuman quality by calling him 'The Strongest' (*saikyō*), and television commercials proclaimed, 'Zatōichi, now no one can beat him' (*Zatōichi, mohaya tekinashi*).

20. Kitano, *Takeshi ga Takeshi o korosu riyū*, p. 318.

21. Kanazawa Makoto, 'Intabyū Kitano Takeshi', *Kinema junpō* no. 1389 (15 September 2003), p. 35.

22. Henrik Sylow, 'Kitano at the IFFR 04', <www.kitanotakeshi.com/index.php? content=resources&id=53>.

23. Nishida Rie, 'Eiga *Zatōichi*, honmono wa dochira', *Asahi shinbun*, 22 September 2003.

24. See some of the comments for the film on the Internet Movie Database, <www.imdb.com>.

25. See Sugawara Fumio, 'Kitano *Zatōichi* wa goraku eiga no kessaku', *Mainichi*

shinbun, 26 September 2003.

26. Ahn Min Hwa, 'Zatōichi', *Bandaly* 3 (March 2004), pp. 91–106.

27. Hideboh, the leader of the Stripes, studied under Gregory Hines. See Ciment, 'Créer un tempo', and the British pressbook for *Zatoichi*.

28. That association is made, for instance, by Ian Whitney, 'Zatōichi', <www.duallens.com/index.asp?reviewId=40204>.

29. Kitano, *Takeshi ga Takeshi o korosu riyū*, p. 318.

30. Bryan Walsh, 'Striking a New Beat', *Time Asia*, 8 September 2003, <www.time.com/time/asia/magazine/article/0,13673,501030915-483348,00.html>.

31. Kitano, *Takeshi ga Takeshi o korosu riyū*, pp. 318, 324–5.

32. These are Shibuya Yōichi's words in introducing his interview with Kitano: Kitano, *Takeshi ga Takeshi o korosu riyū*, p. 304.

33. Walsh, 'Striking a New Beat'.

34. Stephen Appelbaum, 'Blind Fury', *Total DVD* 65 (July 2004), p. 25.

35. Ueno Kōshi, 'Akushon toshite no chanbara to iu meikakuna senryaku ishiki o kanjiru', *Kinema junpō* no. 1389 (15 September 2003), p. 43.

36. Yoshioka Tatsuya, 'Zatōichi mite Nihon no kokoro shiru', *Asahi shinbun*, Ōsaka morning edition, 20 September 2003.

37. See Ciment, 'Créer un tempo'.

38. Shinkichi's lesson in swordfighting is also Kitano's lesson in the problems of *tate*. What Shinkichi wants to teach is the *tate* of old-style *jidaigeki*, where swords bang against each other; his friends, however (like Kitano), soon

figure out it is much more effective to aim for the body.

39. Ciment, 'Créer un tempo'.

40. Mizuta, 'The Blind Swordsman: Zatoichi'.

41. Appelbaum, 'Blind Fury', p. 26.

42. Quoted in the British pressbook.

43. As some critics, like Katsuta Tomomi, noted: 'Shinema no shūmatsu', *Mainichi shinbun*, evening edition, 5 September 2003.

44. The English subtitles – 'Even with my eyes wide open, I can't see a thing' – are misleading. The comment here is actually universal, emphasising how all of us are limited in sight.

Takeshis' Conclusion

1. Kitano Takeshi, 'Takeshi's Message', *Sōryoku tokushū Kitano Takeshi* (Tokyo: Kadokawa Shoten, 2005), p. 15.

2. Kitano Takeshi, 'Face: Kitano Takeshi', *Kinema junpō* no. 1443 (15 November 2005), p. 4.

3. See Yamane Sadao's 'Kitano eigagun no mori no naka e' in the official pamphlet.

4. Mori Masayuki, 'Shinkasuru Kitano eiga', *Sōryokū tokushū Kitano Takeshi*, pp. 67–71.

5. See the interview with Kitano in the official pamphlet for *Takeshis'*, p. 13.

6. See Akimoto Tetsuji's comments in '*Takeshis*' hihyō', *Sōryoku tokushū Kitano Takeshi*, p. 100.

7. See, for instance, Nomura Masaaki's 'Jūrai no eiga no rūru o kowasō to iu kokoromi', or Watanabe Sachiko's 'Eiga to geijutsu ni taisuru shinkenna aichaku', in *Kinema junpō* no. 1443 (15 November 2005), pp. 157–9.

8. See Kitano, 'Face: Kitano Takeshi', and Mori, 'Shinkasuru Kitano eiga'.

9. Stuart Hall, 'Old and New Identities, Old and New Ethnicities', in Anthony D. King (ed.), *Culture, Globalization and the World System* (London: Macmillan, 1991), pp. 41–69.

10. A phrase that begins the introduction of the official pamphlet.

11. See Kikuchi Maruyoshi's 'Mottomo warakariyasuku, mottomo omoshiroku natte shimatta "jikken"' in the official pamphlet.

SELECT BIBLIOGRAPHY

Books and Long Articles

Abe, Casio. *Beat Takeshi vs. Takeshi Kitano* (New York: Kaya Press, 2005).

Abe Kazushige. '"Hana" to "bi" no aida ni nani ga aru no ka', *Ronza* no. 32 (December 1997).

——. 'Kako no sairai to baka shōjiki', *Bungakkai* vol. 56 no. 12 (December 2002).

——. 'Kitano Takeshi *Sonachine* to *Kizzu ritān*', *Kokubungaku* vol. 42 no. 4 (March 1997).

Ahn Min Hwa. 'Zatōichi,' *Bandaly* no. 3 (March 2004).

Barcaroli, Luciano, *et al.* (eds). *Il cinema nero di Takeshi Kitano* (Milan: Ubulibri, 2001).

Bīto Takeshi. *Takeshi-kun, hai!* (Tokyo: Shinchōsha, 1984).

——. *Watashi wa sekai de kirawareru* (Tokyo: Shinchōsha, 1999).

—— (ed.). *Komanechi! 2: Brother daitokushū* (Tokyo: Shinchōsha, 2000).

Buccheri, Vincenzo. *Takeshi Kitano* (Milan: Editrice Il castoro, 2001).

Buiré, Jean-François. 'Hana-Bi', *Lycéens au cinéma* (2000–1).

Ciment, Michel. 'Créer un tempo', *Positif* no. 513 (November 2003).

Davis, Bob. 'Takeshi Kitano', *Senses of Cinema*, <www.sensesofcinema.com/contents/directors/03/kitano.html>.

Davis, Darrell. 'Reigniting Japanese Tradition with *Hana-Bi*', *Cinema Journal* vol. 40 no. 4 (Summer 2001).

Fadda, Michele, and Rinaldo Censi (eds). *Kitano Beat Takeshi* (Parma: Stefano Sorbini, 1998).

Gerow, Aaron. 'A Scene at the Threshold: Liminality in the Films of Kitano Takeshi', *Asian Cinema* vol. 10 no. 2 (Spring/Summer 1999).

Hase Masato. *Eizō to iu shinpi to kairaku* (Tokyo: Ibunsha, 2000).

Horike Yoshitsugu. 'Jitensha no kioku', *Yuriika* vol. 28 no. 12 (October 1996).

Jacobs, Brian (ed.). 'Beat' Takeshi Kitano* (London: Tadao Press, 1999).

Jousse, Thierry. 'Kitano le maître-fou', *Trafic* no. 25 (Spring 1998).

Kitano Takeshi. 'Dai 1-kai Kyoto Eigasai "Kitano Takeshi, gakusei to kataru"', *Kinema junpō* no. 1293 (5 October 1999).

——. 'Hana-bi, Kitano Takeshi', *Studio Voice* no. 263 (November 1997).

——. 'Kitano Takeshi eigajutsu', *Switch* vol. 9 no. 4 (September 1991).

——. 'Mizuumi mitaina umi ga ii',
Cahiers du cinema Japon no. 23
(March 1998).

——. *Takeshi ga Takeshi o korosu riyū*
(Tokyo: Rokkingu On, 2003).

——. 'Venechia o seisu', *Brutus* no. 396
(15 October 1997).

——. *Asakusa Kid* (Paris: Serpent à
plumes, 2001).

——. *Rencontres du septième art* (Paris:
Arléa, 2000).

—— (ed.). *Komanechi! Bīto Takeshi
zenkiroku* (Tokyo: Shinchōsha, 1998).

'Kitano Takeshi soshite/arui wa Bīto
Takeshi', *Yuriika* (rinji zōkan) vol. 30
no. 3 (February 1998).

McDonald, Keiko I. *Reading a Japanese
Film* (Honolulu: University of Hawaii
Press, 2006).

Mes, Tom and Jasper Sharp. *The
Midnight Eye Guide to New Japanese
Film* (Berkeley, CA: Stone Bridge
Press, 2005).

Miyahara Kōjirō. 'Tasha no shōgeki,
shōgeki no tasha', in Uchida Ryōzō
(ed.), *Imēji no naka no shakai* (Tokyo:
Tokyo Daigaku Shuppankai, 1998).

Miyao Daisuke. 'Blue vs. Red: Takeshi
Kitano's Color Scheme' *Post Script*,
vol. 18 no. 1 (Autumn 1998).

——. 'Telephilia vs. Cinephilia = Beat
Takeshi vs. Takeshi Kitano',
Framework vol. 45 no. 2 (Autumn
2004).

Mutō Kiichi. *Shinema de hīrō: Kantoku
hen* (Tokyo: Chikuma Shobō, 1995).

Niizawa Hiroko. *Bīto Takeshi ron*
(Tokyo: Gakuyō Shobō, 1995).

Okuyama Kazuyoshi. 'Bīto Takeshi e no
ketsubetsu', *Bungei shunjū* vol. 71
no. 9 (1993).

Ōta Shōichi. *Shakai wa warau* (Tokyo:
Seikyūsha, 2002).

Rayns, Tony. 'Flowers and Fire', *Sight
and Sound* vol. 7 no. 12 (December
1997).

——. 'The Harder Way.' *Sight and Sound*
vol. 6 no. 6 (1996), p. 24.

——. 'Kids Return', *Sight and Sound*
vol. 7 no. 5 (1997).

——. 'Papa Yakuza', *Sight and Sound*
vol. 9 no. 6 (June 1999).

——. 'Puppet Love', *Sight and Sound*
vol. 13 no. 6 (June 2003).

——. '3-4 x Jugatsu', *Sight and Sound*
vol. 4 no. 8 (August 1994).

——. 'To Die in America', *Sight and
Sound* vol. 11 no. 4 (April 2001).

Saruwatari Manabu. 'Kitano
Takeshi/Bīto Takeshi no sekai',
*Tōhoku kōgyō daigaku kiyō II Jinbun
shakai kagaku hen* 22 (2002).

——. 'Kitano Takeshi *Dolls* shiron',
*Tōhoku Kōgyō Daigaku kiyō II:
Jinbun shakai kagaku hen* 25 (March
2005).

Schilling, Mark. *Contemporary Japanese
Film* (New York: Weatherhill,
1999).

Sera Toshikazu. *Sono eiga ni haka wa
nai* (Okayama: Kibito Shuppan,
2000).

Sharp, Jasper. 'Sono otoko, kyobo ni tsuki Violent Cop', in Justin Bowyer (ed.), *The Cinema of Japan and Korea* (London: Wallflower, 2004).

Shinozaki Makoto. 'Fukigen ni tatakaitsuzukeru monotachi', *Cahiers du cinema Japon* no. 0 (Summer 1991).

Smith, Gavin. 'Takeshi Talks', *Film Comment* vol. 34 no. 2 (March/April 1998).

Sōryoku tokushō Kitano Takeshi (Tokyo: Kadokawa Shoten, 2005).

Stephens, Chuck. 'Comedy plus Massacre', *Film Comment* vol. 31 no. 1 (January–February 1995).

Suzuki Hitoshi. *Gamen no tanjō* (Tokyo: Misuzu Shobō, 2002).

Tsutsumi Ryuichiro. 'Finding an Alter Ego: The Triple-Double Structure of *Brother*', *Iconics* 8 (2006).

Ueno Kōshi. *Eiga zenbun* (Tokyo: Ritoru Moa, 1998).

Umemoto Yōichi. 'Umerareyō tosuru kūhaku no fūkei', *Cahiers du cinema Japon* no. 31 (2001).

Yamane Sadao. *Eiga no bō* (Tokyo: Misuzu Shobō, 1996).

Yodogawa Nagaharu (ed.), *Kitano Takeshi* (Tokyo: Kinema Junpōsha, 1998).

Yomota Inuhiko. *Nihon eiga no radikaruna ishi* (Tokyo: Iwanami Shoten, 1999).

Yonezawa Kazuyuki (ed.). *Masters of Takeshi* (Tokyo: Shūeisha, 1999).

Special Magazine Sections

The following issues featured several articles and/or interviews about Kitano's films.

Eiga geijutsu: 363 (Winter 1991), 368 (Summer 1993), 375 (Spring 1995), 379 (Summer 1996),

Kinema junpō: 1016 (15 August 1989), 1067–8 (1–15 October 1991), 1108 (15 June 1993), 1153 (1 February 1995), 1198 (1 August 1996), 1285 (1 June 1999), 1324 (15 January 2001), 1366 (15 October 2002), 1389 (15 September 2003), 1443 (15 November 2005).

Shinario: 45.9 (September 1989), 49.7 (July 1993), 54.2 (February 1998).

Internet Sites

KitanoTakeshi.com: <kitanotakeshi.com>.

Office Kitano: <www.office-kitano.co.jp>.

Takeshi Kitano: <www.takeshikitano.net>.

Takeshi no idenshi: <page.freett.com/idenshi>.

FILMOGRAPHY

Violent Cop (Sono otoko, kyōbō ni tsuki, 1989)
Based on the idea by Okuyama Kazuyoshi
Screenplay: Nozawa Hisashi
Photography: Sasakibara Yasushi
Lighting: Takaya Hitoshi
Editor: Kamiya Nobutake
Music: Kume Daisaku
Sound Designer: Horiuchi Senji
Production Designer: Mochizuki Masateru
Assistant Directors: Tenma Toshihiro and Tsukinoki Takashi
Cast: Bīto [Beat] Takeshi (Azuma), Hakuryū (Kiyohiro), Kawakami Maiko (Akari), Sano Shirō (Yoshinari), Kishibe Ittoku (Nitō), Ashikawa Makoto (Kikuchi), Yoshizawa Ken (Shinkai), Hiraizumi Sei (Iwaki)
Production: Okuyama Kazuyoshi, Nabeshima Hisao, Yoshida Takio and Ichiyama Shōzō
Production Company: Shōchiku Fuji
Running Time: 103 minutes
Colour

Boiling Point (3–4xjūgatsu, 1990)
Screenplay: Kitano Takeshi
Photography: Yanagijima Katsumi
Lighting: Takaya Hitoshi
Editor: Taniguchi Toshio
Sound Designer: Horiuchi Senji
Production Designer: Sasaki Osamu
Costume Designers: Kawasaki Kenji and Kubota Kaoru
Assistant Directors: Tenma Toshihiro and Yoshikawa Takeshi
Cast: Ono Masahiko (Masaki), Ishida Yuriko (Sayaka), Iguchi Takahito (Iguchi), Iizuka Minoru (Kazuo), Ashikawa Makoto (Akira), Igawa Hisashi (Ōtomo), Bengaru (Mutō), Tokashiki Katsuo (Tamaki), Bīto [Beat] Takeshi (Uehara)
Production: Okuyama Kazuyoshi, Nabeshima Hisao, Yoshida Takio and Mori Masayuki
Production Company: Bandai and Shōchiku Fuji
Running Time: 96 minutes
Colour

A Scene at the Sea (Ano natsu, ichiban shizukana umi., 1991)
Screenplay: Kitano Takeshi
Photography: Yanagijima Katsumi
Lighting: Takaya Hitoshi

Editor: Kitano Takeshi
Music: Hisaishi Jō
Sound Designer: Horiuchi Senji
Production Designer: Sasaki Osamu
Costume Designer: Shimoda Machiko
Assistant Directors: Tenma Toshihiro
    and Kitahama Masahiro
Cast: Maki Kurōdo [Claude] (Shigeru),
    Ōshima Hiroko (Takako), Kawahara
    Sabu (Tamukai), Fujiwara Toshizō
    (Nakajima), Terajima Susumu (man
    in pickup truck), Koiso Katsuya and
    Matsui Toshio (soccer youths)
Production: Tachi Yukio, Kitano
    Takeshi, Mori Masayuki and Yoshida
    Takio
Production Company: Office Kitano
    and Tōtsū
Running Time: 101 minutes
Colour

Sonatine (Sonachine, 1993)

Screenplay: Kitano Takeshi
Photography: Yanagijima Katsumi
Lighting: Takaya Hitoshi
Editor: Kitano Takeshi
Music: Hisaishi Jō
Sound Designer: Horiuchi Senji
Production Designer: Sasaki Osamu
Assistant Directors: Tenma Toshihiro
    and Kitahama Masahiro
Cast: Bīto [Beat] Takeshi (Murakawa),
    Kokumai Aya (Miyuki), Watanabe
    Tetsu (Uechi), Katsumura Masanobu

(Ryōji), Terajima Susumu (Ken),
Ōsugi Ren (Katagiri), Zushi Tonbo
(Kitajima), Yajima Ken'ichi
(Takahashi), Minakata Eiji (the
    hitman)
Production: Okuyama Kazuyoshi, Mori
    Masayuki, Nabeshima Hisao and
    Yoshida Takio
Production Company: Bandai Visual
    and Shōchiku Daiichi Kōgyō
Running Time: 94 minutes
Colour

Getting Any? (Minnā yatteru ka!, 1994, released 1995)

Screenplay: Kitano Takeshi
Photography: Yanagijima Katsumi
Lighting: Takaya Hitoshi
Editors: Kitano Takeshi and Ōta
    Yoshinori
Music: Koike Hidehiko
Sound Designer: Horiuchi Senji
Production Designer: Isoda Norihiro
Costume Designer: Iwasaki Fumio
Assistant Director: Shimizu Hiroshi
Cast: Dankan (Asao), Hidari Tokieda
    (Asao's mother), Kobayashi Akiji
    (World Defense Force Chief), Yūki
    Tetsuya (gang boss), Terajima
    Susumu (wounded yakuza), Ōsugi
    Ren (thin hitman), Gadarukanaru
    [Guadalcanal] Taka (pilot), Minakata
    Eiji (enemy boss), Bīto [Beat]
    Takeshi (scientist)

Production: Mori Masayuki, Nabeshima Hisao, Tsuge Yasushi and Yoshida Takio

Production Company: Bandai Visual and Office Kitano

Running Time: 110 minutes

Colour

Kids Return (Kizzu ritān, 1996)

Screenplay: Kitano Takeshi

Photography: Yanagijima Katsumi

Lighting: Takaya Hitoshi

Editors: Kitano Takeshi and Ōta Yoshinori

Music: Hisaishi Jō

Sound Designer: Horiuchi Senji

Production Designer: Isoda Norihiro

Costume Designer: Iwasaki Fumio

Assistant Director: Shimizu Hiroshi

Cast: Kaneko Ken (Masaru), Andō Masanobu (Shinji), Morimoto Reo (their teacher), Yamaya Hatsuo (boxing gym manager), Ishibashi Ryō (yakuza boss), Terajima Susumu (yakuza lieutenant), Kashiwaya Michisuke (Hiroshi), Daike Yūko (Sachiko), Moro Morooka (Hayashi)

Production: Mori Masayuki, Tsuge Yasushi and Yoshida Takio

Production Company: Office Kitano and Bandai Visual

Running Time: 108 minutes

Colour

Hana-Bi (a.k.a. Fireworks, 1997, released 1998)

Screenplay: Kitano Takeshi

Photography: Yamamoto Hideo

Lighting: Takaya Hitoshi

Editors: Kitano Takeshi and Ōta Yoshinori

Music: Hisaishi Jō

Sound Designer: Horiuchi Senji

Production Designer: Isoda Norihiro

Costume Designer: Saito Masami

Assistant Director: Shimizu Hiroshi

Cast: Bīto [Beat] Takeshi (Nishi), Kishimoto Kayoko (Miyuki, his wife), Ōsugi Ren (Horibe), Terajima Susumu (Nakamura), Watanabe Tetsu (Tezuka, the junkman), Hakuryū (Tōjō), Yakushiji Yasuei (the criminal), Ashikawa Makoto (Tanaka), Daike Yūko (Tanaka's wife)

Production: Mori Masayuki, Tsuge Yasushi and Yoshida Takio

Production Company: Bandai Visual, TV Tokyo, Tokyo FM and Office Kitano

Running Time: 103 minutes

Colour

Kikujiro (Kikujirō no natsu, 1999)

Screenplay: Kitano Takeshi

Photography: Yanagijima Katsumi

Lighting: Takaya Hitoshi

Editors: Kitano Takeshi and Ōta Yoshinori

Music: Hisaishi Jō
Sound Designer: Horiuchi Senji
Production Designer: Isoda Norihiro
Costume Designer: Iwasaki Fumio
Assistant Directors: Shimizu Hiroshi
Cast: Bīto [Beat] Takeshi (Kikujirō),
Sekiguchi Yūsuke (Masao),
Kishimoto Kayoko (Miki, Kikujirō's
wife), Yoshiyuki Kazuko (Masao's
grandmother), Gurēto [Great]
Gidayū (fat biker), Ide Rakkyo (bald
biker), Fumie Hosokawa (girl on a
date), Maro Akaji (paedophile),
Daike Yūko (Masao's mother)
Production: Mori Masayuki and
Yoshida Takio
Production Company: Bandai Visual,
Tokyo FM, Nippon Herald and Office
Kitano
Running Time: 121 minutes
Colour

Brother (2000, released 2001)
Screenplay: Kitano Takeshi
Photography: Yanagijima Katsumi
Lighting: Takaya Hitoshi
Editors: Kitano Takeshi and Ōta
Yoshinori
Music: Hisaishi Jō
Sound Designer: Horiuchi Senji
Production Designer: Isoda
Norihiro
Costume Designer: Yamamoto Yōji
Assistant Director: Shimizu Hiroshi

Cast: Bīto [Beat] Takeshi (Yamamoto),
Omar Epps (Denny), Maki Kurōdo
[Claude] (Ken), Katō Masaya
(Shirase), Terajima Susumu (Katō),
Royale Watkins (Jay), Lombardo
Boyar (Mo), Ōsugi Ren (Harada),
Ishibashi Ryō (Ishihara)
Production: Mori Masayuki and Jeremy
Thomas
Production Company: Office Kitano
and Recorded Picture Company
Running Time: 114 minutes
Colour

Dolls (2002)
Screenplay: Kitano Takeshi
Photography: Yanagijima Katsumi
Lighting: Takaya Hitoshi
Editors: Kitano Takeshi and Ōta
Yoshinori
Music: Hisaishi Jō
Sound Designer: Horiuchi Senji
Production Designer: Isoda Norihiro
Costume Designer: Yamamoto Yōji
Assistant Director: Matsukawa
Takashi
Cast: Kanno Miho (Sawako), Nishijima
Hidetoshi (Matsumoto), Mihashi
Tatsuya (Hiro, the gang boss),
Matsubara Chieko (Ryōko), Fukada
Kyōko (Haruna), Takeshige Tsutomu
(Nukui), Kishimoto Kayoko
(Haruna's aunt), Ōsugi Ren
(Haruna's manager)

Production: Mori Masayuki and
    Yoshida Takio
Production Company: Bandai Visual,
    Tokyo FM, TV Tokyo and Office Kitano
Running Time: 113 minutes
Colour

Zatoichi (Zatōichi, 2003)

Screenplay: Kitano Takeshi
Based on the novel by Shimozawa Kan
Photography: Yanagijima Katsumi
Lighting: Takaya Hitoshi
Editors: Kitano Takeshi and Ōta
    Yoshinori
Music: Suzuki Keiichi
Sound Designer: Horiuchi Senji
Production Designer: Isoda Norihiro
Costume Designers: Yamamoto Yōji and
    Kurosawa Kazuko
Assistant Director: Matsukawa Takashi
Cast: Bīto [Beat] Takeshi (Zatōichi),
    Asano Tadanobu (Hattori), Ōgusu
    Michiyo (Oume), Natsukawa Yui
    (Oshino, Hattori's wife),
    Gadarukanaru [Guadalcanal] Taka
    (Shinkichi), Tachibana Daigorō (Osei),
    Daike Yūko (Okinu), Kishibe Ittoku
    (Ginzō), Ishikura Saburō (Ōgiya),
    Emoto Akira (Matoya proprietor)
Production: Saitō Chieko, Mori
    Masayuki and Saitō Tsunehisa
Production Company: Bandai Visual,
    Tokyo FM, Dentsū, TV Asahi, Saitō
    Entertainment and Office Kitano

Running Time: 116 minutes
Colour

Takeshis' (2005)

Screenplay: Kitano Takeshi
Photography: Yanagijima Katsumi
Lighting: Takaya Hitoshi
Editors: Kitano Takeshi and Ōta
    Yoshinori
Music: Nagi
Sound Designer: Horiuchi Senji
Production Designer: Isoda Norihiro
Costume Designer: Yamamoto Yōji
Assistant Director: Matsukawa Takashi
Cast: Bīto [Beat] Takeshi (Beat Takeshi,
    Kitano Takeshi), Kyōno Kotomi (Beat
    Takeshi's lover, Kitano's neighbour),
    Ōsugi Ren (Beat Takeshi's manager,
    taxi driver), Kishimoto Kayoko
    (woman at mah-jongg parlour,
    audition judge, customer, etc.),
    Terajima Susumu (Beat Takeshi's old
    colleague, Kitano's neighbour),
    Watanabe Tetsu (costumer, *rāmen*
    cook, bad actor), Miwa Akihiro
    (Miwa, the singer)
Production: Mori Masayuki and
    Yoshida Takio
Production Company: Bandai Visual,
    Tokyo FM, Dentsū, TV Asahi and
    Office Kitano
Running Time: 110 minutes
Colour

INDEX

Page numbers in *italics* refer to illustrations; those in **bold** indicate a major chapter on the subject, or an entry in the filmography

List of Illustrations

Whilst considerable effort has been made to correctly identify the copyright holder this has not been possible in all cases. We apologise for any apparent negligence and any omissions or corrections brought to our attention will be remedied in any future editions.

Takeshis', Office Kitano; *Kids Return*, Office Kitano/Bandai Visual; *Sonatine*, Bandai Visual/Shochiku Dai-ichi Kogyo/Right Vision Co./Office Kitano; *Violent Cop*, Bandai/Shochiku-Fuji; *Boiling Point*, Bandai/Shochiku Co. Ltd/Fuji; *A Scene at the Sea*, Office Kitano/Totsu Co. Ltd; *Getting Any?*, Office Kitano; *Hana-Bi*, Bandai Visual/TV Tokyo/Tokyo FM/Office Kitano; *Kikujiro*, © Bandai Visual/© Tokyo FM/© Nippon Herald Films/© Office Kitano; *Brother*, © Little Brother Inc.; *Dolls*, © Bandai Visual/© Tokyo FM/© TV Tokyo/© Office Kitano; *Zatoichi*, © Bandai Visual/© Tokyo FM/© Dentsu/© Asahi National Broadcasting/© Saitô Entertainment/© Office Kitano; *Zatoichi and the One-Armed Swordsman*, Consolidated/Katsu Production Company.